Unspoiled Beauty

A Personal Guide to Missouri Wilderness

Charles J. Farmer

D1520633

University of Missouri Press
Columbia and London

Copyright © 1999 by
The Curators of the University of Missouri
University of Missouri Press, Columbia, Missouri 65201
Printed and bound in the United States of America
All rights reserved
5 4 3 2 1   03 02 01 00 99

Library of Congress Cataloging-in-Publication Data

Farmer, Charles J.
   Unspoiled beauty : a personal guide to Missouri wilderness /
Charles J. Farmer.
      p.   cm.
   Includes bibliographical references.
   ISBN 0-8262-1230-1 (alk. paper)
   1. Wilderness areas—Missouri.   I. Title.
QH76.5.M8F37   1999
333.78'2'09778—dc21   99-30420
                                                                              CIP

♾   This paper meets the requirements of the
American National Standard for Permanence of Paper
for Printed Library Materials, Z39.48, 1984.

Cover design: Kristie Lee
Text design: Mindy Shouse
Typesetter: Crane Composition, Inc.
Printer and binder: Walsworth Publishing Company
Typefaces: Giovanni and Palatino

For Brittany and Scotty

Contents

Foreword

WILDERNESS IS A word to conjure with. It draws up images rooted deep in the consciousness. The Old Testament depicts wilderness on the one hand as a place of loneliness and temptation, but also as a refuge of prayer and communion. Our American encounter with the untamed "New World" evoked both experiences. Our forebears struggled against the wilderness, to settle and civilize the land; at the same time it was out of the wilderness that we were to bring forth a new nation. Some part of our national spirit has always found solace in the untrammeled American landscape.

Our national park system grew out of this instinct. And so, later, did the national wilderness system. In 1964 America decided officially that we should always retain at least some remnant of the original wilderness out of which we had built our nation. This wild remnant was to be preserved as a reminder of our national identity and as a source of physical refreshment and inspiration. Part of the wisdom of America's commitment to wilderness is that it offers an antidote to our tendency toward arrogance about the natural world. In wilderness, we restrict ourselves from normal management and development of the land, because we recognize that there is much we still have to learn from nature and that it is only prudent to set some land aside where we intrude as little as possible, where we go not to dominate, manipulate, or improve; but to learn, enjoy, and reflect.

This noble concept was first applied almost exclusively in the great scenic areas of the mountain West. But as we more deeply understood the meaning of wilderness, we saw that a proper wilderness *system* must include representative landscapes from all regions of the country where any qualified lands remained, including Missouri.

No state of our Republic has a richer heritage of wild beauty than Missouri. Most of the lands qualified for Wilderness Act designation are in the Ozark region, where, in many choice and select spots, mature forests of oak and shortleaf pine stretch to the horizon; where massive bluffs of limestone, granite, or sandstone rise up toward the sky; where clear waters flow swiftly over clean gravel beds or mossy bedrock; and where wild animals large and small live out their lives in ancient rhythms little disturbed by man. You can visit these places, alone or with a few companions, and it can enrich your life.

One of the best things about the campaign to protect the remnants of Missouri's wilderness was that a whole generation of Missouri conservationists became much more keenly aware of their home state. Protecting wilderness means proposing specific areas for designation, which requires that the proponents know the areas in depth, their qualifications, boundaries, difficulties, and benefits. Between 1969 and 1984, many Missourians became intensely familiar with the public forests of our state, especially those in the Ozarks, and developed a wonderful knowledge that did enrich their lives. And the result of their effort was congressional action that designated a superb selection of Wilderness Areas in Missouri, areas now protected for coming generations to discover, explore, and enjoy for themselves.

One very helpful assist for those who want to know more about Missouri Wilderness is this fine book by Charlie Farmer. For many years Charlie has been a leading outdoor writer in Missouri; he has, in fact, played a substantial role in building public support of wilderness protection. Few people know the Missouri outdoors better than Charlie. Now he has drawn upon his wealth of personal memories of these special places, and also upon some original historical research, to tell us the story of Missouri Wilderness, the story of the campaign, but especially the story of each area, revealed through his own experiences. And through Charlie's lively and engaging narrative, each reader will have a deepened and refreshed appreciation for Missouri's wild landscape and heritage. You may also feel a renewed commitment to protect and defend that heritage. Such a commitment would greatly please both the author and this writer.

JOHN KAREL

Acknowledgments

W ITHOUT THE HELP and consistent encouragement of Darsan Wang of the Mark Twain National Forest, John Karel, the foremost authority on Missouri Wilderness, and B. Eric Morse, former supervisor of the Mark Twain National Forest, who believed in the project, *Unspoiled Beauty: A Personal Guide to Missouri Wilderness* would be but a fleeting dream.

Also, thanks to Taylor Instrument Company for providing technical assistance.

Unspoiled Beauty

1

History of the Land prior to Wilderness Designation

IN THE BEGINNING, it was all wilderness—pure and simple, Missouri wilderness of the finest kind—Yellowstone quality. The scope of southern Missouri could have and maybe should have been designated a national preserve. Native Americans, the original inhabitants, certainly treated the territory as a sacred place.

The area that would become known as the Ozarks, comprising 55,000 square miles in southern Missouri and northern Arkansas, was a natural treasure filled with forests of shortleaf pine, oak, hickory, and cedar and ten thousand springs bubbling up through limestone cavities to fill crystal pools. It was a land of unspoiled beauty, nature in her most striking dress: towering bluffs, bare glade tops, boulders gouged and sculpted by raging water, and caves that tunneled deep into the earthly unknown.

For ages, the wilderness of southern Missouri remained inaccessible to all but the Indian tribes who hunted there. The land was home to the Osage, Sac, Fox, Oto, Iowa, Missouri, Miami, Kickapoo, Delaware, Shawnee, Kansas and Cherokee tribes at various times. They came for the abundant game. Hidden among the rolling hills were open meadows lush with prairie grass and rich with wildlife; winding through them were sparkling streams brimming with fish.

If a trapper or hunter was determined to explore the area, he had to boat up the Mississippi to the Arkansas River then on to the mouth of the White River. He then had to hike into the interior, carrying what supplies he needed. It took extraordinary resolve, superior boating skills, and a penchant for cross-country walking over rugged terrain; even then an explorer entered the sanctuary slowly and carefully. There was a constant threat from hostile Indians guarding their hunting grounds. Few settlers were up to the challenge. Bottomland suitable for farming was sparse and prone to flooding. There were no supply towns, and no established overland routes or railroads through the heart of the mountainous region to other towns. And so a large part of the Missouri Ozarks remained off the beaten track of the westward migration.

Missouri has belonged to three nations: France, Spain and, as part of the Louisiana Purchase, the United States. Father Jacques Marquette and Louis Joliet, who boated down the Mississippi from the north in 1673, supplied the first written accounts of exploration in Missouri. Robert de LaSalle claimed the area for France in 1682, and the territory was ceded to Spain in 1762. Although Spain held the country for forty years, its influence was slight. The early culture of the state was determined mostly by the French. They established the first permanent settlement, Ste. Genevieve, in the mid–1730s. This settlement survived alone in the massive Upper Louisiana Territory until the establishment of St. Louis as a fur-trading post in 1764. Because of its strategic location, where the Missouri River flows into the Mississippi, St. Louis became the largest settlement in the state.

In 1802, Spain ceded the Louisiana Territory back to France by secret treaty. Napoleon Bonaparte, anxious to rid himself of the vast and troublesome frontier, sold it to the United States in 1803 for fifteen million dollars. A year later, President Thomas Jefferson dispatched the Lewis and Clark expedition to explore the northwestern part of the new territory. Missouri was organized as a territory in 1812 and was admitted to the Union as the twenty-fourth state on August 10, 1821. The state ranks eighteenth in size with a total area of 68,898 square miles. The highest point in the state is 1,772 feet above sea level at Taum Sauk Mountain in Iron County in the St. Francois Mountain area. The lowest point is 230 feet above sea level at the extreme south end of the lowlands of southeastern Missouri.

Sometime after Missouri was organized as a territory, the Osage, one of the most powerful tribes in the Ozarks, signed a treaty with the U.S. government in which they supposedly relinquished their lands. However, they never conceded their hunting rights in the game-rich Ozark territory. The normally peaceful Osage became more protective of their rights and further discouraged attempts at white settlement. When the government forced the tribe further west into Kansas, trappers, hunters, and explorers began filtering into the region in quest of furs, game, and adventure. Most were vagabonds who hunted and trapped, moving where deer, elk, and beavers were plentiful. A few stayed on, built huts or small cabins, and mixed peacefully with the Indians in the area. Several trading posts were established, and for a while, a spirit of cooperation existed between whites and Indians. But with increasing settlement came broken bonds of trust. Skirmishes became common. Government paranoia fueled distrust between whites and Indians. New treaties, most paving the way for an influx of white settlers, sealed the fate of the Osage and Delaware tribes in southern Missouri. Likewise, the fate of the Ozarks was sealed. Within one hundred years, the very heart and soul of the Ozark wilderness would change forever.

There are several theories about the origin of the word *Ozark*. Richard Rhodes, who has written about the Ozarks in *"The Ozarks"*— *The American Wilderness* for Time-Life books, says the region's name seems to be lost in legend. Some have thought Ozarks came from the French name for the tree from which the Indians took wood for their bows. The tree produces green fruit in late summer and fall that are the size of softballs. They are known as Osage Orange or hedge apple trees and were commonly used as field borders or hedge rows around crop fields. The French called them *Bois d'Arc*. Conceivably pronunciation of these words might have been corrupted to become Ozark. It also has been suggested that the word is a corruption of *aux arcs*, "with bows," the name given by the French trappers to the local Quapaw Indians. But authorities on such matters, knowing that the French trappers, like American soldiers, had a penchant for shortening familiar words, believe that when someone asked an Ozark-bound trapper where he was going, he said that he was going toward Arkansas, *aux* Arkansas, *aux* Arks, which eventually became *Ozarks*.

More settlers came from Kentucky and Tennessee than from any other states. Many of these rugged pioneers were of Scottish and Irish descent. Some were subsistence hunters and trappers looking for wildlife. Others were loggers and farmers who sought forests or fertile land.

Water for drinking, fishing, and irrigation was plentiful. There was more fertile bottomland than first met the eye. The abundant spring-fed streams were eventually dammed and river current used to power simple mills built for grinding grain, ginning cotton, and saw-ing logs into lumber. Flour and cornmeal became staples. Small, per-manent settlements sprung up in places where the Osage had once lived and hunted. In 1830, a road was built from Springfield to the mouth of the White River near Swan Creek (near the present town of Forsyth). Taney County was established in 1837, and the 1840 census of that county reveals that there were 3,265 people living in 385 households and building more. Steamboats were hauling goods and logs up the White River to Forsyth. The growing prosperity and in-creasing demands of settlers were not without consequences.

In the winter of 1838–1839, some 17,000 Cherokee Indians were forced to leave their homes in the Southeast and move to Okla-homa. Ill-clothed and sick, about 4,000 of them died along the way. Their route came to be known as the Trail of Tears. In the Ozarks, they followed a trail called the White River Trace, which took them from Arkansas to the James River Fork of the White River in Missouri; they then followed the James on to Springfield and out of the state. Some of the Cherokee escaped the forced march and settled in Missouri. The incident involved the North-ern Cherokee Nation of the Old Louisiana Territory. They have been called the "Lost Tribe." Their forebears were American Indi-ans who started moving west of the Mississippi in the early 1700s, driven by the French and Spanish occupation of the Louisiana Ter-ritory. They settled mainly in southeast Missouri and northern Arkansas. About one hundred years later, they were joined by Cherokee Indians going through Missouri. The Cherokee lived throughout western Missouri until 1825, when the general assem-bly passed legislation essentially outlawing Indians in the state. The law forbade trading with Indians and allowed militia officers to kill Indians found near white settlements.

For the next eighty-four years, until the law was repealed, many of the Cherokee stayed in hiding or dressed and behaved like whites to conceal their identity. In 1983, the tribe was officially recognized by the governor and the Missouri house—the only Indian group to be so distinguished.

Beginning in 1840, increasing numbers of settlers found their way into the Ozarks. Needless to say, only the start of the Civil War allowed this migration. After the war, increasing settlement resumed. Small towns provided services for farmers and loggers, but the refinements common in cities like Springfield, Kansas City, or St. Louis were not always available because of the lack of roads and trains. Still, growth was steady. Then, suddenly, most forms of commerce came to a halt.

The start of the Civil War in 1861 had a pronounced effect on southern Missouri. Battles, like the one at Wilson's Creek near Springfield, and a multitude of skirmishes ended peaceful, progressive living. Most of the men who were able went to war, and those who remained behind were tormented by marauding outlaws. By 1865, the official end of the war, Ozark towns were dying and families fragmented. Many of the original settlers never made it home. The slow healing process began in 1866. To a large extent it was the expansion of the railroad and the laying of track into once-remote places that spurred new life into the Ozark economy. The railroad required wood for ties before new track could be laid. Tie hacking was big business in the hills after the war. There was plenty of wood to cut—a seemingly endless supply of native short-leaf pine, oak, and cedar.

Sadly, the new prosperity lasted only fifty years. By then, most of the trees were gone, and the hills of green had been eroded, transformed into barren, rocky wastelands when their soil and gravel were washed into pristine streams and rivers. The process of revitalizing commerce had inflicted severe, long-lasting wounds on the natural beauty of the deep Ozarks. According to State Forester Marvin D. Brown, of the Missouri Department of Conservation, virtually every acre of Missouri's oak, hickory, and pine forest was logged between 1880 and 1920. Only a few remnant stands of virgin forest managed to survive the onslaught.

It was during Reconstruction that roads were built in the region. By the 1900s, there was a network of roads throughout the Ozarks that made travel easier and faster. More goods and services were made available. From Reconstruction through the early 1930s, prosperity was common throughout the nation. Southern Missouri also rode the crest of good times as more people settled in the area. However, the economy was ailing; a severe downswing took place in 1934 and 1935. The United States had emerged as an industrial nation, but suddenly the country was faced with low production and sales and a high rate of business failures and unemployment. The Great Depression of the 1930s hit hardest in the large eastern cities, but the entire country, including the Ozarks, felt the aftershock.

The natural resource picture was equally gloomy. Ozark forests were destroyed. The shortleaf pine, which had once covered the Ozark region, was nonexistent. The trees had been exterminated by loggers supplying lumber for the building industry. With soil-holding trees and vegetation gone, the ravages of erosion had turned rolling green hills into barren, rocky moonscapes basically devoid of life. Once-clear waterways had become clogged. Fish were dying. Deer and turkeys were virtually wiped out due to loss of habitat and unregulated hunting. Had it not been for a relatively few strong voices "crying in the wilderness," Missouri's forests could have been permanently destroyed. Concerned conservationists, most of them fishermen, hunters, and resource managers, brought the plight of the land to the attention of their representatives in state government, who in turn petitioned the federal government for help.

The U.S. Forest Service connects environmental damage to the Ozarks with its settlement in the early 1800s. Fortunes boomed with early lead and silver mining. The harvesting of oak and pine, which covered the Ozarks for unbroken miles, followed close on the heels of mining. At the turn of the century, the largest pine mill in the world was operated at Grandin, Missouri. Companies selected high-quality trees for their products, and only stunted trees, those of poor quality for milling lumber, remained. When logging operations were completed, areas were frequently burned, killing the remaining trees. Fast-spreading wildfire left charred brush and slash in its wake. Timber harvesters moved on, leaving bare hillsides prone to erosion. Farmers moved in; they believed that burning the woods stimulated the growth of grasses and improved grazing conditions. Instead, upland soil was depleted and failed rapidly under the plow. Cattle and hogs competed with wildlife for what food would grow. The burning and overgrazing interfered with the establishment and growth of new trees and further increased erosion. Streams that had once been deep and fast were muddy and sluggish.

During the great Mississippi Valley flood of 1927, over 38 percent of the water came from the Ozarks, which constitute a meager 4 percent of the river basin. These were lands few people wanted fifty years ago. The Ozarks was on the brink of ecological disaster. Something had to be done. Conditions were so dismal that some Missourians believed that attempts at reforestation were pointless. Fortunately, enough resource managers and citizens to influence the government disagreed, and in 1931 measures were taken to correct the years of environmental abuse.

Concerned conservationists from the University of Missouri and influential citizens of the state requested that national forests be established to restore productivity to Missouri's wild forestland. In 1933, the state passed legislation enabling the U.S. Forest Service to start defining areas to be protected and revived. A letter from the secretary of war established the National Forest Reservation Commission.

The commission's first purchase was made in 1934: 10,443 acres of scarred Ozark land for $2.20 an acre. Shortly after, 359,225 acres were purchased at $1.95 an acre, for a total cost of about $723,000 for both purchases. By 1945, about 1.25 million acres had been approved for purchase.

Upon the creation of the Mark Twain National Forest, the U.S. Forest Service began to lead the Ozarks down the road to recovery. Deer and turkeys were released and protected in certain areas as seed stock. It was estimated that by 1930, the statewide population of deer had dwindled to sixty thousand. The Missouri deer herd is now estimated to be well over five million. Flocks of turkeys are flourishing throughout the state. Professional resource managers acknowledge that there are more deer and turkeys in Missouri today than there were one hundred years ago.

The environmental impact of timber harvesting was carefully evaluated and regulated. Professional forest management has virtually guaranteed the prohibition of unscrupulous logging on public forests in the state. The creation of Roosevelt's "Tree Army," a youth work program called the Civilian Conservation Corps, was a grand success. The corps provided the manpower, and the new national forest provided plenty of work. The CCC planted trees; built dams, roads, and recreation areas; and fought fires. In 1937, under the guidance of the newly created Missouri Department of Conservation, CCC workers also helped restock and protect deer and turkeys in the Ozarks. From these early beginnings, the Mark Twain National Forest has grown in size and improved in quality. Public forests now represent 68 percent of federal land, 49 percent of public land, and 2 percent of all forestland in Missouri.

It was fortunate that restoration began in the early 1930s, for the worst crisis in U.S. history was yet to come. The most devastating global military conflict in human history began in 1939 as a European conflict between Germany and an Anglo-French coalition. World War II strained the nation's resources. Life for many was put on hold until 1945, when the war officially ended. During that time, however, Ozark forests literally began sprouting new life, and wildlife rebounded.

After the war, the U.S. Army Corps of Engineers built fourteen reservoirs on rivers in the Ozarks, flooding the best cropland, recreating the landscape, and changing the socioeconomic structure of the region forever, according to Ozarks historian Robert Flanders. There would have been more dams, artificial lakes, and federal pork barrel projects had it not been for a small but highly vocal and active group of conservationists who decried the demise of Ozarks streams, some of the finest spring-fed, clear-water riverways in the nation.

Bitter fights ensued to save the Current and Buffalo Rivers, contested primarily by urban conservationists who treasured free-flowing waters for the wildlife they attracted and the leisure opportunities they provided—canoeing, fishing, and camping. There are 11,500 miles of clear, sparkling streams and rivers contained within the Ozarks. Also on the Corps of Engineers' list were the Jacks Fork, Eleven Point, and North Fork Rivers. Conservationists and journalists from St. Louis, Kansas City, and Columbia once again mobilized forces and saved those waters from being dammed. The Current, Buffalo, Jacks Fork, and Eleven Point are now permanently protected as National Scenic Riverways managed by the National Park Service. Most of the North Fork of the White River is intact within Missouri.

Almost all the rest of the once-mighty White River was dammed to create a series of lakes: Lake Taneycomo in 1913, Norfork Lake in 1941, Bull Shoals Lake in 1947, Table Rock Lake in 1958, and, finally, Beaver Lake, upstream from Table Rock, in 1966. Much of the James River, a famous float fishing stream before Table Rock and Springfield Lakes were created, had lost its original character and good fishing. While no one realized it then, there is little doubt now that some of the wildest and most picturesque lands in the Ozarks were lost forever to development and overuse. In their place, man-made lakes have since created a profitable tourist and recreation trade.

As early as 1897, when the Forest Reserve Management Act was

Gifford Pinchot became head of the division of forestry of the Department of Agriculture in 1898. In 1905 the Forest Service was created, and Pinchot became its first chief.

passed, and in 1911, when the Weeks Act was enacted, the importance of forests in flood protection was recognized by foresters—largely based in the U.S. Forest Service—but not by the Army Corps of Engineers. The latter advocated flood control through use of dams and levees. The first Forest Service chief, Gifford Pinchot, believed that the Corps' position undermined at the time one of the key arguments for creating additional forest reserves and national forests. The issue of flood control was important because of the need to gain political support in the East for purchase of forestland.

Ozark reforestation and the resurgence of wildlife is a success story of splendid magnitude. Through the efforts of Mark Twain National Forest's management, the Civilian Conservation Corps, the Missouri Department of Conservation, and concerned citizen conservationists, second-growth forest attained much of the beauty, bounty, and productivity of original stands. Oak-hickory forests dominate the southern Missouri woodlands today. While a large number of majestic shortleaf pine trees were harvested in the late 1800s, old logging methods did not have the same effect as modern clear-cutting, in which trees that have no commercial value are also removed. The result was that many areas of the Ozarks did not lose their authentic wild character. Although greatly outnumbered by

Prominent early conservationists Bernard Frank, Harvey Broome, Bob Marshall, and Benton MacKaye who set the stage for the preservation of unique wilderness. *Courtesy the Wilderness Society.*

deciduous trees, remnant stands of pines, the stately sentinels of Ozark ridgetops, are a welcome and necessary evergreen force in the forest tapestry.

The rebirth of Ozark forests is one of the state's finest conservation triumphs. So overwhelmingly successful was rehabilitation, there is little doubt many Missourians believe existing unbroken stands of public forest are virgin originals. For naturalists, hunters, campers, fishermen, hikers, and birders—conservationists all—the victory was one to be savored. Beneficiaries are future generations who receive the lasting gift of national forests. But for many of those who had struggled to revive the forests, the best was yet to come. The health of public forests in the Ozarks had soared beautifully in a forty-year growth period. The crown jewels of American forests, including the Mark Twain National Forest, were championed by three Forest Service employees who later gained prominence as national environmental and forest recreation leaders. Aldo Leopold (1886–1948), Arthur Carhart (1892–1978), and Robert Marshall (1901–1939) designed and helped implement a wilderness policy for the Forest Service in the 1920s and 1930s. The Wilderness Act of September 3, 1964, forever bonded their efforts, as congressionally designated lands were brought into the system.

Founders and members of the Wilderness Society George Marshall (member), Olaus Murie (member and officer), Harvey Broome (founder), Bernard Frank (founder), and Ernest Griffith (member and officer). *Courtesy the Wilderness Society.*

The act contained a formal definition: "A wilderness is hereby recognized as an area where the earth and its community of life are untrammeled by man, where man himself is a visitor and does not remain." The word *wilderness* is used both as a concept of wild lands and as a statutory legal entity describing officially designated Wilderness Areas. Fortunately for Missouri and other eastern-region states, there were no hard-core congressionally designated Wilderness qualifications requiring virgin timber and tracts that had never been inhabited by humans. For if that had been the case, the second-growth public forests of the Ozarks and many other eastern states would never have qualified.

It was the power of regeneration, healing aided by man, that restored the forest to its former beauty. Once trammeled to near-exhaustion, the abused land was tended, and wounds eventually healed. There would be subtle signs of past habitation—homestead sites, logging roads, wire fences, planted daffodils blooming every spring, rock fences and old water wells. These were minor blemishes compared to the overall beauty of lands to be preserved.

Olaus Murie addressing a group in 1953. Next to him are Robert F. Griggs and Bernard Frank. *Courtesy the Wilderness Society.*

Historically, they serve as poignant symbols of the nation's heritage. Despite past abuses, the finest mountain lands in Missouri before 1800 had regained much of their former beauty by 1960. The uniquely beautiful forest settings, filled with springs, streams, bluffs, caves, glades, and vistas, stood out from the rest.

Citizen conservationists—hunters, fishermen, campers, hikers, birders—and resource professionals identified these treasures. Those areas they chose and rallied for were elevated into seven congressionally designated Wilderness Areas managed by the U.S. Forest Service and one area managed by the U.S. Fish and Wildlife Service, for a total of eight. The fight for Missouri Wilderness was a difficult one that was carried out by relatively few men and women, who realized the physical, mental, and spiritual need for protected wild places. After the grassroots door-to-door political campaign, the treasures of Bell Mountain, Devil's Backbone, Hercules Glades, Irish, Mingo, Paddy Creek, Piney Creek, and Rockpile were preserved forever. From a forest once devastated rose a splendid 71,358-acre wilderness in Missouri—treasures earned, treasures saved.

2

The Birth of Missouri Wilderness— Battles and Victories

AFTER WORLD WAR II, there was a dramatic increase in commercial use of public forest, including grazing, mining, and logging. At the same time there was a growing emphasis on increased recreational activity in the national forest system. A significant number of forest recreationists believed the Forest Service was drifting away from the balancing of recreation with commerce, leaning toward serving timber industry needs first. Hikers, hunters, naturalists, campers, and fishermen began lobbying for safeguards that would protect existing forests that exhibited a "wilderness character." Senator Hubert H. Humphrey (1907–1964) introduced a "study bill" in 1956, which set out a Wilderness Society proposal for allocations on the national forests. The Forest Service countered with the Multiple Use–Sustained Yield Act of 1960 to prevent any monopolizing of the resource base.

Wilderness advocates reacted to this strategy by seeking passage of legislation that became the 1964 Wilderness Act. The natural resource base was shrinking in the face of accelerated demand for housing, and the Forest Service was less able to appease conflicting factions by granting each group an exclusive piece of the forest. Wilderness was not compatible with timber harvesting, and the remaining old-growth timber was increasingly found in roadless

13

President Lyndon Johnson signing the Wilderness Act, September 3, 1964, which set the stage for federally designated Wilderness throughout the nation. *Courtesy the Wilderness Society.*

areas and environmentally sensitive zones, such as high-elevation watersheds.

The Wilderness Act allowed Congress to establish wilderness areas in national forests. A ten-year study to select sites, Roadless Area Reviews and Evaluations (RARE I and RARE II), stemmed from compliance work required by the act. Public involvement in Forest Service policy originated with the 1970 National Environmental Policy Act (NEPA), signed January 1 by President Richard Nixon. This act reversed the direction of the Forest Service's mission; it stopped development and returned to stewardship of forestland. The Forest Service had always consulted with special-interest groups, but after NEPA, Congress and the public became directly involved in daily operations of the agency. The act allowed lawsuits to be filed against the Forest Service if it failed to prepare environmental impact studies (EIS) on proposed major actions by federal agencies. Early challenges in which environmentalists made use of NEPA include cases of excessive timber harvests on the Bitteroot National Forest (Montana) in 1969 and clear-cutting on the Monongahela National Forest (West Virginia) in 1973. It became apparent the public no longer held the view that the professional forester knew best how to manage the national forests.

According to *The Wilderness Movement and the National Forests* by Dennis M. Roth, between the fall of 1971 and the summer of 1972, the Forest Service inventoried and studied 1,449 roadless areas, containing 55.9 million acres. The agency held 300 meetings and received more than 50,000 written and oral comments, which, at the time, made RARE I the most extensive public-involvement effort ever undertaken by the federal government. The Forest Service selected 274 areas, amounting to 12.3 million acres, for temporary protection and further study.

The Sierra Club and the Wilderness Society charged that RARE I had been done too quickly, that areas had been split arbitrarily into smaller units to lower their wilderness quality rating, and that the entire study was biased toward commodity values. The Forest Service later conceded that RARE I was flawed, but with the passage of time and cooling of emotions, environmentalists acknowledged its importance.

After RARE I, the public gained a greater say in land-use practices through a series of laws, including the 1973 Endangered Species Act, the 1974 Forest and Rangeland Renewable Resources Planning Act, and the 1976 National Forest Management Act, which requires the Forest Service to involve the public in its decision making and hire people trained in professions other than forestry and engineering. Still, as late as 1960, 90 percent of professional positions in the Forest Service were filled with foresters.

Citizen conservationists from across the nation had drawn their inspiration from pioneers of wilderness preservation like John Muir, Henry David Thoreau, Teddy Roosevelt, Gifford Pinchot, Aldo Leopold, Arthur Carhart, and Bob Marshall. Without those visionaries and the invaluable support they garnered from national conservation groups such as the Wilderness Society, Sierra Club, and Izaak Walton League, the Forest Service would undoubtedly have continued to evaluate and manage land based on commodity values. Many potential wilderness areas would have been lost to business interests.

On this strong foundation, the Missouri wilderness campaign was built. A precedent had been set by ten years of RARE I and RARE II. Although far from perfect in terms of definition and

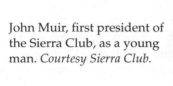

John Muir, first president of
the Sierra Club, as a young
man. *Courtesy Sierra Club.*

compliance, Roadless Area Reviews and Evaluations provided the
necessary guidelines to define and preserve Missouri wilderness.

A Guiding Light for Missouri Wilderness

From his college days, John Karel had been an active leader on environmental issues. While at the University of Missouri–Columbia,
Karel earned a bachelor of arts in American intellectual history and a
master of science in wildlife management, and he cofounded the Missouri Wilderness Coalition (MWC) with Don Pierce, a graduate student of the University of Missouri. The purpose of MWC was to form
an extensive informal communications network as a working alliance
of conservation organizations and individual activists. Its function
was to coordinate the flow of information in the embattled atmosphere
of the wilderness legislative campaign. The concept worked! The modern Missouri wilderness campaign began in 1969 with a resolution
passed by the board of directors of the Missouri Conservation Federation, requesting that the Forest Service identify potential Wilderness or
Wild Areas on national forestland. From that time forward, there has
been an organized effort to identify and protect such areas.

According to Karel, 1976 was a landmark year for wilderness in

Missouri. In October, Congress enacted Public Law 94-557, designating Missouri's first official wilderness areas, Mingo (managed by the U.S. Fish and Wildlife Service) and Hercules Glades (managed by the U.S. Forest Service). In addition, four wilderness study areas were set aside: Bell Mountain, Rockpile Mountain, Paddy Creek, and Piney Creek.

In "Building Missouri Citizen Support," written for *The Living Wilderness* magazine, published by the Wilderness Society in 1978, John Karel defined RARE II as it pertained to wilderness designation efforts in Missouri:

> First came the inventory phase. The summer of 1977 found many Missourians tramping the backwoods of the Mark Twain Forest, meeting over kitchen tables with topographic maps, debating the merits of various areas and conscientiously referring back to the official inventory criteria.
>
> As in most states, many Missouri conservationists were too busy that summer reviewing national forest lands to attend the Forest Service's RARE II workshops. Fortunately for us, and in contrast to some other states, opponents of Missouri wilderness also attended lightly.
>
> On September 13, 1977, the MWC presented Tom Roederer, Mark Twain National Forest Supervisor, with a package of 11 suggested additions to the inventory of roadless areas, complete with precise descriptions, supporting documentation and maps. Care had gone into our selection and proposal process. Moreover, a core of citizens was becoming intimately familiar with RARE II and with the forest.
>
> On September 23, the Forest Service announced that two of our areas, Swan Creek and Big Creek had been added to the inventory. Nine of the proposals had been rejected. Mark Twain Forest's final inventory consisted of 10 areas, encompassing 74,634 public acres—less than 5 percent of the forest.
>
> This was a psychological milestone. Our heads were cleared of the seductive illusion that the new Jimmy Carter administration, though pro conservation, could balance the Forest Service's traditional outlook in one stroke. From this point on, we approached RARE II with an increased sense of our responsibility to shape goals for the forest, to inform the public accurately and to alert the state's congressional delegation to our concerns.

Karel and MWC's statewide wilderness leaders met often at the organization's headquarters in Columbia, Missouri. The meetings catalyzed the coalition's perception of RARE II as the logical vehicle for most wilderness issues in the state. A good RARE II campaign would draw public attention to all the proposed areas; build recognition and support, especially of new volunteers; and ready the delegation for legislative action.

In May 1977, three Missourians attended the Eastern Wilderness

President Theodore Roosevelt and John Muir. *Courtesy Sierra Club.*

John Karel, leader of the Missouri
Wilderness movement.

Leaders' Conference, cosponsored by the Wilderness Society and
the Sierra Club in Roanoke, Virginia. The RARE II situation was
reviewed in depth. Following that conference, two MWC participants traveled to Washington D.C. to brief the Missouri congressional delegation on forthcoming wilderness goals and strategies.
Various coalition affiliates from across the state thought it best to go
back into the field to conduct their own evaluation phase. On June
17, at Montauk State Park, the investigative teams reported to
MWC leaders. An important resolution came out of that meeting.
The coalition identified thirteen areas of Mark Twain National Forest with irreplaceable wilderness values. Six of those areas were
supported for immediate inclusion into the national wilderness
preservation system. They were Irish, Bell Mountain, Rockpile
Mountain, Paddy Creek, Piney Creek, and Devil's Backbone. The
rest, Lower Rock Creek, Swan Creek, Van East Mountain, Smith
Creek, Spring Creek, North Fork, and Big Spring Addition, were
listed as areas with confirmed wilderness potential deserving full
study.

   Shortly afterward, Forest Service EIS were released throughout
the country. John Karel believed the range of alternatives for the inventoried Mark Twain selections was more balanced than those for

many other areas of the nation. Still, the text displayed a pervasive antiwilderness slant. Some of the passages seemed designed to arouse opposition. For example, the EIS repeatedly stated that one area, Piney Creek, included some of the better timber-producing sites in the Cassville Ranger District, clearly implying that wilderness designation would have an adverse impact on local logging operations. "Only deep in the appendix of the EIS," Karel stated, "does one find statistics showing that, in reality, wilderness designation for Piney Creek would have no effect on local timber production and employment."

The response from the national conservation leadership was a battle cry: "Organize and fight!" As a result of the Montauk meeting, RARE II coordinators were designated for all major populations centers. Each proposed wilderness unit was assigned a champion. Leaders or entire groups saw to it that conservationists turned out at each RARE II open house scheduled by the Forest Service. Campaign leaders assigned volunteers their congressional contacts. There were others whose support was needed, and a letter-writing campaign was begun. Karel himself wrote close to two hundred letters urging the protection of Missouri wilderness. Meanwhile, St. Louis leaders hit upon a strategy for generating a large number of letters on the draft EIS that would reach the Forest Service before the October deadline. They came up with the idea of declaring September "RARE II Outings Month." More than six thousand copies of a four-page report on RARE II in Missouri, called "Summer of Decision," were distributed across the state. Karel was glad that RARE II in Missouri did not generate the extreme controversy that prompts the kind of blow-by-blow press coverage that occurred in most other states. On the contrary, MWC enjoyed excellent editorial support. The favorable coverage spurred many Missourians to action; hundreds of factual, well-written letters were directed to the Forest Service's regional forester in Milwaukee.

RARE II was vital to the preservation of Missouri wilderness. It focused the energies of wilderness supporters on a set of issues. The inventory of potential wilderness areas led to a new vision of Mark Twain Forest's potential. Despite inventory disputes with the Forest Service over wilderness attribute ratings (W.A.R.), differences in interpretations, and socioeconomic concerns that surfaced in the draft EIS, MWC held firm. A number of new areas that came under scrutiny were later recognized as bona fide de facto wilderness.

At the same time, the search for wilderness revealed the finite extent of the remaining wild Ozarks. The strenuous exploration that went into the inventory phase of RARE II put many Missourians in much closer touch with their land and its communities of life. Karel summed it up this way: "More of us now appreciate the rich if not always spectacular beauty of Missouri's wildlands. We are emerging from our participation in RARE II a more knowledgeable and confident group of conservationists. It became clear that only an aroused and vigorous citizenry can save the Missouri wilderness."

Letters, Words, Actions Made the Difference

Don Pierce, a Missouri Wilderness Coalition leader, described the struggle to protect Missouri wilderness:

> Through thick and thin, we thoroughly enjoyed the wilderness campaigns. Everybody chipped in. There were no real chiefs. Everyone had a job and they did it. One of our goals was getting the word out to the public. The Forest Service received over 1,300 public opinion input letters from Missouri citizens concerning 10 roadless areas that were reviewed. The results of that input showed that 93% were in favor of wilderness designation; 3% were opposed and the remaining 4% opted for further planning.

In the battle over designating Missouri wilderness, activists were divided into camps: those who wanted the last few remnants of "eastern" wilderness preserved, and those who believed that public forestland should be exploited for commercial gain. Early on, wilderness supporters realized the campaign could very well turn into a dogfight. On paper, the issues pitted urban conservationists, environmental groups, and big city and federal lawmakers against small town and rural residents, forest commodity users, and local politicians who rallied for mining and logging jobs in addition to keeping the federal government at bay.

Members of the Missouri Wilderness Coalition knew that to be successful they had to work correctly and quickly within the state and federal political system. Coalition leaders desperately wanted to avoid being labeled environmental extremists who were horning in on the lives and culture of the citizens who lived near, and perhaps utilized, existing forest and potential Wilderness Areas. Of prime importance were efforts to educate both rural and urban residents about the positive impact designated wilderness would have for all citizens of the state.

In early disputes over wilderness inventory, workers became aware of another potential roadblock. The Forest Service, specifically Mark Twain Forest supervisors, though consistently courteous, displayed a persistent philosophic resistance to wilderness preservation. On November 10, 1975, Mark Twain Forest supervisor Donald L. Rollens sent a letter to Missouri congressman Gene Taylor in which he stated that wilderness designations would eliminate the opportunity to harvest timber. Rollens wrote, "We are reluctant to defer our normal management plans especially in Piney Creek and Paddy Creek. We believe we have a well designed management program (at those areas) which responds to the need for sustained production of resources while also providing the public with high quality recreation areas." John Karel recalls that the Forest Service seemed to be trying to undermine the inclusion in the Wilderness system of Hercules Glades, Irish, Bell Mountain, and Rockpile Mountain in addition to Piney Creek and Paddy Creek.

The Sierra Club filed a "no logging" request on December 31, 1975, after Rollens lifted an administrative "hold" placed on timber cutting and other commodity activities in the areas. The supervisor claimed that the decision to resume harvesting was made because none of the affected areas had ever been mentioned in any of the legislative proposals. The Missouri Wilderness Coalition later proved that Rollens was wrong in his assessment. An article in the *Springfield Daily News,* dated February 11, 1976, was headlined "Forest Service Rejects Sierra Club Appeal."

In May 1978, Dave Foreman, wilderness affairs coordinator for the Wilderness Society, warned state campaign leaders of Forest Service resistance. Foreman wrote, "If you have dealt with the Forest Service or Bureau of Land Management in efforts to designate a wilderness area which they opposed on lands they manage, then you probably have heard their concern that over-eager citizen conservationists are degrading the National Wilderness Preservation System by including inferior areas in it." The Forest Service seemed bent on initiating timber-management plans on two study areas: Piney Creek and Paddy Creek, which could have negatively affected their eventual inclusion in the wilderness preservation system. Today the unique areas are regarded as two of the finest in Missouri's Wilderness system.

Lawmakers Supported Wilderness

Through a consistent, fact-filled, and intelligent letter-writing and telephone campaign, the MWC made allies of many of the most influential and respected lawmakers in the state. Among them was Senator Thomas F. Eagleton. In a letter to John Karel, dated March 12, 1973, concerning the Eastern Omnibus Wilderness Bill S316, Eagleton wrote, "I am pleased to advise you that I have added my name as a co-sponsor of S316. I have felt for some time that the state of Missouri should have wilderness areas selected from the outstanding natural areas in the state and formally designate these areas as wilderness by an Act of Congress. Please be assured that I will give this bill my vigorous and sympathetic support."

On October 15, 1975, John Karel received a letter from Senator Stuart Symington. It read, "I am very much in favor of the National Wilderness Preservation System and I am working on proposed boundaries and the addition of Paddy and Piney Creek study areas along with Senator Eagleton and other members of the Missouri delegation."

A letter from Governor Christopher Bond, November 25, 1975, to Donald Rollens favored inclusion of Bell Mountain, Rockpile Mountain, Paddy Creek, Hercules Glades, Piney Creek, and Irish into the Wilderness system. Bond said,

> It has come to our attention that several of these areas may be subject to management activities, including timber sales, which could adversely affect their consideration for inclusion in the National Wilderness Preservation System. I sincerely hope the wilderness option for these few areas will not be lost and request that the Forest Service protect the wilderness character and values of these areas until Congress has full and complete opportunity to determine their suitability for wilderness designation.

Governor Bond's letter was instrumental in persuading the Forest Service not to initiate management activities in wilderness study areas.

Victories in 1975 and 1976 for designated eastern Wilderness Areas in Alabama, Arkansas, Florida, Georgia, Kentucky, New Hampshire, North Carolina, South Carolina, Virginia, Tennessee, Vermont, West Virginia, and Wisconsin served as a catalyst for a fundamental revival of the Missouri wilderness campaign.

In April 1977, Senator John C. Danforth, a staunch wilderness supporter, introduced Senate Bill 1285, designating 17,562 acres of the Mark Twain National Forest as the Irish Wilderness. "Every place I go," Danforth said, "people are concerned about the Irish Wilderness. I grew up hearing about the beauty of the area and float trips on the Eleven Point River from my father."

Representative Harold Volkmer led the charge in the House for Irish Wilderness designation. Not all of Missouri's representative supported it. Congressman Bill Emerson from Cape Girardeau voted against the plan, claiming it would limit lead and zinc mining and thus limit the growth of the economically depressed area. "Local people don't want federal protection," he said. Representative Richard Ichord joined Emerson in opposing to the designation.

Resistance was not limited to the federal level. State Representative Gene Oakley from the 148th District said, "In Oregon County where the Irish Wilderness is located, the fight has pitted neighbor against neighbor; county judge against county judge. Feelings run high. The battle between the whims of preservationist groups and those who need to feed their children appears to be over. We the people have lost."

Representative John Sieberling was instrumental in paving the way for Missouri wilderness and the Senate passage of HR5487, known as the Colorado Wilderness Bill, which included Bell Mountain, Rockpile Mountain, Piney Creek, and Devil's Backbone areas in Missouri. Tom Eagleton helped push the bill through. In an October 7, 1983, letter to Robert Lindholm, a conservationist and former Missouri assistant attorney general, Danforth praises Sieberling's efforts on behalf of the Irish Wilderness as monumental. He said, "I truly believe that John Seiberling should receive some sort of prize from Missouri environmentalists. He has gone out of his way on behalf of the Irish Wilderness. If we get that bill passed it will be because of John. We in Missouri owe him a great debt of gratitude."

The U.S. Fish and Wildlife Service had recommended that none of the 21,640–acre Mingo National Wildlife Refuge be placed in the wilderness preservation system; however, some citizens and legislators however felt that Mingo's unique cypress and tupelo swamp was worthy of permanent protection. Fish and Wildlife then offered seventeen hundred acres for wilderness. Congressman Bill Burleson and Senator Tom Eagleton rejected that offer and battled, along with conservationists, to obtain eight thousand acres. Along with

Burleson and Eagleton, Dr. Lee Fredrickson was a principal author of the proposal to make Mingo a Wilderness Area. Fredrickson is a professional waterfowl biologist who works at Duck Creek Wildlife Area, managed by the Missouri Department of Conservation, adjacent to Mingo. He, along with Burleson and Eagleton, testified at House and Senate hearings on behalf of Mingo Wilderness. Bill Burleson gained credit among the conservation community for paving the way for the House vote to include Bell Mountain and Rockpile Mountain in the national preservation system.

The support for wilderness designation from elected officials and lawmakers cannot be overemphasized. A typical response can be found in a letter from Governor Joseph Teasdale dated January 26, 1979, supporting all MWC wilderness recommendations and disagreeing with the nonwilderness classification of Swan Creek, Spring Creek, Lower Rock Creek, and Van East Mountain. The governor cited strong public support for including these areas in the system. Government leaders were frequently torn between providing forest commodity jobs and land preservation. But in this case, many lawmakers went out on the limb for what they believed and what their constituents wanted. The constant communication provided by John Karel and the Missouri Wilderness Coalition played a vital role in inspiring workers in the field and gaining legislative support.

Under Karel's leadership, the Missouri Wilderness Coalition turned the combination of involved citizens and supportive lawmakers into a potent force for the preservation of Missouri wilderness. The MWC's success set a new and valuable precedent for wilderness campaigns to follow. And the 1990 Rangeland Renewable Resources Planning Act (RPA) made adding more Missouri land to the national wilderness preservation system an attainable goal.

Since the national wilderness preservation system was created in 1964, Congress has designated a total of 91 million acres of wilderness. Of that total, the Forest Service manages 32 million acres in 354 designated Wilderness Areas. Wilderness now totals 17 percent of all national forest system land. The 1990 RPA Program proposes designating an additional 7 million acres of wilderness in the national forest system, bringing the total to 39 million by the year 2040.

It is important to recognize those who were instrumental in laying a solid wilderness foundation in Missouri. A Wilderness Area can only be created by an act of Congress. Because of the efforts of the following people, eight congressionally designated Wilderness Areas, containing 71,358 acres of the most pristine land in the state, have been preserved.

In wildness is the preservation of the world.

HENRY DAVID THOREAU

Missouri Wilderness Honor Roll

To the men and women who helped save the best of Missouri's natural heritage and appreciation to all those who wrote letters, newspaper articles, and attended wilderness meetings:

- Jean Ann Allen
- Bill Bates
- Dave Bedan
- Jim Berlin
- Dick Bolling
- Margaret Broadaway
- Betty Campbell
- Senator John C. Danforth
- Reid Detchon
- Ernie Dickerman
- Leo Drey
- Senator Thomas F. Eagleton
- Wilson "Poncho" Elliot
- Dorothy Ellis
- Dr. Leigh Frederickson
- Darwin Hindman
- Greg Iffrig
- Mark Kaiser
- John Karel
- Julie McQuary
- Rindy O'Brien
- Ron Olsen
- Ed Pembleton
- Don Pierce
- Roger Pryor
- Charley Putnam
- Dan Saults
- Sandy Schlafke
- Ed Stegner
- Kay Stewart
- Paul Stupperich
- Senator Stuart Symington
- Representative James Symington
- Mary Ann Turner
- Representative Harold Volkmer
- Alan Wheat
- Tom Williams
- Jim Young

Bill Bates, a tireless worker in the campaign for protected Wilderness, particularly Piney Creek and Hercules Glades.

Roger Pryor, tireless leader and executive director of the Missouri Coalition for the Environment.

3

Bell Mountain Wilderness

The long fight to save wild beauty represents democracy at its best. It requires citizens to practice the hardest of virtues, self-restraint.

EDWIN WAY TEALE

MY FRIEND AND I crossed Highway A near Ottery Creek and climbed the shadowy, switchback trail into the Bell Mountain Wilderness. It took us only a few moments of hiking to sense the untrammeled magic of the place—quiet, mysterious, and brooding as though the oak, hickory, and shortleaf pine trees towering above guarded dramatic and often sad secrets from the past. The wilderness is like a cathedral. As you step into the forest, and the trees seem to close in behind you, like a heavy, ornate door shutting, you find a remarkable peace and contentment that nourishes heavenly thoughts and well-defined dreams.

This time though, the tranquility was shattered forty paces up the narrow trail. The ground shook, dogwood leaves fluttered, and a buglelike scream assaulted my ears and seemed to echo forever. I looked ahead wide-eyed and spotted in a fleeting glimpse an eerie mosaic of red, white, and blue splashing through the oak trees. It was the head of the gobbler. I watched as, long, brushy beard dangling, he lifted awkwardly off the ground, frantically beating wings gradually raising the heavy black bird to just barely above the treetops. My heart was still pounding. The turkey must have first seen us through the trees as we leaned into the slope, beginning our climb up the mountain. To the tom, maybe we looked like a pair of hens lured by his charms. It was April mating season, and he did what came naturally. But the thunderous double and triple gobble had been so close and so loud he sounded more like a bull elephant than a lovesick boss gobbler.

Minutes later, after the shock wore off, my partner and I stood grinning and shaking our heads. Missouri's turkey hunting season would open in four days. That bird would make a fine trophy for some hunter who displayed a lot more composure than we had. Old longbeards like that one don't forget close encounters with humans. Chances are he would keep his mouth under control until after the two-week season ended. We regarded the turkey encounter as a good omen. What a welcome to Bell Mountain Wilderness!

The 9,027-acre Wilderness was officially included in the national wilderness preservation system by Public Law 96-560 on December 22, 1980. The area is part of the St. Francois Mountains, one of the oldest landforms in North America. This mountain range covers several counties in southeastern Missouri and includes the state's highest elevations and most ancient rocks.

Bell Wilderness is named for a family that once lived and farmed along the ridgetop that is now known as Bell Mountain. Elevations range from 1,702 feet at the peak to 970 feet in Joe's Creek drainage. Local relief is about 600 feet and is characterized by steep felsite (a dense igneous rock consisting almost entirely of feldspar and quartz) and rhyolite (a very acid volcanic rock that is the lava form of granite) outcroppings. Both Bell Mountain and Lindsey Mountain (1,662 feet) offer excellent views of the surrounding area. The associated granite glades provide a variety of fascinating plant and animal life.

Wilderness Areas, especially those found in eastern wilderness, such as Bell Mountain, are far from being elitist destinations. Opponents of federal preservation commonly use the argument that only superfit individuals with plenty of free time on their hands can enjoy the values and solitude that wilderness provides. Nothing is further from the truth.

Many people enjoy simply knowing wilderness exists. Others, including myself, find pleasure hiking through it or camping at easily accessible roadside trailheads. The beauty of designated Wild Areas lies in the multitude of options available to forest users of all tastes, ages, and physical abilities. Overnight camping close to the road can be as satisfying as extended backpack camps. Short hikes of two hours or less can be as refreshing as long ones. Wilderness advocates use the land for fishing, hunting, walking, shooting photos of wildlife, and bird-watching. Nearly everybody who has experienced the wilderness becomes addicted to its spiritual and physical healing powers. When we are bathed in solitude we grow in many new directions.

It is the marriage of the soul with Nature that makes the intellect fruitful, and gives birth to imagination.

THOREAU, JOURNAL, AUGUST 21, 1851.

You may accuse me of being a wilderness elitist after hearing what I have to say. In reality, I preach no such snobbery. For wilderness is truly not about miles hiked or mountains climbed. It is about pristine beauty consumed, savored, and harnessed to real life. With me, there's a philosophy attached to each and every Wilderness Area I visit, something that's vitally important to me and to many other adventurers. It is simply this: No wilderness experience is complete until you have set a sleeping bag overnight or several nights on wild ground. There is this desire to experience wilderness day and night. There is the need to eat, drink, sleep, and live in the wild in order to more fully understand and connect the wilderness soul. There is much adventure, and appreciation of wilderness, to be found between sunset and sunrise.

I drove alone from my home in Ozark to the Ottery Creek Trailhead in mid-May. My first two-day backpacking trip in Bell Mountain would be a solitary one. While good companions can add immensely to the pleasures of a wilderness trek, there is something to be said for hiking and camping alone, not all the time, but often enough for a decent chance to try to learn or relearn one's body and soul. The therapy of silence is best practiced in wilderness.

My own solitary hikes produce a heightened awareness of natural surroundings. Senses tune sharp and alert. Introspection is common and quite welcome in contrast to a city world laden with nonstop chatter and forced entertainment There are more occasions to stop, explore, reflect, and savor; pause to hear, feel, touch, and smell when alone in the wilderness.

The day was cool and sunny at mid-morning, near perfect conditions for climbing to the top of Bell Mountain with a pack weighing around forty pounds. Earlier that morning, I had the option of camping high or low. I nearly chose the unique beauty of Shut-in Creek, which flows in bottomland gorges between Bell and Lindsey Mountains. It was a toss-up until the very last minute when I locked the truck at the trailhead.

The view from the top of Bell Mountain could very well rank first in the state. John Karel, a Missouri Wilderness expert, would agree. Karel's description of the scenic vista to be seen from the top sums it up best:

> The landscapes visible from the top of the mountain are not only beautiful, but also of great scientific interest. To the east, just across Shut-in Creek rises first of all glade-flanked Lindsey Mountain. Beyond Lindsey to the south and east rise the "tall peaks" of the St. Francois uplift: Goggins, High Top, Proffit, Church, Wildcat and Taum Sauk Mountains.
>
> Until comparatively recently, this region was the deepest stronghold of wilderness in the St. Francois range and perhaps in the whole Ozark Highland. As early as 1949, these peaks were proposed as a wilderness of 100,000 acres. At the time not one paved or improved road penetrated the region. Bell Mountain was included in that proposal.
>
> Most of the vista skyline visible today still reflects a wild and rugged character, but visible in the distance is the man-made pumped-storage reservoir that in 1960 violated the heart of the wild country. From Bell's crest it is possible to scan what remains of the wilderness and draw personal conclusions about whether the remnant enclaves should be protected.

So it was for me that high adventure won out over low that morning in choosing the spot to stake my small backpack tent to the ground and live high like the turkey vultures that commonly cruise low over Bell's crest. I would camp and explore the top, 1,702 feet high. Maybe I would hear turkeys gobble early and late in the day from the thrones of Missouri's highest mountaintops. I would welcome the yelps of coyotes and the serenade of barred owls . . . "Who cooks for you, who cooks for you all!" I could hoot back to them and draw these owls close to my fire as I have done in the past.

I looked forward to watching the changing light from dawn to sunset and photographing its effect on mountain majesty that so dominated the landscape below, a green carpet unrolled. It would be a good change for someone who is nearly always hunting, fishing, and hiking to simply sit still, to watch, listen, and feel from a temporary home atop the mountain. I was having a sort of light-duty vision quest, with no intention of mimicking the sacred journeys of Native Americans who climbed, and continue to climb, to mountaintops alone, carrying only the bare necessities for three or four days. They are seeking spiritual oneness in order to be healed and receive good medicine for the future. I believe in the power of unspoiled mountaintops myself. They inject fresh faith and hope into the mind because of their unrestricted view of the heavens. There is little doubt that native peoples of all ages have savored the view from the top of Bell Mountain, and for this reason and others, I was looking forward to camping there.

There is a trailhead located on Forest Road 2228, which can be accessed from Highway A about a half-mile south of Highway 32. A separate two-mile section begins at the end of Forest Road 2359 on the east side and leads to the top of Lindsey Mountain. The Ozark Trail is concurrent with the Bell Mountain Trail for about a mile into the Wilderness. Then the Bell Mountain Trail turns north and begins a gradual ridgetop ascent most of the way. The only steep part of the route is the last definitive seven or eight hundred yards up mountain to the top of Bell. The moderate trail gradient allows comfortable hiking for anybody in reasonably good physical condition, even carrying a loaded backpack. Hiking early in the cool of a well-shaded, predominately oak and hickory forest is enjoyable exercise and yields a comfortable feeling of well-being. That last short surge to the top challenges legs and lungs, but the climber knows the serious climbing won't last long, and the anticipation of a spectacular view tends to keep legs springy and motivation in high gear.

My walk in was delightfully peaceful. As on most of the wilderness hikes I've taken in Missouri, there was absolutely no competition for trail space. In fact, during the next two days, my only company was wary, quiet wildlife. This was fine with me. I have hiked trails in massive Wilderness Areas throughout the West. Odd as it may seem, I often see more hikers, hunters, and fishermen there than I do in my home state. Eastern wilderness like Missouri's may not have the vastness and spectacular beauty of the West's wild lands, but the hiker is blessed with abundant solitude. There are not the high numbers of commercial outfitters and highly publicized tourist destinations found in the West, a remarkable fact, considering that eastern wilderness is commonly located near large population centers.

At the time of RARE I and RARE II, there was much discussion of the worth of eastern wilderness candidates. The Forest Service, in particular, was critical of state and national wilderness proponents who listed areas that were close to big cities. The government viewed these candidates as tainted because they were too close to the noise, air pollution, city lights, and pulse of major population centers. Eventually, the Forest Service was proved wrong and these areas were incorporated into the national wilderness preservation system. Today, wilderness supporters and the Forest Service believe that "city wilderness" is some of the most valuable within the system. Wilderness Areas are preserved sanctuaries and natural resource classrooms close to the city. They serve as natural laboratories and study sites for teachers and students. The flora and fauna of wild lands serve as indicators of environmental quality. Most important, they are anchors in the rapidly changing ocean of time. They define the human connection as it relates to heritage, history, legends, and lore. In every piece of wilderness there is human history. There is a preserved sense of the past that will become more valuable as population soars and rural lands shrink. If nothing else, wilderness is freedom for all!

In Piney Creek Wilderness and Hercules Glades Wilderness are preserved the area's two finest examples of southwest Missouri forest, glade and stream habitat. The flood of development and tourism in the once-sleepy fishing village of Branson has changed the face of the land in southwest Missouri. About thirty miles separates each Wilderness, Hercules Glades to the east and Piney Creek to the west, from the city's chaotic agenda of development and programmed entertainment.

Remaining Wilderness Areas in Missouri, including Bell Mountain, have plenty of distance, relatively speaking, from Missouri's major population centers—Kansas City, St. Louis, and Springfield. Bell Mountain, Paddy Creek, Rockpile Mountain, Devil's Backbone, Mingo, and Irish Wilderness are tucked away in rural areas, some of the most out-of-the-way locations in the state. It takes a good road map and significant drive time to reach these spots. Like the search for any hidden treasures, the journey in quest of wilderness is always worth the drive.

My backpacking trip to Bell Mountain in May was leisurely. Trees and shrubs along the trail wore the fresh, vibrant green of spring. There was a time when I would not have noticed. When I first started backpacking thirty years ago in Wyoming, I approached hiking as a footrace to whatever lake, stream, or hunting area I was headed. My focus then was narrow, aimed pretty much at bagging game and catching fish. I was, for the most part, a consumer on a mission. Along the trail, I searched for deer prints and turkey scratchings but passed up wildflowers and songbirds. At water's edge, I zeroed in on fish habitat and treated catching fish as though my next meal depended on it. A few times it did. Back then I scoffed at the recreational hikers' advice to slow down and "smell the roses."

I suppose it's part of the maturation process, but several years ago I finally realized how much I was missing by always charging ahead. I also realized, the older I became, the more it made sense to pace foot travel and conserve energy. Hunting and fishing are still important components of my outdoor adventure, but now I connect more with my surroundings because everything in nature is connected. My new philosophy has enabled me to better understand and appreciate the treasure of wilderness. This awakening I feel has made me a more observant hiker, hunter, and fisherman.

An electronic pedometer, attached to my belt near the buckle, indicated I had reached the two-mile mark on the Bell Mountain Trail. I could easily have kept on walking but decided to take a break. I had not seen or heard any wildlife, save for a solitary gray squirrel, since the hike began. This is not unusual in a Wilderness Area where birds and animals are more sensitive to the presence of man and their surroundings. Those hikers going through wilderness for the first time commonly expect a junglelike orchestration of bird and animal calls. Most often that's not the case in deep forest because dominant old-growth trees don't harbor the diversity of bird life found in young forests. There are times, especially at dawn, when such events do occur. Wild turkeys, whippoorwills, crows, owls, pileated woodpeckers, coyotes, and squirrels occasionally sound off in a semblance of togetherness from ridgetops, hillsides, and bottomland. Each bird and animal seems to spur another on in a kind of wild chorus that sometimes greets the break of day or some unknown (to man at least) atmospheric oddity. The opening flashes of lightning and booms of thunder in a spring storm sometimes initiate this serenade. Wild turkeys, for sure, seem to take pleasure in gobbling to thunder gods. Otherwise, the wilderness is often strikingly quiet, as if birds and animals are nowhere to be found. Oftentimes though, stopping throughout the day to sit still and listen for ten or fifteen minutes can yield sporadic surprises.

Unleashing the pack felt good. No matter how well designed and comfortable the new models are, it is always a relief to slide them off the shoulders and use them for backrests. Dressed in hiking shorts and a T-shirt, I stretched out on a thick cushion of last year's fallen oak leaves. Chiggers were still a few weeks away and ticks had not been particularly bothersome. A column of sunshine funneled through the treetops and bathed me in near-perfect warmth. It would have been easy to take a nap. I devoured a chocolate chip granola bar and washed it down with water from one of the two thirty-two–ounce plastic Nalgene bottles I carried. These containers are popular with hikers and packers because they are durable and don't leak even after years of use and abuse.

The stillness of Bell was overwhelming. If it weren't for the occasional rustling of oak leaves, I could very well have been contained in a glass biosphere. A few minutes later, the silence was abruptly shattered by the screeching of a bird I recognized immediately. I did not see the pileated woodpecker making the racket, but from the sound of the call, it was close. I shifted slowly from the backpack rest and craned my neck for a glance at this big, red-crested woodpecker. When I did, the bird took off from a nearby oak, squawking as it flew awkwardly through the trees to a spot twenty yards away. The red-and-white triangular head of this uncommon and consistently wary bird flashed brightly between limbs and leaves. Missourians are fortunate to have a stable population of these large woodpeckers, which grow to fifteen inches in length. I see and hear plenty of them during wilderness turkey and deer hunts. Visitors to Bell Mountain, and other wild territories in the state, who stay still and blend into their surroundings are likely to observe this bird.

A gray squirrel appeared and scampered within three feet of my right foot. I thought for a moment he would jump the distance and land on a human limb. The animal had that kind of curious glow in his eyes. But after a tentative step toward me, something, maybe the glare from my sunglasses, made the creature bound away in a rush of scattered leaves. I heard a flock of crows off in the distance. Then quiet returned as the sun rose higher in the sky. It was time to hit the trail, reach the summit, and set up camp.

Where the trail dipped in between ridgetops, the vegetation thickened to crowded oak and hickory saplings and boney stands

An old hunting stand in a tree in Bell Mountain Wilderness. *Author's collection.*

of sumac, dogwood, and redbud. These saddles of land in the wilderness are popular crossing spots for whitetail deer. I set up tree stands at these locations in October and November for archery and rifle deer season seasons, respectively. I fully expected to surprise a deer during the quiet ascent to the top of Bell. But whitetails are elusive critters with keen survival instincts. They can appear and disappear like ghosts. They chose not to show themselves.

I did find turkey scratchings in the leaf litter. Some of the soil scratchings were dry and bleached out. Others were dark and fresh, possibly made late yesterday afternoon or early this morning, recent enough that the musty scent of humus was detectable. The wild turkey scratches out leaves in order to uncover nuts, insects, and other foods in the soil. Birds commonly follow ridgetop trails, where mature white oak trees are common. In late summer, the mast crop falls from the trees onto the ground. White oak acorns are a favorite food of turkeys and deer.

Within the last decade, armadillos have migrated north into southern Missouri. They are found in all of the state's Wilderness Areas. Some hikers confuse armadillo rooting tracks with turkey scratchings. Armadillos seek out grubs, beetles, worms, and a variety of insects under the leaves. They root for food as they walk, using their armor-encased bodies, made up of small bony plates, and their sharp foreleg claws. They leave narrow, mostly straight trails of disturbed leaves as they walk and feed. Turkey scratchings are wider, more pie-shaped, and feature more of a meandering track in the leaves. Turkeys commonly scratch down to bare soil, piling leaves in small mounds behind the scratching as they walk. Turkey scat is sometimes present on the ground in the scratched-out area. Gobbler scat is shaped like a cheese curl approximately one and a half inches long; hen scat resembles popcorn.

There are several places along the Bell Trail where confusing paths, some as distinctive as the true trail, others less obvious, veer off the main route or fork one way or the other. These spots can cause temporary setbacks. As greenup and vegetation take hold during warm weather, trails may be disguised and more difficult to follow. The hiker who is not paying attention can veer off course without realizing it. This is why a compass and a topographic map of the area are essential. When there is a question about what trail to take, always trust map and compass over a hunch, gut feeling, or position of the sun. I have followed all three in the past and have learned to trust my compass; I even carry a spare.

Some Wilderness Areas have signs at trail junctions, and they may show mileage information to various destinations. Signing, like other man-made intrusions, is generally kept to a minimum. The only sign I found in Bell was at a junction with a one-mile segment of Missouri's Ozark Trail. That sign was an official green-on-white rectangle and overlapping "O-T" symbol. In Missouri Wilderness Areas, hikers may find only wooden posts to show where a sign was. Forest Service signs, typically rustic, unpainted wood, have often been torn down and destroyed or packed out as souvenirs. While this thievery is unfortunate and punishable by a stiff fine, it is difficult to stop. It is best not to depend on trail markers. Always refer to compass and map. Rustic visitor registration desks at wilderness trailheads have, on occasion, also fallen victim to vandalism.

The spot on Bell Trail where the path takes on a steep, uphill slant is unmistakable. With a great deal of enjoyment, I attacked the mountain, knowing full well the rewards on top would be worth the beads of sweat on my forehead. When I reached the crest, two familiar man-made landmarks remained just as I had remembered them. The skeleton of an old disassembled fire tower of 1940s vintage and the concrete blocks that were part of its foundation remained as a human connection to Bell Wilderness. Every Missouri Wilderness has its own connection with past human activity. And while some may argue that this condition taints the true meaning of wilderness, I disagree. Whether it be a former fire tower, concrete or stone foundations, overgrown logging roads, decaying log cabins, rock or wire fences, or patches of once-planted daffodils, it ties wilderness to human history. That history is a part of the American heritage, my heritage. I stop and look at the signs of civilization and wonder how it was to live in the days of horse-drawn wagons or newly invented automobiles. What was it like to eke a living from the land and raise a family without modern conveniences? I watch each year as the forest reclaims the land and most vestiges of man's presence erode away, leaving few permanent reminders—utility lines, wildlife ponds, old mines—behind.

I quickly walk east of the tower and reach open glade—the escarpment of Bell Mountain is the highest. John Karel describes it well:

> It is the most spectacular portion of the wilderness and a focal point of interest. This east-facing slope rises steeply 700 feet up from the valley of Shut-in Creek to a boulder-strewn crest where open, igneous barrens create an aspect of "timberline" country. The top of this crest above Shut-in Creek is within a few feet of being the highest elevation in the Missouri Ozarks. With open views on all sides, it provides one of our breathtaking natural vistas.

The barrens or glades that John Karel describes are prairielike openings in limestone areas. They stand out in sharp and unique contrast to the surrounding forest of oak, hickory, and cedar. Massive, rose-hued boulders are scattered here and there. Below some of them, in small crevices, are fire scars and remnants of burnt wood left by careless campers. The wind can blow amazingly hard on top, and the cold in early spring and late fall is surprisingly harsh. Still, I would not have built a fire in one of those crevices and scarred it. There are other places for a small fires. The monumental rocks on top of Bell, I feel, are sacred.

I stood for five minutes fixed on the view from all directions. I was so engrossed in the expanse of wildness before me that I nearly jumped out of my pack when a flock of ten mourning doves flushed in unison from a gnarled and thick-headed cedar tree thirty feet from where I stood. Apparently the doves had found a roost tree to their liking—one that was bathed in sunshine and probably provided some warmth. It was then that I realized how much warmer it was on top compared to the shady forest below where I had hiked. I could actually feel warmth radiating from the rocky ground and massive boulders that surrounded me.

I set my tent back some distance from the rim, inside a fringe of cedar trees and scattered sumac shrubs. Together with red oaks they provided most of the cover. This location afforded a windbreak and shade yet still offered a spectacular panorama of mountain ranges framed by cedar boughs. The weather was clear. My spot would not have been a good choice during unsettled weather with the chance of thunder and lightning. If such a storm moved in, I would break camp quickly and set up further down the mountain on a level terrace of land. For now, I had found the perfect setting. After a quick lunch of hard salami, cheese, Tang, and GORP ("good old raisins and peanuts" with shredded coconut and M&Ms thrown in), I explored the plateau-type terrain at the top of Bell. Brown and purple rhyolites, felsites, and ash-flow tuffs that had originated as liquid magma, forced up to the surface more than a billion years ago, dominated the dry desertlike landscape. I circled the crest and found a good viewing spot for late afternoon and evening, when I would watch the sun set over the Joe's Creek drainage.

After the short tour of the mountaintop, I loaded my daypack with a full water bottle and snacks, then proceeded to hike down the northeast face of Bell into Shut-in Creek. The northeastern point of the mountain offers a "softer" descent into the creek bottom than the southeastern escarpment. There is no established trail to the bottom, but the hike both up and down is fairly simple.

I had just begun the descent when I spotted what looked like a child's toy sitting on an outcropping of rose-hued boulder twenty feet from where I stood. It was, at first glance, a brilliant aqua-and-green-colored dinosaur about eight or nine inches long. When I stepped closer to the toy, it awkwardly jerked its head and tail. The coloration of this particular eastern collared lizard was the most dramatic I had ever seen. The male is more colorful than the female, and the brightness of coloration can vary between young and old lizards. This lizard was a work of art. I slowly reached for the small point-and-shoot thirty-five millimeter camera in my belt pouch, hoping to get close enough for a decent picture. I longed for my full-size Nikon with its telephoto capability. From where I stood, I could have framed the entire lizard with the big camera; however I had chosen to bring the smaller camera for its light weight.

This lizard, fairly common on glade areas of most Missouri wilderness, runs on its hind legs like a dinosaur. We played tag among the boulders for ten minutes. At one point, when I was seven feet away, about as close as I could get, he looked at me and opened his mouth. I knew better than to try getting closer. The pugnacious eastern collared lizard, when forced to defend itself, will sometimes hold its ground in preparation for inflicting a not-to-be-forgotten bite. I didn't allow him to clamp down on one of my fingers, but I did manage to snap off three good shots of him perched on different rocks. The prints show a most handsome "miniature dinosaur" in a setting that looks amazingly prehistoric. Considering where I was, it seemed a fitting discovery.

I worked my way down the mountain through boulders and grassy terraces filled with cedars. Some of the terraces held shallow pools of water. Carpets of emerald grass, wilderness landscape of unsurpassed beauty, grew on the terraces and under the shady monuments of knobby, stunted oak trees. Beds of viola pedata, bird's-foot violet, grew profusely in these natural rock-garden beds. Wild sweet william, indian paintbrush, and black-eyed susan stood out like prom-night bouquets. The finest and most fragrant beauty is wild—no artificial preservatives!

The open terraces and garden fields gave way to a splendid mix of white and red oak, hickory, sugar maple, white ash, and to a lesser extent, basswood and dogwood. The perfect forest, now untouched by the lumberman's chainsaw and free of prescribed commercial management techniques, was doing very well. Shady cool, even in mid-afternoon, this is the travel zone of wild turkeys and whitetail deer—the place of food and hiding cover. The forest zone, as I call it, is for dreaming and talking to the trees. I sat there for a few minutes admiring trunks, limbs, and leaves. Then I hiked down to the bottom and, as my map had indicated earlier, found the Shut-in Creek Trail coursing north and south.

Wilderness bottomland has a special quality to it—moist, aromatic, and junglelike, rich with grasses, flowers, ferns, mushrooms, may apples, blackberry thickets, spice bushes, sycamores, and river birches. It is in the bottoms of every designated Wilderness in the state that one of life's rarest and most precious resources can be experienced—solitude! There is full-fledged insulation from traffic noise and other man-made audio clutter, utter silence save for birdsong, the gurgle of streams, and the faint rustling of leaves in the breeze.

I trailed north at a leisurely pace and found "shut-ins," or gorges, along the stream course. Shut-in Creek, like Joe's Creek, Bell's other perennial stream, is spring fed throughout its length. The bottom-land streams of other Wilderness Areas are intermittent and usually dry up in summer and fall; only Bell's are constant. Another unique feature of the bottoms are the steep talus slopes that intersect the stream course at several locations. Rocks and boulders along the stream are commonly carpeted with green and gray moss and lichens. A mix of trees, many of them river birch, grow thick near the water's edge.

I saw fresh beaver-chewed sticks scattered here and there. Ele-phant-shaped, rose-tinted boulders and slate blue slab rocks, simi-lar to those found at nearby Johnson's Shut-Ins and Elephant Rocks State Parks, have created gorges, miniature waterfalls, and bathtub-size pools of cold, clear water. The actual size of the pools reminded me of those just upstream from Mina Sauk Falls in Taum Sauk Mountain State Park, also close to Bell Mountain. Some rock pools were rounded out smooth and were just the right depth for dan-gling your feet or wading in, with water therapeutically ideal for tired feet that had been confined within beefy hiking boots for most of the day.

I went a step further, shedding everything. Bracing my arms be-hind me, I slid gingerly from the base of a smooth rock into the pool until I was sitting on the gravel bottom with water up to my neck. The water was cold but gloriously invigorating. It was for me an-other refreshing lesson in wilderness therapy, one of many that keep me looking at the good side of life, just me and a shut-in pool deep in the wilderness. A minute later I completely submerged, then I climbed out of the pool and let the sun dry me. I had a feeling I was not the first to bathe in Shut-in Creek, nor would I be the last. A sun-dried hiker is a happy camper. I smiled and whispered to myself, "Close to heaven . . . really close to heaven."

I walked another mile down the trail, thoroughly enjoying some of the most unique scenery in the state of Missouri. Close to 4 P.M. it was time to head back up to camp. As usual, I had a difficult time abandoning the path, believing full well I would miss something important. But I was hungry and wanted to eat before watching the sun set over Joe's Creek drainage to the west. I chose a different route going back, spotting both shadbush (serviceberry), fire pink, and jack-in-the-pulpit halfway up the mountain in the forest zone. I ended up on top about a quarter mile from camp.

My backpack dinner, cooked over a lightweight, single-burner pack stove, began with a cup of chicken noodle soup, followed by macaroni and cheese, hot tea, and dessert, consisting of five Oreo cookies. I had brought along a dozen cookies packed in a plastic bag, which were somewhat of a luxury, considering that every bit of space in a pack matters. When dunked in tea though, they were worth their weight in gold.

Not long after eating, I found the perfect west-facing boulder for watching the sunset. It resembled an easy chair. A small, packable, soft-sided camp chair, popular with backpackers these days, fit the seat of the "stone chair" and added just the right amount of wilderness luxury. Through a small opening in the trees, I watched the rosy disk of sun flatten out like hot wax over the profile of sullen green trees and melt into the mountain. At that point it was easy to envision the syrupy flow of magma erupting from the earth and the molten evolution of the St. Francois Mountains.

Again I turn to John Karel's description of the land:

> Compared to some other regions of the country, the "Mountains of St. Francois" are not awesomely high, but these mellowed, lobate mountains have instead the beauty of great age, the magnetism of enduring stability in the face of temporal change. The igneous bedrock of these mountains was formed under molten conditions and remains the "crystalline core" of the entire Ozark dome. Made up of a variety of granites, rhyolites and basalts, they represent exhumed Precambrian lava. Although many questions about the exact geomorphology of these mountains are still debated by geologists, it is apparent to even the casual observer that drainage patterns and general topography in this region are radically different from the rest of the Ozarks. Much of this special character results from the stubborn resistance of igneous rock to water erosion as compared with the younger sedimentary rocks that compose most of the Ozark plateau.

I left the rock chair and made the short walk back to camp. Dusk had turned the mountaintop shadowy and more mysterious than it was in daylight. After sundown a cool breeze came from the west. I put on a jacket and sat down in the soft chair. I hesitated to light a fire, as though the flames would somehow disturb the tranquility, but I soon changed my mind, gathered a bundle of deadfall sticks, and dropped them into a small fire ring that somebody had already built about twenty yards from where I had pitched my tent. When I bent down to light the starter mound of "twiggies" (tiny, dead twigs), I was caught off guard by a sudden gust of wind, or so I thought. The wind turned out to be a flock of doves flying and landing in a nearby cedar tree. Whether it was the same flock I had flushed from a different tree earlier in the day I'll never know, but if I were betting, I'd say it was. For some reason, those birds liked the top of Bell Mountain.

When you spend the night in a Wilderness Area, you notice an aura different from that of other camping places. Wilderness is quiet in the day and even quieter at night. As far as I knew, I was the only human in Bell Mountain Wilderness that night. Next week would be the Memorial Day weekend holiday, and chances were good, if I elected to camp there again, that I would have the place to myself. It is being alone in darkness, at the top of a mountain, stirring a small fire, that transports men, women, and children back to their roots. There is a trace of aloneness, maybe even a tiny flicker of fear. But it is precisely this bonding with solitude that makes us grow and continue to explore nature and life regardless of our age. There is no better therapy anywhere. And I have immersed myself in it many times when faced with challenges or difficult decisions.

I sat by the fire until my eyelids drooped. After smothering the coals with dirt, I walked to the tent, and before unzipping the flap, I looked to the heavens. The stars seemed brighter and closer, as well they should. The boulders along the eastern edge of the mountain had lost their glow; they were now dark and moody like worried elephants ready to charge. I have backpacked and camped in many parts of the world, and the top of Bell ranks with the best of them. I lay in the sleeping bag for a few minutes, recapping the day's adventure before I drifted off. At 4 A.M., while it was still dark, I heard coyotes yipping below the mountain. Their howls echoed below camp for several minutes. I envisioned them loping together in a pack, mouths open and shifty eyes glowing pale yellow. They were hunting something, maybe a rabbit. Or maybe they were running and howling just for the fun of it. Then suddenly it was silent, maybe a kill. I fell back to sleep.

At sunrise, I awoke and peered out of the tent. I slipped on hiking boots and walked east to the edge of the mountain. Billowing gray clouds were forming to the south. After a balmy May day yesterday, it appeared the clouds would soon blot out the sun. I disassembled the tent quickly and stowed it in its waterproof carry sack. If it started raining and the tent got wet, I would have to pack it away wet and then dry it at home—a chore I always found bothersome.

After packing, I boiled water on the stove and poured some of it into a small plastic bowl filled with two envelopes of "peaches and cream" instant oatmeal. I finished breakfast with a cup of tea and the remaining cookies.

I hiked off the mountain and out of the wilderness under threatening skies. A half-mile before I reached the trailhead where the truck was parked, thunder boomed and a bolt of lightning knifed through the dark clouds. Almost simultaneously, a turkey gobbled loud and clear close by. He sounded like a boss tom. By mid-May, most gobblers and hens in the Ozarks are through mating. This longbeard was proclaiming either his pleasure or his displeasure at the approaching storm. I never saw the bird, but his voice sounded familiar, and it was a joy hearing him.

When I unlocked the doors of the truck and stowed my pack, the first drops of rain splattered the yellow pine dust that had settled on the windshield. The storm smelled fresh and inviting. Bell Mountain's fauna and flora would certainly benefit from the flush of rain. Shut-in Creek would build water volume quickly in a deluge. As beautiful as it is in normal weather, heavy rain would turn the narrow valley bottom into a raging beast and make camping dangerous. It could take you and your tent for an unforgettable ride.

The driver's seat felt luxurious, as it always does after a pack trip. For a moment, I envisioned last evening's sunset and the cozy "rock chair" from which I had watched it. And I thought about Bell and the many times I had planted lug soles on its wild paths and about how that primitive place made me feel totally alive. Best of all, my sleeping with Bell had sealed the bond between us. And once the bond is made with wilderness, it is forever lasting. I would miss her and vowed to return soon.

4

Devil's Backbone Wilderness

In God's wilderness lies the hope of the world—the great, fresh, un-blighted, unredeemed wilderness, the falling harness of civilization drops off and the wounds heal.

JOHN MUIR

WHY NOT ANGEL'S Backbone or Saint's Backbone—something bright and heavenly? The devil has no place hiking game trails in such a divine work of nature. Is it a foreboding place? Heavens no!

The wilderness takes its name from a long, spiny, north-south "backbone" about nine hundred feet above Crooked Creek. Despite its hellish name, the hike on top is heavenly, and below the devilish ridge snakes a generous portion of rugged wilderness belly.

Thomas R. Beveridge, an author published by the Missouri Department of Natural Resources, explains why many Missouri names include "devil." He says that settlers from the Appalachian highlands were largely of Scotch-Irish descent. Their concern with the devil was undoubtedly, in many cases, a result of Calvinistic influences. Beveridge says the preoccupation of pioneer Missourians with the devil is dramatized by the dozens of natural features considered to be creations, haunts, or even corporeal parts of the devil. There are more than eighty natural features in Missouri that are "officially" named after the devil. Devil's Backbone Wilderness is one of them. No natural surface features involving angels were found. This is in sharp contrast to the western United States, where Latin-American influence predominated, and the names of features often include allusions to angels and heaven.

Folklore born and buried in the wilderness is worth preserving. The shadowy haunts and spooky "hollers" seemed to early settlers to be the work of the devil. When you hike into Devil's Backbone today, you might experience the odd feeling that someone or something is watching, especially if you are supernaturally inclined. Noises just off the trail—running, walking, or shuffling sounds—are hard to explain. Naturally, you believe them to be wild turkeys, deer, or squirrels scampering in the leaf litter. But for some strange reason, there is rarely any clear proof of what's making those sounds. Animals and birds fail to materialize. So you continue walking, telling yourself there is nothing to fear. The ghosts of Devil's Backbone, and the mysterious legends conjured there, are buried deep in forest ground. Or are they?

My first visit to Devil's Backbone Wilderness was during a three-day spring turkey hunt in 1987. This was no ordinary turkey hunt, and I remember those days in late April as if they just occurred. It was one of those memorable trips that was seasoned with good people, splendid scenery, high adventure, diversity, and success. Ron Kruger, a magazine editor, had asked me if I would be interested in joining him and hunting guide Joe Hollingshad on a mule-back turkey hunt in Devil's Backbone. Riding mules anywhere makes for adventure. But using a mule for transportation in the wilderness had that certain "buried treasure" ring to it. The action actually started before we rode into hunting camp, when Ron and I met Joe and Gina Hollingshad at their dairy farm near Dora.

After brief introductions, the Hollingshads led three saddled mules from the corral to the farmyard, where Ron and I waited. The animals seemed docile enough, but when Ron tried to swing his leg over "Dolly's" saddle, she bolted, and Ron, who claims no previous rodeo experience, bailed off without hesitation and landed squarely on two feet. He managed a wry grin and a hearty "wow." Joe fixed the bit in Dolly's mouth, apparently the source of the problem, and told Ron to try again. This time he got into the saddle. I mounted a pure white mule named Ajax without incident. Joe took control of a large, handsome mule named Alvis. We said goodbye to Gina and began the nine-mile ride to camp.

It took but fifteen minutes on muleback to access the McGarr Ridge Wilderness Trail off Highway CC. We would ride in a south-westerly direction until we reached camp on the east bank of the North Fork River. Some of the finest public land for hunting wild turkeys in the state, and the nation for that matter, is found on the Mark Twain National Forest in south central Missouri. The Wilderness Areas within the system offer the adventurous an edge be-cause relatively few hunters penetrate the steep ridges of the forest, where no motors are allowed. There are easier places to hunt turkeys, where vehicular access is permitted. Having dealt with mules before on various backcountry trips, I figured the balky crea-tures, including Ajax, would probably spring some surprises whether we liked it or not. I was right. Halfway into the ride, we crossed Crooked Creek, a main tributary of the North Fork. The crossing looked simple enough; the water ranged from one foot to stirrup-deep near the opposite bank. Joe was in the lead when we splashed our way across. His mule had no problems getting to the other side and climbing up a moderately steep bank onto the flat, heavily vegetated land above.

Ajax ignored my attempts to get him to follow Joe's mule and opted for a different route, one that led to the bank's most precari-ous-looking perch, chock-full of brush and low-hanging trees. Using a series of lunges and sideslips, accompanied by loud bray-ing, my mule reached the top but was stopped short of getting us both on flat land by a wall of vegetation. Before us was a web of thick grapevines; behind us, about one inch from Ajax's rump, was a ten-foot drop. I faced being hanged by the grapevines or doing an awkward back flip, with a camera dangling around my neck, into the frigid water of the creek. Bailing off was my only chance. To make matters worse, two feet away, Ron's mule was surging up the bank behind Ajax and me.

Ajax was getting more nervous by the second and so was I. Eject-ing from the saddle the best I could, and taking a camera body hard to the chin in the process, I somehow managed to land on my two feet. Just barely. Solid ground brought immediate relief. I managed to lead the white mule through the jungle and into the clearing, where Joe waited with a half-cocked grin and a lightly oiled com-pliment: "You made it." Ron followed seconds later, shaking his head while mouthing his customary exclamation, "Wow!" The look, part astonishment, part fear, on his face soon gave way to the utter joy of arriving at the clearing in one piece. I knew how he felt. Through some unsophisticated instinct between their huge ears, mules, I think, sometimes sense when their riders have had enough punishment for one day. The rest of the ride to camp lacked the rodeo drama of the initial charge into Devil's Backbone. We settled comfortably into the trail and the magnificent scenery around us.

While weaving our way along a path through thick, emerald bottomland grasses, Ron suddenly reined his mule to a stop and suggested we take a photo break. He slid off Dolly and was removing the lens cap from his camera when a patch of grass exploded ten feet away. Dolly and Ajax spooked as a hen turkey rose laboriously from her hiding spot. There was no grace in her liftoff, just pure determination to gain altitude and escape the intruders.

Ron was so shaken by the bird's getaway that he never lifted the camera to shoot. The turkey noisily cleared the treetops and vanished out of sight. We all sensed that the hen was probably on her nest. He walked gingerly to the spot where the launch had taken place and confirmed the presence of a simple, shallow impression in the grass filled with a dozen white eggs—size grade A large. We took turns photographing the wonders of nature and motherhood and then beat a hasty retreat from the spot so the hen could resume incubation. For Ron and me the turkey nest sighting was a first. Joe told us if we had not stopped along the trail, the hen would have remained motionless and allowed us to ride by. We wanted her to return as quickly as possible.

For a while the trail continued to snake through lush hollows filled with grass and wildflowers, then it abruptly reared up on horseshoe switchbacks laced with oak, dogwood, redbud, walnut, hickory, and shortleaf pine trees. As occasionally happens, the dogwoods and redbuds were both blooming. Redbuds usually show first and dogwoods follow. The showy white of dogwood flowers and the pink wash of eastern redbud taken together was one of nature's finest art exhibits.

Save for a smattering of old rusted and flattened tin beverage cans, there was very little evidence of hard use or abuse in Devil's Backbone. In Missouri, as in other states, the overwhelming majority of citizens prefer motorized locomotion over foot power. There are certainly no waiting lines at trailheads. For those who enjoy walking and camping in unspoiled places, solitude in the Backbone is abundant.

Our mule train was moving right along with very little conversation among the riders. Each one of us was comfortable alone with his thoughts. My musing made me laugh out loud at something that Kruger had complained about several miles back. When he heard me laugh, the editor turned around. "What's so funny?" "You," I said. "You wishing that you could keep your mule walking in the straight line."

Having been behind Ron and Dolly since the creek crossing, I noticed that about every ten steps, Kruger would vigorously rein hard to the right and shout some words I won't mention. That was because every ten steps the mule veered to the left as though she were metal drawn off the trail by a magnet. Dolly no doubt had a diagonal personality, and if Ron would have allowed the mule freedom of choice he could have very well "diagonaled" from southern Missouri to Washington State. She was some mule!

The big tent near the water's edge appeared like a mirage. Saddle numb the past few miles, I had lost track of time and figured we had more riding ahead of us. But there it was, tucked in the trees with the North Fork gurgling softly thirty yards away. The low sun painted the bluff across the river a pale yellow. Campfire smoke curled slowly around the limbs of a broad, friendly cedar tree. The aroma of grilled meat and fried onions overwhelmed fragrant cedar, but nobody was complaining. Ron groaned as he dismounted. "If you don't mind, I think I'll walk tomorrow," he announced to nobody in particular.

The man responsible for the succulent aroma rising from the fire was Don Schnable, a friend of Joe's who would serve as camp cook over the next three days. Schnable had packed in camp the day before. There were steaks cooked over hickory coals on an open grill. On the camp stove, a large cast-iron skillet brimmed with potatoes and onions. Ears of corn simmered in a pot on another burner. A plastic milk crate submerged in an ice-cold spring about the size of a kitchen sink held a generous supply of cold drinks. Kruger and I were told to help ourselves.

I've spent a lot of quality time in Missouri Wilderness Areas more or less "roughing it" with basic backpack equipment and simple food. I enjoy the bare-bones approach when communing with nature. After two or three days, body and mind respond positively to no-frills outdoor living. It's like shedding unwanted baggage. There's no phone, no fax, no dot coms, no motors. There is no finer method for gaining or regaining a zest for life and no better therapy for fine-tuning the dulled senses of a city-worn mind and body.

But I certainly had no reservations about roughing it in style occasionally. Beasts of burden can make that happen. Joe Hollingshad's mules provided the muscle power without violating the sanctity of wilderness. What the guides created reminded me of an African safari camp, complete with table, chairs, fine food, and drink plus a strong sense of backcountry luxury. After the long, bumpy ride into camp, the refinements felt just fine. The welcome banquet that followed proved to be as tasty as the aroma that had preceded it.

We lingered around the table, drinking coffee and puffing long, mild cigars that Ron passed out after dinner. Without much prodding, talk turned to turkey hunting, the prognosis and plans for the morning hunt. Breakfast would be served at 4 A.M. We would leave camp by five and hike about a mile to a ridge where Joe had been hearing gobblers since the season began.

After plans were made, we had about an hour of daylight left. Just enough time to sample an inviting bluff hole on the other side of the river. Ron pulled on a pair of chest waders and headed to the river with his fly rod. I used one of the two canoes that Joe had paddled into camp a few days ago. Devil's Backbone Wilderness is uniquely blessed with the presence of the North Fork River, one of Missouri's finest float and fishing streams. Each of the options for getting to camp, paddling, hiking, or riding, offers adventure with a different perspective on the wonders of this unique treasure.

I used a light-action spinning rod and reel with an assortment of small spinners and 1/32–ounce lead jigs with soft plastic bodies. My favorite colors for Ozark streams are black and brown, which imitate live crayfish and hellgrammites—favorite foods of smallmouth bass, rock bass, locally called "goggle-eye," and panfish. The river also holds good populations of brown and rainbow trout.

Ron quickly discovered that the river's surprisingly deep water prevented him from reaching the promising water below the bluff. With the canoe I was able position myself in a back eddy close to the bluff. Ron is a fine fly caster, but I had the edge on him. Within twenty minutes I had landed and released a dozen fish, two of them smallmouth that exceeded the twelve-inch length limit. The rest were hand-sized rock bass. I told my partner if he wanted to join me in the boat I'd put my rod down and paddle him into position for reaching fish with his fly rod. He agreed. After I stroked the canoe back to the shallow bank, Ron waded across and took his seat in the bow. Dusk was upon us. But now the fly rodder could show off his skills. Using a streamer-type fly called a Clauser minnow, he caught either a smallmouth or rock bass on nearly every cast. He was grinning from ear to ear when we called it quits. We both agreed that tomorrow we would keep some of the rock bass and longear sunfish for a camp fish fry.

Joe and Don had a roaring fire crackling and a fresh pot of coffee on the stove when we returned. Down in the river bottom, the damp night air was cool. The lightweight fleece camouflage jacket I pulled from my duffel felt good. A barred owl up on the ridge sounded its nasal nine-note proclamation. Tomorrow we would imitate that same call and try to "shock" a tom into gobbling. As smart as wild turkeys are, they are commonly fooled into giving away their positions by the calls of owls and crows. If turkeys ever learned to keep their mouths shut, most hunters, including myself, would be hard-pressed to locate them.

Before bunking down in individual tents, the four of us sat around the fire, mesmerized by the dancing flames mostly and feeling good about where we were and what we would be doing in the morning. Joe was a man of carefully chosen words, but when he spoke of the beauty and the bounty of fish, game, and scenery in Devil's Backbone, his voice had filled with emotion. He had grown up within a mile of the forest, and he knew every ridge and hollow in the area's 6,595 acres. There was the distinct possibility that as an avid hunter, fisherman, and amateur naturalist, he knew the Backbone better than anybody else.

He told fascinating stories of deer, turkeys, mountain lions, timber rattlers, and wild pigs. Being the consummate editor, Ron, who had been slouching in his chair and thoroughly relaxed, was forced to scramble for notebook and pen to record the guide's recollections. Upon returning, he questioned the presence of wild lions. Joe responded with certainty: "They're here!" I believed him. Ron wasn't so sure.

Ron was the first to excuse himself from the fire ring an hour later. His day had begun at 4 A.M. with the drive from St. Louis. That, combined with the long ride to camp on a crossways mule, had done him in. I followed a short time later. Bedding down on a foam pad and snuggling into cocoon-shaped sleeping bag, I swiftly found slumber, pleasant transport into the world of dreams.

The murmur of low voices, the hiss of the Coleman stove, and the smell of frying sausage eased me into a pleasant awakening. I dressed quickly in the coolness, unzipped the tent flap, and frog-walked through the low entry. Ron was already up and sitting close to the fire. Don kept watch over a frying pan full of sausage patties. Joe was pulling on a camouflage vest. Stars glittered in the blackness. When the fried eggs were done, we ate as though we had never eaten. Strong, black camp coffee provided a sensual stimulus that efficiently removed the cobwebs left over from a good night's sleep. We did not linger at the table but instead readied our shotguns and hunting gear.

We had a long, uphill hike ahead of us but took our time for the sake of moving quietly through the woods. The gradual ascending grade was not particularly taxing. It felt good to walk even though I could feel the effects of yesterday's mule ride in my buttocks and thighs. I figured by the end of the morning the saddle soreness would work itself out. Ron and I were happy about Joe's decision to hike rather than ride to the hunting area. Ron admitted he was pretty sore all over—even his arms and hands hurt from trying to keep Dolly on the trail.

The black of night was grudgingly giving way to the misty vagueness of false dawn. We stopped every few minutes to listen for the birds that sang early. There is a pattern to the melody in the spring woods, and it usually starts with whippoorwills, fades into barred owls, and sometimes reaches a blood-pumping crescendo with the first lovesick turkey of the morning. This can happen during false dawn. Or it may not happen until true dawn when the sun breaks over the ridges. No two hunts are ever the same. Wild turkeys have mastered a wide array of diversionary instincts.

There was no hint of breeze—perfect for hearing the reveille of barred owls and crows—those winged antagonizers that spur toms into gobbling while they are still perched in evening roost trees. Despite perfect conditions, the forest remained unusually quiet. We reached the top of the ridge and stood there for a few moments. Suddenly, one gobble, then another echoed from the ridge across the river from camp. Joe moved in close to where Ron and I stood. "I thought about heading over there this morning," he whispered, "but decided on this spot instead. It was a toss-up." The gobbling continued with one bird cutting off the other in the middle of a throaty plea for the company of hens. Then we heard a third turkey gobble across the river. "Wouldn't you know it," the guide muttered in a disgusted tone of voice. For a moment Joe stood there, no doubt debating the merits of turning around and heading back along the route we had just followed so we could eventually cross the river. A few seconds later he turned and motioned us to follow him. We would continue with the original plan. Gobbling from across the river continued loud and clear.

We were on the ridge where Joe had been hearing gobblers for the past week. We could tell by the look on his face that he was concerned about the sudden stillness of birds that had been so vocal. There was a slight chance they could have been spooked by other hunters. But he had seen no evidence of vehicles at the trailhead, nor had he recently crossed tracks with any other humans in this section of Devil's Backbone.

We stood silently at the spot where we had first topped the ridge. There was no sense barging ahead and possibly flushing turkeys that simply had a case of lockjaw. Joe's patience was remarkable, no doubt reinforced by his confidence in that specific spot. So we stood there and waited almost twenty minutes. Up until that time the only gobbling had come from across the river. Then it happened—a faint gobble rose below the ridge where we stood. Thirty seconds later, the turkey gobbled again.

"Let's close the gap on that bird," Joe whispered. We walked as fast as our legs could carry us for about thirty seconds, then stopped and listened. This time the gobble rang out loud and clear. The bird was moving in our direction. Joe motioned for Ron and me to spread out about forty yards apart and find a comfortable place to set up. He would call from about thirty yards behind us. I headed right and Ron left. The forest was popcorn dry, and every step I took made me think that wherever the turkey was he could probably hear me. I quickly settled against the base of an oak tree that would serve as a backrest and a backdrop to enhance my camouflage. It wasn't the ideal place, but it had to do. I had a feeling the tom was on his way.

We set up short of the ridge crest on a wide flat populated with mature oak, hickory, sassafras, dogwood, and redbud. It was a wide-open place with plenty of routes for a turkey to take. Suddenly Joe's voice call split the silence. The double-sounding hen yelp sounded so good I wondered if a live hen hadn't circled behind us. The gobbler responded immediately. He was getting close.

Some turkey hunters make the mistake of over-calling because they love to hear the tom gobble. In a natural situation, the hen travels to the gobbler. Hunters try to sound so much like real hens that the gobblers break their habit and do the searching. Apparently our guide chose not to call anymore, feeling that the tom was working his way into shooting range. Again, Joe displayed his patience. It took another twenty minutes before the gobbler showed himself. He was coming from left to right. The bird must have walked by Ron, possibly out of shotgun range or camouflaged by the weeds and shrubs. The turkey kept angling toward me. I had the semiautomatic twelve-gauge shotgun in the ready position braced on my knee. It seemed like he was taking forever to close the gap. Then I lost sight of him. I was afraid the bird had spotted me and done an about-face.

At least twenty seconds passed. He should have been right in front of me now, about thirty yards away. I waited. Suddenly he appeared close to where I thought he would. His red wattles and ivory crown were glowing in the soft light of morning. He stopped behind a tree, hiding most of his body. He craned his neck one way, then the other, searching for the "hen" he had heard. Quickly the tom turned around and retraced several steps. I sensed he was spooked by something. But he turned again, walking past the tree where he had stopped a minute ago. The gobbler paused in the open, looking around for a companion. He had made a fatal mistake. The twelve-gauge roared, and the kill was clean and swift. He was a fine mature gobbler that weighed about twenty pounds.

Neither Joe nor Ron had seen the bird walk in. Ron had set up in front of a small rise for better camouflage. Although he said he could hear the turkey walking in the dry leaves, the bird must have stepped behind the rise and then angled toward my position. I credited Joe's double-sounding hen yelp for hooking the gobbler's curiosity and passion.

It was mid-morning. On a good turkey day, toms commonly gobble until noon or so. But at 10 A.M. this particular day all was quiet save for the raspy cawing of crows. In Missouri, the spring season closes at 1 P.M. each day. Some say it's to protect hens on the nest from intruding hunters. The real reason probably has more to do with enforcement of the turkey hunting regulations—making sure hunters check in their harvested birds the same day they shoot them, during daylight hours. Even though we didn't hear any turkeys, it was still early enough in the day to stand a good chance of calling in a gobbler. Now it was Ron's turn. Joe showed us another prime location, and we set up. It was near the head of a wide, gently sloping point that nurtured a beautiful stand of mature white oak trees. There were abundant fresh turkey scratchings in the leaf litter.

Ron was in a favorable position about twenty-five yards forward of where Joe and I sat with our backs up against a pair of wide oak trees. Joe sounded his double hen yelp, and I scratched clucks and purrs with a fiberglass peg on my slate call. After thirty minutes of intermittent calling and stone-still waiting, we gave up on the spot. Joe already had another idea. We would work our way slowly back to camp, pausing often to listen and perhaps do some random calling at likely locations. If nothing happened along the way, we would leave Ron at a special spot along the trail that our guide was familiar with, a unique location where turkeys congregated early in the afternoon when temperatures rose. It was a wildlife pond that had been dug by the Forest Service back in the 1950s, well before the area became designated Wilderness. Nearly all of Missouri's Wilderness Areas have these man-made ponds. They provide a reliable source of water for animal life. Shortleaf pines that were planted as seedlings around those ponds are now forty years old and they, along with native grasses, shrubs like sumac, and other trees like redbud and dogwood, provide both shade and cover. It is common to find deer, turkey, and raccoon tracks in the soft earth surrounding these forest oases.

We eventually reached the pond, having had no luck hearing or calling turkeys. Ron had confidence in Joe's plan. It was a mile back to camp along the main trail, so there was no chance of his getting lost. While Ron was hunting, Joe and I would head back to camp, take one of the canoes, and paddle four miles downstream so we could check my turkey in at a conservation department station before it closed at 3 P.M. One of Joe's trucks was parked at the take-out spot, so we could drive the rest of the way to the store that served as the check station. After checking the bird, cleaning it, and storing the gobbler in Joe's walk-in cooler, we would put the canoe in above camp at the North Fork campground and float about two miles downstream to our tent camp. I was looking forward to the change of pace. We said goodby to Ron and bid him good luck.

After drinking coffee with Don back at camp, we loaded the

gobbler and a couple of spinning rods and paddled downstream. Rainbow Spring entered the North Fork a mile below camp, and the cold, clear water holds a good population of brown trout. In between paddle strokes from the bow I was able to make several casts using a number two bronze-bladed in-line spinner. It was in the middle of one shallow water riffle at Rainbow Spring that I hooked and landed my only catch, a colorful, stubby brown trout that nailed the Roostertail spinner. The fish, which I released, was about ten inches long.

After checking the turkey and field dressing it back at Joe and Gina's farm, we drove to the North Fork campground and launched the canoe. It was close to 4 P.M. when we ground to a halt in the shallow water in front of camp. After beaching the boat, we found Ron and Don sitting comfortably around the campfire. The delicious smell of a pot roast simmering in the cast-iron dutch oven reminded me of a farmhouse kitchen on a lazy Sunday afternoon. I was hoping Ron had bagged a turkey.

They had heard us coming and before I could ask Ron about his hunt, he blurted out, "You're not going to believe this—but it's true. Right, Don?" They stared each other in the eyes, and whatever it was, the cook agreed without hesitation.

"We had a mountain lion go right through camp. About an hour ago. Right through there. We saw him big as life." Joe and I looked at each other and grinned. "See, what did I tell you last night and you didn't much believe me," Joe said. "I do now," Ron snapped. "He was only ten yards away and never broke stride. Never even looked at us as far as I could tell."

Joe told us that while he had spotted mountain lions in Devil's Backbone on several occasions, he had never seen one this close to the river. The best look he had ever had at a lion was on the Collins Ridge Trail two years ago in November. He was riding Alvis and towing Ajax. The latter was carrying camping equipment in preparation for firearms deer season. The lion bounded across the trail fifteen yards in front of the guide and his mules. Miraculously, Alvis and Ajax never spooked. Joe, however, had been looking off to the right for no particular reason. First he saw a blur through the trees, and his mind registered deer. But something didn't jive. When the lion hit the clearing in full stride, Joe focused squarely on him, seeing his tawny form and long tail flowing gracefully behind. There was no sign of a collar or an indentation on the skin where a collar had been. "That ol' boy was nobody's runaway pet. I'd bet my life on it," he said.

The Missouri Department of Conservation (MDC) had long denied the existence of both mountain lions and black bears in Missouri. The agency finally admitted that bears were migrating from northern Arkansas into southern Missouri, but most of the lion sightings in the state, all originating in southern Missouri, were dismissed by the department as somebody's pets gone astray. It wasn't until 1996 and 1997 that MDC grudgingly confessed there was a possibility that wild mountain lions (also called cougars, pumas, and panthers) could exist in the remote areas of the Ozarks. With abundant populations of whitetail deer and turkeys already in place and growing, the food base that could sustain lions was certainly a reality.

Joe felt that sightings had become more frequent since the 1980s due to the establishment of designated Wilderness. While relatively small in acreage compared to western wilderness, large blocks of prime, protected habitat in the east make suitable homes for lions and bears. Both carnivores are native to the state. They disappeared because of unregulated hunting practices and widespread forest habitat destruction. Now that there is again suitable habitat and ample food, they are returning. Currently no hunting is allowed for either species.

The next morning, before dawn, the three of us crossed the river in a canoe. We would climb, under a veil of darkness, the steep, trailless ridge where the turkeys had been so vocal the day before. For fear of spooking the birds, we left our flashlights off, which made the going tricky. Saplings swatted us where it hurt. Greenbriar thorns clawed at our ankles. We sweated freely. But it was the only way to get on top of gobbler ridge. The only opportunity to set up in good position and hope that the birds were again feeling talkative.

An hour later, after trying two locations without success, we settled into the third zone. It was there we heard gobbling for the first time. And now we watched Ron crawl on his belly through the grass and trees in order to close the distance between him and the gobbler. Neither Joe nor I approved of the tactic. It was dangerous. Ron had altered his silhouette, and he now looked very much like a turkey himself. And what if there happened to be another hunter moving in on the bird who mistook Ron for the gobbler? Joe whispered to me that Ron would probably spook the bird. He should have waited patiently for the gobbler to come to the call.

Thirty seconds later, when Ron was out of sight, a shotgun blast shattered the morning stillness. For what seemed like an eternity, there was no movement. Then we spotted Ron walking quickly up-hill onto a thin secondary ridge covered with oak saplings. By the time we reached Ron, he was kneeling down by his trophy and grinning from ear to ear. He told us the gobbler had been sur-rounded by hens, and he could not get a clear shot at him. That's why he had crawled. When he stopped moving, the tom was nowhere in sight, but he could hear the hens yelping and clucking. Then the longbeard showed himself big and bold.

It had taken nearly three hours from the time we first set up that morning for Ron to finish the hunt. At the check station later, Ron's turkey was officially weighed at 22½ pounds. The bird had an 11½-inch beard and 1¼-inch spurs. He was a true boss tom who'd had a generous harem of hens at his side. Ron was elated, even after the long hike and short canoe ride back to camp.

On the way back we came across a whitetail deer skeleton that was completely intact. The buck wore a thick, symmetrical eight-point rack. It is unusual to find a complete skeleton. Coyotes and ro-dents generally pick and gnaw the bones apart; however, this deer had fallen into a most inaccessible spot near the bottom. I tied the skull and antlers onto my daypack. Joe didn't seem that impressed with the rack. "We've got heads in the Backbone that make that one look like a baby." The man of few words was indirectly inviting us back in the fall to hunt deer with bow and arrow.

We stayed in camp another day, spending most of the time fish-ing for bass and trout. The next day we packed out. Ron elected to canoe out with Don. Joe let me ride Alvis, "the cadillac of mules," as he put it. The guide rode Dolly on a remarkably straight course with Ajax in tow. During the ride I thought a lot about the Devil's Backbone Wilderness—the hunting, fishing, camping, and hiking it had provided over the past few days. Some people travel thou-sands of miles to find the solitude and quality outdoor adventure that we enjoyed close to home. Smooth-gaited Alvis made it easy for me to daydream along the way. Actually, I was deep into the pleasure of planning another trip to the Backbone. This time I would bring my family. We would backpack in and camp and fish along the river. Mid-October, when the sugar maples turn bright yellow, and dogwood berries are shiny crimson, would be a perfect time. Now that I had experienced the stunning beauty of Devil's Backbone myself, I wanted to share it with others.

Each Missouri Wilderness Area has a distinct "personality." On Devil's Backbone elevations range from 1,020 feet to about 680 feet along the North Fork of the White River. The North Fork flows through the Wilderness for approximately one and a half miles. Blue Spring, Amber Spring, and McGarr Spring are high-quality permanent water sources that provide water to the river year-round. Eighteen man-made wildlife ponds provide water in upland areas where natural water sources are deficient. In spring, it is easy to find these ponds, even when they are hidden in vegetation, by the high piping whistle of a spring peeper, a chorus frog found throughout the Ozarks. These tiny brown or gray frogs sing night and day, and although they whistle loud and clear, they are rarely seen. Spring in Ozark wilderness would not be the same without the peepers' fluted serenade.

The forest is dominated by a variety of oak, hickory and shortleaf pine. In the spring, as the peepers pipe their music, dogwood, redbud, and wild azaleas dress Devil's Backbone in spectacular color. Rhododendron roseum, or azalea, is found primarily along the North Fork River. Native Ozarkians commonly call this fragrant woody shrub honeysuckle. There are small scattered limestone glades throughout the forest. These openings in an otherwise "crowded" forest habitat are ideal for taking a break—sitting and watching wilderness vistas and occasionally catching a glimpse of a coyote or red-tailed hawk. Glades are the trailheads of dreams. The wildlife species are typical of forests throughout the Ozarks. This includes, in addition to the animals I've already mentioned, red and gray fox, bobcat, and striped skunk, great horned owl, bald eagle (late fall and winter) great blue heron, green heron, a small population of ruffed grouse, and various songbirds. Beaver and muskrat are found along the North Fork River and in permanent creeks.

Among the reptiles found in the area, two are poisonous snakes, the copperhead and eastern timber rattler. The rattlesnake is encountered by humans infrequently. Copperheads are more numerous, but they are rarely seen because their tan and gray hourglass markings allow them to blend so well into leaf litter and rocks. For the most part, copperheads are silent. Although some of them do vibrate their tails when alarmed, they have no rattles that sound warnings. In over twenty years of hiking, camping, and hunting in Missouri Wilderness Areas, I have encountered only three poisonous snakes. I saw all three in Piney Creek Wilderness during spring turkey seasons. One was a five-and-a-half-foot timber rattler coiled on quarter-size pieces of rock halfway down a steep ridge. The other two were copperheads, about twelve to fifteen inches each, both at trailheads. Fortunately, the timber rattler gave me plenty of warning with its buzzing tail. I have never been bitten by a snake.

Evidence of man's early presence at Devil's Backbone is seen in its approximately twenty-four miles of old settlement and logging roads, wildlife ponds, wildlife food plots, and segments of utility right-of-ways. Today, there are very few "new" signs of man save for infrequent trail maintenance, mainly the clearing away of trees that have fallen. In areas of high horse use, once-soft, quiet trails thick with leaves have been scarred by horseshoes kicking up rocks and the resultant trail erosion.

If there be a serious problem in the seven Wilderness Areas managed by the U.S. Forest Service in Missouri, it is that since 1994 there has only been one ranger at a time assigned to the Mark Twain National Forest, one ranger to patrol 63,628 acres of designated wild lands. Congressionally mandated downsizing and staff cuts in the Mark Twain, as well as in other federal forests, have severely diminished manpower. While the wilderness is self-sustaining and virtually free of heavy-handed timber management prescriptions, there remains the need to guard the lands from real and perceived abuses. Such violations include motorized traffic, illegal timber harvesting, excessive horse use on fragile trails, vandalism of signs and trailhead stations, and dumping of trash. The daily presence of a wilderness ranger for all the areas is not necessary. But maintaining contact with wilderness users on a regular basis is important, as is ensuring the safety of trails. Increasing numbers of wilderness users may have a serious impact on the very values they seek. To assure that these values remain intact, visible wilderness rangers can monitor and evaluate the low-impact manners of visitors and observe firsthand whether or not wilderness regulations are obeyed. Rangers are effective disseminators of educational information that enhances the recreational experiences of visitors. The wilderness ranger is a goodwill ambassador who can spot many potential problems before the damage is done.

Devil's Backbone was designated a Wilderness on December 22, 1980. It is a place of unique beauty and solitude, a backcountry sanctuary that will look pretty much the same one hundred years from now. It will have no malls, no housing developments, and no "No Trespassing" signs.

A friend and I visited the Backbone recently. It was mid-May, and the forest world was a deep emerald green in the misty lushness of spring. We had four designated trailheads to choose from: Blue Spring Trail from the North Fork Recreation Area (known locally as Hammond Camp), Collins Ridge, McGarr Ridge, or Raccoon Hollow. We chose McGarr because of its remoteness. Our goal was simple. We wanted a day hike that would take us down past Crooked Creek and a short bushwhack to whatever part of the North Fork was most conducive for soaking up sunshine and dangling our feet in spring-fed waters. Our small packs held sandwiches—ham and cheese on rye—Oreo cookies, water bottles filled to the brim, and four granola bars each, just in case.

With light loads, we moved at a brisk pace, mostly downhill. It was spring, and there was spring in our steps. We scanned either side of the narrow, rocky trail as we hiked. We were hunters without guns searching for the glint of an eyeball, the flicker of a brown ear, the red, white, and blue of a tom turkey's head and neck. We heard plenty of that rumbling off in the forest so typical of the Backbone. It was the sound of wildlife we thought, but we never saw it.

Down off the mountain we strode, reaching level ground thick with grass, weeds, blackberry bramble, and wildflowers. There's no forest down in the bottoms. We couldn't see the North Fork, but we knew it was there, hidden by willow trees and shrubs. A faint narrow path materialized before us. So we followed it, bending low under the maze of limbs until finally we broke out into the open and beheld the glistening North Fork. The river's rolling current was streaked with varying shades of emerald green and aqua blue. We stood transfixed and silent for several minutes, totally alone with our thoughts. The only sound was the quiet gurgling of gentle riffles.

The narrow path we followed had a purpose. It ended undramatically at water's edge but provided a perfect spot for lounging. A large, smooth rock the size of a bathtub had been warmed by the sun. Although lacking the softness of an easy chair, the rock was the throne from which our feet dangled effortlessly in the North Fork's chilly water. It was a place for reflection . . . and a near-perfect picnic spot.

We had finished our sandwiches and most of the cookies when suddenly two canoes appeared. The floaters, two young couples, paddled midstream and waved to us. We waved back and watched as they disappeared around a downstream bend in the river. They were the first and last people in the wilderness that day. We lingered for an hour or more, content with the river's company and the sun's soothing warmth. Then we hiked back up into the hills under the canopy of late afternoon shade. Thigh muscles worked overtime, but muscle power felt good. A trek into the Devil's Backbone Wilderness need not be a major expedition. A simple day trip has the power to replenish, to get body and mind up and humming.

5

Hercules Glades Wilderness

The more civilized man becomes, the more he needs and craves a great background of forest wildness, to which he may return like a contrite prodigal from the husks of an artificial life.

ELLEN BURNS SHERMAN

EACH MISSOURI Wilderness is unique. But two of them, Hercules Glades and Mingo, are vastly different from the rest. Both lie in the southern part of the state, Hercules Glades in the west, Mingo in the east. They were Missouri's first designated Wilderness Areas, chosen in 1976. Mingo, unlike the other Wilderness Areas, is managed by the U.S. Fish and Wildlife Service. Hercules Glades is under the authority of the Forest Service, and it's the area I'll discuss in this chapter.

Hercules Glades' 12,315 acres is situated where the Ozark Mountains meet the prairie. Named for the tiny village of Hercules just outside the northeast boundary of the wilderness off Highway 125, it is located in Taney County, twenty miles east of Forsyth and sixty miles southeast of Springfield. Most of the forty-two miles of trails on Hercules run near Long Creek and within its surrounding mountains.

The eastern trailhead is located at Hercules Lookout Tower off Highway 125. It has toilets, campsites, and picnic tables and, because it is the highest point in the area, 1,382 feet, offers a panoramic view of the wilderness. If you climb to the top of the tower you can see a long ridge extending westward to Beaver Creek, a fine float fishing stream, which empties into Bull Shoals Lake. Both Upper and Lower Pilot Knob are visible in the distance. South of this ridge is Long Creek and its tributaries. It is approximately five miles from the lookout tower to the west trailhead.

Glades occur in several states in the southeastern and central United States. Robert H. Mohlenbrock, professor of botany at Southern Illinois University at Carbondale, defines glades, such as the ones in Hercules, as forest openings with exposed rocks. "Some people call them balds or knobs, while others refer to them as barrens," he says. There are six types of glades found in Missouri. Those with limestone and dolomite are the most common. Others have as their bases chert, sandstone, shale, and igneous rocks. Missouri glades, found in all the state's Wilderness Areas except Mingo, cover more than 400,000 acres. They range in size from a few hundred square feet to several hundred acres. Almost all of them are surrounded by dense, oak-dominated forests, but trees within the glade are typically eastern red cedar. Soil in the glades is not deep enough for oaks. Most glades face south and west, and the hot summer sun strikes them directly, creating an arid and generally inhospitable habitat. Mohlenbrock says, "Not even summer thundershowers moisten the ground. The water runs rapidly off shallow soil." It is the size, plant diversity, and longevity of the glades in Hercules, combined with its dense stands of oak, hickory, cedar, gum, walnut, dogwood, redbud, hawthorn, sassafras, persimmon, butternut, maple, sycamore, smoke, and fringe trees that make it unique.

I made my first trip into Hercules Glades shortly after it received Wilderness designation, not as a hiker or camper, but as a quail hunter. I was driving south on Highway 125 during a scouting mission when a covey of bobwhites rose from one side of the highway and flew perilously close over and around the hood and windshield of my truck. Most of the birds landed on the other side of the road about thirty yards from a Hercules Glades Wilderness sign not far from the lookout tower access.

I pulled off the highway, leashed Cheyenne, the Brittany spaniel riding in the travel kennel, and uncased my shotgun. At a safe distance from the road, I unsnapped the leash and allowed the Brittany to pick up the fresh scent of quail. He became birdy almost immediately, so I loaded the over-under and followed about fifteen yards behind him. Within two or three minutes, he jammed on the brakes and locked into a classic point in a weedy patch of sumac and blackberry bramble. One bobwhite flushed under the dog's nose in a frenzy of beating wings. When the bird leveled off at ten feet high and fifteen yards away, I fired. One down. Cheyenne rushed to retrieve and flushed a pair of quail before he reached the downed bird. Miraculously I held my composure and doubled, something I had not done in years.

The dog and I eventually found three more singles, one of which I shot cleanly. Four quail in under ten minutes is a record for me. My first contact with Hercules Glades was a memorable one. We walked back to the truck, where I unloaded and cased the gun, kenneled Cheyenne, and drove south another hour before doubling back on the same highway. This time I stopped at the tower and climbed to the top. The November day had turned raw, and I could feel the structure swaying ominously as I scanned the forest and bare knobs of the land below, different from any forest I had seen before.

I knew I would return to this place—maybe to hunt quail, deer, turkeys, or squirrels. Just as important, after reading a Forest Service pamphlet at the rustic registration desk, I wanted to explore the entire area. Knowing that Long Creek ran a west-east course through the heart of the Wilderness was of special interest. Waterways are the lifeblood of the land. To find them nestled and gurgling unspoiled in the heart of the forest is rare and precious.

On two other occasions, I tried to duplicate the first wilderness quail hunt. Cheyenne and I never found birds, but we had fun trying. Hercules is not exactly the picture of classic bobwhite habitat. Scruffy perimeter coverts of weeds, brush, sumac, and blackberry hold birds when the quail population is at a cyclical high. And there are a few inner fields around wildlife ponds where I occasionally flush quail. The southern Ozarks provided good habitat when farmers raised grain crops there. Now, private lands adjacent to Hercules have been converted to pasture and dairy farming, and there is not enough food and cover for quail.

I hear deer and turkey hunting are pretty good in Hercules, although I have never hunted there. I have seen both whitetails and gobblers during early-spring and midwinter hikes. One of these years I may forego the two other Missouri Wilderness Areas I hunt regularly and give Hercules a try. I can visualize sitting at the edge of the oak forest, looking out on Coy Bald, waiting for a buck to step into a clearing.

But hunting is not all there is to do on Hercules Glades. If you enjoy watching wildlife, you will find plenty of it. Aside from whitetails, turkeys, and quail, there are raccoons, cottontail rabbits, gray and fox squirrels, skunks, foxes, numerous songbirds, road-runners, lizards, including the colorful collared lizard, tarantulas and stinger-tailed scorpions. You might also encounter the occasional copperhead and timber or pygmy rattlesnake. The grassland glades certainly have a Southwest desert connection.

One September, about two years after my quail hunt in Hercules, my family and I were headed out for an early morning hike. Our choice was a four-mile loop around Pees Hollow on the northeast section. We were half a mile from the Hercules Tower Trailhead, driving on Highway 125, when I noticed something in the road ahead. It look like an asphalt truck had spilled some of its load on the highway. There were black golf-ball–size globs covering much of the surface. I slowed down. I was nearly on top of them when I thought I saw one of the globs moving. Then my wife, who normally remains calm, screamed. The kids jumped up from the backseat to look through the windows. My brain finally translated lifeless balls of asphalt into big, crawling, hairy spiders: tarantulas!

I pulled the car onto the shoulder. From that position, we counted nearly one hundred tarantulas. But there were many more than that. We finally worked up enough nerve to get out of the vehicle for a closer look. I knew that tarantulas were typically sluggish, and the ones on the road ahead did seem to be moving slowly. And while they can inflict a sharp bite in some instances, they are not poisonous. In fact, some people keep them as pets.

The hairy critters were moving off one side of the road and heading into the wilderness fringe. There were traveling in a mass about twenty yards wide. Some of the tarantulas had been flattened by cars and trucks. My daughter and son, both under eight years old at the time, shrieked when they saw them. The parade of giant spiders did resemble a scene from a horror movie. We stood and watched the procession for ten minutes—my wife and I amazed at the relatively organized and seemingly endless line crossing the road and going into the woods.

We drove away from the spot, knowing full well we would contribute to the casualty count of tarantulas. There was simply no way around them. We had driven to Hercules to hike, and we wanted to get started while the air was still cool. The image of those spiders remained with us throughout our four-hour walk. After a picnic lunch at the tower campground, we headed back home. As we approached the place where the tarantulas had crossed, we could see the procession was over. The spiders were no doubt somewhere in Hercules Glades, going wherever they needed to go. Maybe they were getting an early start for autumn and winter survival. It was difficult to block out the nightmarish thought of setting up camp in the wilderness that night and somehow being in the path of hundreds of tarantulas going who knew where. We saw that a significant number had been killed by passing motorists. We wondered how many other travelers had been awed by this show of nature.

To the best of my recollection, the spider march occurred in 1983. And if I'm not mistaken, winter that year was unusually harsh, with snow laying on the ground for almost a month. Although I have no scientific evidence, I am convinced that the band of giant spiders had sensed the coming of a difficult winter that year. They somehow gathered together to migrate for the winter, and in their path was a treacherous, man-made highway. Those who crossed safely may very well have made it to their safe haven—a place, I suppose, that only tarantulas know about.

I make at least one or two trips to Hercules each fall. I go mainly to hike and shoot photos but partly in hopes of experiencing another tarantula migration. I have not seen another tarantula migration, nor have I ever come across another tarantula in Hercules Glades. The only one I've seen since that day was near Beaver Creek, not far from the Wilderness, while I was on a late-summer camping trip.

Hercules Glades is forty-six miles from my home in Ozark, Missouri. (Piney Creek Wilderness is forty-seven miles away.) I feel blessed by this close proximity. No matter how heavy my physical and mental baggage, I know I am an unhurried hour's drive on winding roads away from peaceful sanctuary. I can drive an hour, hike an hour, then drive back home under the soothing influence of wilderness medicine. It does not take a major expedition to produce sufficient elixir of wilderness for an enduring uplift. Solitude, silence, fragrance, nature, independence, and exercise are miracle ingredients.

It was on March 21 and 22, 1995, that a friend decided we needed a strong dose of Hercules Glades. Temperatures had hovered in the sixties and seventies for the past ten days, and the time was right for an overnight backpacking trip. After lunch at the Hercules campground, we readied our gear and were just on the verge of heading to the trailhead when a car with Kansas license plates pulled into the parking spot next to us.

I recognized the logo of my alma mater on the back bumper. I had graduated from Kansas State University in 1966. Three young men emerged from the compact car and began stretching. I initiated a conversation by asking how everything was in Manhattan, the cozy city where K-State is located. They all smiled and assured me that everything was in pretty good shape there. Then one of them came over and introduced himself.

He explained that they were on spring break and wanted to devote their vacation to hiking and camping in the mountains. They had driven from Manhattan to Colorado but found the higher elevations packed with deep snow. All the alpine lakes were still frozen. One of the guys in the group had heard that southern Missouri had Wilderness Areas, so they had doubled back across Kansas and headed for the Ozarks. They'd obtained a list of areas from the Forest Service and narrowed the options down to Hercules Glades and Piney Creek so they would not have to drive any further east. They had chosen Hercules for no other reason than the name.

The spokesman for the group asked me about hiking and camping in the wilderness, and I told him he could not have picked a better time. Long Creek was full of water, and he and his friends more or less had the wilderness to themselves. I had an extra trail map and gave it to him. We talked about trails, camping areas, and the falls on Long Creek. He asked whether the glades were worth exploring, and I assured him they were. Finally he asked me how safe it was to leave his vehicle in the parking lot because he had heard in Colorado that car break-ins were a problem at popular trailheads. I told him that in all my years of hiking, camping, hunting, and fishing Missouri Wilderness Areas, I have never had anybody tamper with my vehicles. A short time later, my partner and I bid the Kansans goodbye and wished them an adventurous spring break.

Little did we know that we would cross trails with the students twice in the days ahead.

It felt good to finally get on the trail. Stepping over that imaginary line that separates wilderness from non-wilderness—backcountry from civilization—is like being reborn. At last you are free! Legs do what they are supposed to do. The path ribboned its way along the top of the ridge through cedar, red and white oaks, and a shadowy, stately stand of shortleaf pine. The easy walking on top lasted only about twenty minutes. We would be dropping down into the Long Creek valley and eventually reach Long Creek itself. The creek trail is my favorite because it parallels running water, especially in late winter and spring when the stream is running flush. Some parts of the creek dry up during summer.

The steep ascents and descents on Long Creek Trail show evidence of heavy horse use. Rutted trails and displaced rocks, ranging from the size of golf balls to that of baseballs, present a moderate challenge on the downhill, more so than on uphill climbs, and the heavier the backpack, the greater the difficulty. Stepping on one of those "baseballs" the wrong way, a hiker easily can be thrown off balance. A turned ankle or an unexpected tumble can dampen or ruin a trip. The best approach, aside from wearing comfortable, well-fitting hiking boots with lug soles and plenty of ankle support, is to proceed slowly, knowing that when you reach bottomland the trail will be much improved. Using a hiking staff will increase your stability.

It was on the downhill that I became aware of my pack's weight and the hasty loading job I had done back at the trailhead. Generally, I try to cull nonessential items. As a big eater and something of an equipment freak though, this is often easier said than done. The only real difference in packing for an overnighter and for a week-long camp is the quantity of food and the fuel for the pack stove. Grub weight is not all that significant when using dehydrated foods that have been transferred from rigid packaging to compactible, reusable plastic bags. The extra weight typically comes in the form of clothing, binoculars, camera, film, fishing tackle (at times), an extra pair of shoes or sandals for camp, water purifiers, rain gear, sleeping pads, kitchen utensils, and tent.

There are spartan packers, moderate types, and those who pack to excess. I fall somewhere between moderate and excessive. I would like to become more streamlined, but apparently it's not in my genes. I estimated my pack that day at forty-five pounds. Usually I know exactly what my pack weighs because I weigh in, pack and all, before I leave home, then I just subtract my weight. On this trip I had done all of the packing at the trailhead.

I was overburdened. I could feel the strain on my shoulders, hips, thighs, and ankles during the steep descent. So I took longer than usual to reach the bottom. Even at that, there was absolutely no guilt that I had packed in two frozen T-bone steaks, prebaked potatoes, onion, fresh mushrooms, cheese, and a 1994 bottle of Cabernet Sauvignon. They were simply the makings of a feast to be had later that evening in celebration of wilderness adventure. Still the bottom was a welcome sight.

We made our way to a bathtub-size spring just ten yards off the trail but hidden in a cluster of sharp-spined honey locust trees. There's only one thing better than donning a pack with all the essentials for living and heading into the wilderness. That is unharnessing cargo from the torso and taking the day's first legitimate break. The immediate effect on load-free shoulders is the strange but welcome sensation of weightlessness. We removed hiking boots, liner socks, and hiking socks then sat on flat rocks by the pool and immersed our feet in frigid, clear water. Inch-long crayfish darted in every direction. Fortunately, they were not interested in toes.

The wilderness contains a multitude of treasures—some dynamic, others hidden. This spring was a find. It seemed to us there could be no better place in the world to soak feet that were hot, tired, and cramped. While the water soothed our aching arches, insteps, and toes, we ate our first granola bars of the day and washed them down with water from our bottles. Then we leaned back against our packs for a few minutes to let the air dry our feet. Just when we were about to put on socks and shoes, we heard footsteps behind us. The hikers from Kansas had caught up with us. I was about to issue a greeting, but they never slowed down. They passed within ten yards of where we sat without seeing us. They were three young men on a mission, trying to "get there" and missing one of the small treasures.

We lingered at the spring for nearly thirty minutes then resumed the trail with what seemed like more energy than we'd had at the start. Every pack trip has a "break-in" period that tests physical endurance and mental conditioning. After all, most of us come fresh from the city or suburbia with high expectations of endless energy.

A warm-up is generally required for peak physical and mental performance.

We took the trail at an easy pace. A sojourn in the forest is a time for introspection. We wandered, each of us lost in his own thoughts, emerging from contemplation to observe the life around us, refer to guidebooks on flowers and trees, and shoot a few pictures. The mild day fairly melted away smoothly. For us there was hushed wilderness and the gurgling current of Long Creek. The only intrusion was created by a type-A belted kingfisher, who labored from one snag tree to another, chattering at us and trying to drive us away.

Around 3 P.M. we began looking for the perfect camping spot. Finding it was a challenge, because most of the good spots on either side of Long Creek already had fire rings and ample evidence of human presence. Fortunately taste in camps differs from hiker to hiker. We did not need a view of the creek, nor did we require a fire ring. An hour later, we found a spot south of Long Creek. The location was in transition zone between a stand of gnarled cedar trees and a parklike opening dominated by mature white oak trees. We could just barely see the silver slice of creek below. The terrace where we set the tent was flat as a table. Miraculously, there was no sign of past campers.

There is satisfaction in finding pristine ground that shows no bite of a tent peg or scar of a fire. And there is an obligation to leave it as you found it. To avoid marking vegetation or rocks, the cook fire can be elevated with a small, inexpensive metal grill with legs and grate. The grill weighs about a pound and easily can be wrapped in a recycled plastic grocery bag and lashed to a backpack. The grill and a lightweight, single-burner backpack stove are adequate for all cooking, including brewing strong camp coffee and heating water for tea. A cozy after-dinner campfire can be built in the same grill, minus the cooking grate. No-trace wilderness camping and hiking is about going the extra measure to preserve the natural beauty of the land.

After pitching the tent, we gathered twigs and larger pieces of wood for the fire. Once the twigs were burning, we added the pieces of wood to raise a mound of coals that would warm the spuds and sear the steaks medium rare. I pulled the corkscrew from one of the side compartments of my pack and carefully opened the wine, which was, according to my temperature gauge, a fitting sixty degrees—"room" temperature. Dale had brought a pair of plastic wineglasses, the kind with removable stems. Crystal would have been more appropriate for wilderness celebration, but plastic served nicely in a pinch. We toasted Hercules Glades and the men and women who had worked long and hard to assure its preservation, especially two persistent and effective crusaders: Bill Bates and Buzz Darby.

If it had been two or three weeks later, around the time of turkey season, we probably could have foraged enough morel mushrooms to layer our steaks. Morels grow in all the state's Wilderness Areas. The timing was off a bit, and we settled for the store-bought variety mixed with diced onions and sautéed in butter. Despite its being a blatant violation of backpacking's spartan, pack-light regulations, I find a large measure of satisfaction in producing an elegant meal or two on camping trips.

Actually there are no set rules. If you feel the eating and drinking are worth the carrying and cooking, by all means indulge. Meals prepared and savored in the woods are far more memorable and delectable than those eaten at home or at restaurants. And all those delicious foods you carried in are easily burned as calories on the hike out. Your pack feels much lighter on the return trip.

Our late-afternoon dinner capped a good day. As the sun set, the temperature dropped. We donned jackets and built up the fire in the grill pan. We moved our soft-sided camp chairs nearer the campfire. The chairs have metal frames to which are attached nylon shells stuffed with foam. They fold up for storage in sacks, and the bags can be tied to a pack frame. They provide good back support and insulation against the cold ground. The weight of this luxury is 23.3 ounces, including stuff sack. Our time sitting around the fire and solving the problems of the world has doubled since we made the chairs standard equipment. That alone makes it worth carrying the extra ounces.

I mentioned the soaking pool as one of the gifts of wilderness. Black night, unbroken by artificial light, is another. The half-moon glows spectacularly. The constellations Big Dipper, Little Dipper, Lyra, and Cepheus—faded or invisible when competing with city lights—are dazzling.

Around 9 P.M., while Dale and I were feeding the fire dry, down-fall sticks, a chorus of barred owls burst into song halfway up the ridge. Their nasal harmony—"Who cooks for you, who cooks for you all" was a nine-note greeting to night, stars, moon, and each other I suppose. Owl mating had started and would continue through April.

I learned to hoot like an owl from Rob Keck, a champion turkey caller and owl hooter. Hooting like a barred owl shocks turkey gobblers into gobbling. The voice call is important for locating long-beards in the spring, and it is also fun to call owls into camp. Of course the birds take their vocalization much more seriously.

It is not my intention to deceive them, but in reality I do just that. I call and an owl answers. I call again a minute later and the bird replies, this time from much closer. I call a third time, and I hear the soft swoosh of wings somewhere beyond the glow of firelight. The owl is close. Probably staring down at us. I hoot again, and this time he flies to the limb of an oak tree just above us. He sees us. We see him. He bobs his head in circles, confused by the view below. A few seconds later the owl rises from the limb, strokes twice with powerful wings, and glides away into the darkness. I wonder what owls think of this game?

The day's activity, although by no means a disciplined march toward some faraway destination, had taken its toll. The pleasant fatigue plus our full bellies had us yawning. When the small fire burnt itself out, we headed for the tent and bore down into the cozy confines of mummy-style sleeping bags. We talked a few minutes more, recalling the beauty of the day and planning hiking destinations in the morning. Then we drifted off to the land of dreams.

I woke at 7:30. Sunlight had yet to penetrate Long Creek's bottoms. It was cold, and I would have pulled the sleeping bag's built-in hood over my head and curled back to sleep if it hadn't been for the thought of fresh-perked coffee. I had lashed a small, four-cup pot to the pack for just such an occasion. There was no going back to sleep. I dressed quickly and eased out of the tent. Twenty minutes later Dale woke to the aroma of the black brew, and I delivered a cup to him room-service style while he basked in the warmth of his sleeping bag. The first shaft of sun made its way slowly down the ridge and settled on the frost-covered tent fly. Breakfast was simple. Coffee, Tang, and two packages each of "peaches and cream" instant oatmeal.

We left our camp intact, electing to fill daypacks with snacks and water for go-light hiking and exploration of the Long Creek Trail. Later we planned to do some bushwhacking off the trail just for the adventure of finding new places. It felt good walking without full packs. The cool morning was ideal for striding out and covering ground. For the first fifteen minutes the trail was flat. Then we came to a rocky, steep, and narrow downhill path that veered away from the creek. We began the descent, grateful for minimum cargo. About halfway down, Dale and I heard a sound like falling rocks coming from the trail above us. We stopped and looked back up the hill but saw nothing out of the ordinary. The switchback trail prevented us from seeing more that thirty yards behind us. The noise was getting louder.

Then I recognized the sound of hoofbeats. At first I thought they could be made by deer who had spooked after scenting our tracks. Dale resumed walking, but I stayed put. Suddenly a horse and rider appeared. I yelled to Dale. The horseman, riding at full gallop and seemingly out of control, did not appear to see us. He was followed by three more riders. We scrambled off the trail to avoid being trampled. The horses and riders thundered by us without slowing. I figured one of those horses was going to take a tumble. The third rider lost his baseball cap to an overhanging branch. He reined the horse to an abrupt halt on the rocks and called out for the others to wait.

Dale and I were shocked. No experienced rider gallops his horse down a stony, looping trail. The man who had lost his hat sat on his horse not fifteen feet away and said nothing to us. Two of the others had returned to him, and they all seemed to be waiting for the third. I would probably have retrieved his hat for him had he offered a friendly greeting or an apology. But except for glancing our way once or twice, they all acted as though we didn't exist. The rider who had been first down the hill doubled back, dismounted, and picked up the hat. No one spoke. The four slowly rode off without looking back. Perhaps they had lost control of their horses on the steep trail and were too embarrassed to admit it. Maybe they were under the influence of something that made them act weird and wild. We could only speculate. All Dale and I knew for sure was that we had come close to disaster in peaceful Hercules Glades.

We had mixed emotions about following the band of riders, but we decided to stick to the trail for a half-mile or so. The topo map showed a fork up ahead; we would choose the way without hoofprints. Then, we would bushwhack our way back to camp and pack out. We ended up hiking about eight more miles, most of it off the trail. We lingered at the falls on Long Creek, and we sat for awhile on top of Coy Bald, admiring the unique topography of Hercules.

It was time to leave. We broke camp and hiked out to Hercules Tower. In the parking lot we saw two pickup trucks with horse trailers. We were tempted to write a note about trail etiquette and leave it for the four wild horsemen of Hercules, but we didn't. I could imagine those guys chasing us on horseback to the ends of the earth.

Ordinarily, you meet the nicest people in the wilderness. They are there for many of the same reasons you are. The experts on an individual area can be particularly interesting people. I remember a trip I planned with the help of Mark Twain National Forest Recreation Specialist Darsan Wang. Darsan suggested I take an ecology hike through Hercules Glades with Forest Service ecologist Lynda Richards. I called Lynda to set up a time and place to meet.

She suggested the first Saturday in June because the "wine-scented" Missouri evening primrose was likely to be in full bloom then. The glades would be radiantly alive with color. Somehow I had missed the yellow primrose during my many hikes into Hercules. I was anxious to learn more about the area's ecology.

Saturday arrived, clear and cool. I met Lynda at 8 A.M. at the Coy Bald Trailhead, the west entrance to Hercules. We introduced ourselves, signed in at the rustic registration desk, and got on the trail. From that point on, I saw Hercules through Lynda's eyes. She led the way down the narrow trail, a woman on a mission, scanning both sides of the path ahead for fauna that most people, including myself, would not recognize. We stopped often so that she and I could stoop down for a closer look at noseburn, pagoda mint, calamint, sensitive briar, and purple penstemon. In a hushed voice, as though not wishing to disturb the plants, Lynda described them as if she knew each and every one personally. Her respect for wild things was both inspirational and soothing.

"See the stinging hairs on noseburn [*Tragia urticifolia*]," she whispered. "Look at the calamint [*Satureja arkansana*] and its tiny blue flowered mint. You have to be careful of sensitive briar's [*Schrankia uncinata*] recurved spines. Purple penstemon [*Perstemon cobaea*] looks like big snapdragons." Rarely did we walk ten steps without inspecting something new and unusual. I began to realize how much I had missed during past wilderness hikes.

There were exotic plants in the wilderness along with the natives. They included *Sericea lespedeza*, multiflora rose, and oxeye daisy.

We saw June mushrooms, including bolete, a mushroom that stains blue, and charterelle. The morels had already peaked in April and early May. But not everything was at ground level. During our eight-mile hike we identified twelve different trees and shrubs, including chinkapin, post, black, white, and blackjack oak; smoke tree, winged elm, possumhaw, fragrant Sumac, rough-leafed dogwood, and ninebark.

One of the highlights of the day came when the trail abruptly broke out of deep forest into the open spaciousness of Coy Bald glade. Such a dramatic change of scenery is one of the unique features of Hercules Glades. I could sense Lynda's excitement as she stepped up the pace. She was searching for the huge yellow blooms and big flanged pods of the Missouri evening primrose, sometimes nicknamed the "glade lily." Other species of primrose grow in Missouri, such as the evening primrose, showy evening primrose, and cutleaved evening primrose. But the Missouri evening primrose (*Oenothera macrocarpa*, formerly *O. missouriensis*) is queen of the glades.

We had covered about seventy yards of the glade without finding the flower of dreams. I heard a hint of panic in my hiking partner's voice. Then we rounded an assembly of dwarfed cedar trees, and there before us was a flower garden of immense proportions and glowing beauty. We knelt down to admire the sunny petals of the large blooms.

Surrounded by trophy flowers, some three inches across, we were able to relax. Lynda's mission had been accomplished. We sat on flat limestone rocks and had snacks. The flowery glade was the perfect setting for relaxing and savoring the unspoiled beauty of the wilderness. Now that we'd turned our attention from the plant life, we noticed large, dramatic thunderheads were stacking up to the west. We joked about the possibility of getting wet but quickly dismissed the notion; the sun was still shining brightly and billowing clouds still ruled the sky.

We left Coy Bald and continued on the miniature "Missouri Bootheel loop trail" that would take us down to Long Creek and a spot that is often called the most dramatic feature in the wilderness. The falls at the bottom of the loop consist of six- and ten-foot cascades that gurgle across rock shelves and rush through a dolomite cleft. Springs and seeps are numerous in this picture-postcard spot. The springs create ideal growing conditions for a variety of mosses, ferns, and flowering plants.

The character of the falls changes with the seasons. Long Creek is usually overflowing with water in winter and early spring, and the falls roar dramatically then. In late spring, summer, and early fall, there is scarcely any water, and the falls barely produce a cascade. I have visited the site several times in winter, when the seeps from hillside cliffs along the creek and falls create enormous ice swords, giving the area an arctic look. One late-February day stands out in my memory. I was hiking down to Long Creek from the Blair Bridge access when I heard what sounded like thunder. But the sky was a spectacular, cloudless deep blue. The closer I got to the creek, the louder the thunder was. When I broke out into the open near the creek, the sound was continuous. When I reached the bank, I looked across the creek, and just then an ice lance that extended from the top of an overhang on the cliff nearly to the bottom broke off. The falling ice, one segment as big around as a utility pole, hit the boulders with a sound like a cannon blast. The thunder I had been hearing through the trees was the sound of enormous icicles thawing and pulling away from the cliff. Every few minutes another column of ice would break away and crash to the ground.

But there was no such drama on the pleasant June day that Lynda and I took our ecology hike. We poked around the falls for nearly an hour. Shortly after we arrived, we met two brothers, the oldest probably twelve, who lived within two miles of Hercules Glades off Highway 125. The falls on Long Creek were a favorite swimming spot for them, and they hiked in often during spring and summer. Unlike some youngsters who grow up near beautiful places without realizing what they have, this sociable pair obviously appreciated their wilderness playground. They enthusiastically relayed to us stories of deer, wild turkeys, bobcats, roadrunners, collared lizards, and tarantulas. The kids seemed well informed about wildlife and woodsmanship.

When we left them, we crossed Long Creek and followed the trail as it looped north and then west. This route would eventually take us back to the Coy Bald Trailhead. About twenty minutes later, we ran into a group of Boy Scouts and their two adult leaders. They had camped overnight on Upper Pilot Knob and seemed to be enjoying everything about the adventure. Each boy had his own walking stick, and all their backpacks were decorated with camp patches and feathers. One of the boys said they had found a large patch of Missouri evening primrose in the glade where they

"Ice swords" hanging on a bluff over Long Creek in Hercules Glades Wilderness. *Author's collection.*

camped. Lynda was duly impressed. We bid them good-bye and good luck. Shortly afterward I told Lynda how impressed I was, impressed that men and women take the time to teach kids about the outdoors and that the kids are so appreciative of having a place like Hercules Glades in which to roam, camp, and learn.

As we continued our hike, we noticed that the thunderheads we had seen from the top of Coy Bald had taken over the sky. It began to rain, and we quickened our pace. Neither one of us had brought rain suits. There had been no forecast of rain to break the serene weather pattern of the last week. There was no reason to plan for rain, except that you should always plan for rain. I advise others heading outdoors to pack rain gear even when the sun is shining. Today's rain suits are compact and add little weight to a pack. They are good insurance.

We hoped the storm would blow over, but it intensified. Thunder boomed and lighting flashed as the rain fell in sheets despite the thick forest canopy. The drops, nearly cold enough to turn to hail, pricked like pins. When we reached the crossing at Long Creek, the water was thigh-high and the current fast. We had to go through it to get to the steep ridge where the vehicles were parked. As we crossed, a flash of lighting seemed to reach toward us. We ran through the remaining stretch of water, feeling relieved when we reached the bank. Both of us were shivering after the crossing, and we welcomed the steep hill that lay before us. The climb would generate body warmth. About halfway up, the rain stopped, and the sun sheepishly broke through the clouds. When we got back to the trucks we looked at each other and began laughing uncontrollably. We both looked, and felt, as if we had just climbed out of the tank of a washing machine. We said good-bye.

A week letter I received a letter from Lynda. She had not suffered so much as a sniffle from the drenching we received on our hike. She sent me a list she had made up of every plant, grass, bird, insect, and butterfly we had observed that day. I have reproduced the list below, minus the fauna already mentioned, for you to think about when you hike through the wilderness. Even if you've been there many times, I bet you'll find things on this list you've never seen before.

Lynda opened up a whole new world for me on our hike in 1995. I was convinced after spending the day with her that a knowledge of flora and fauna makes any wilderness activity more pleasurable.

Whether you are hiking, camping, backpacking, bird-watching, hunting, or fishing, you can increase your enjoyment and satisfaction by learning to appreciate the connectedness of all life in the wilderness. These days I take my time on the trail, looking around at what I'm passing. Since I can't match Lynda's ability to identify nearly everything I see, I carry a few guidebooks in my pack. A particular favorite is Edgar Denison's *Missouri Wildflowers*.

Flowers

- Missouri black-eyed susan
- Carolina larkspur
- Blue false indigo
- Green-flowered milkweed
- Wild petunia
- Pale purple coneflower
- Yellow coneflower
- Indian paintbrush
- Self-heal or heal-all
- Pagoda mint or Ohio horsemint
- Wild phlox or wild sweet william
- Wild rose
- Coreopsis
- Prairie clover
- Climbing milkweed
- Greyback grape
- Spiderwort
  (note: "only saw one")

Insects and Butterflies

- Golden rose beetle
- Sylphid beetles
  (note: "both these beetles found on an old deer carcass")
- Red admiral butterflies
  (note: "saw several at the waterfall")

Birds

- Prairie warbler
- Field sparrow
  (note: "warbler and sparrow are common glade birds")
- Red-eyed vireo
  (note: "a woodland bird that calls "Here I am . . . where are you?"")

Grasses

- Little bluestem
- Indian grass
- Eastern gama grass

The 12,315–acre Hercules Glades Wilderness is second only to the Irish Wilderness in size. It is, like all of Missouri's designated Wilderness, steeped in history and legend. Early settlers raised cotton within the current Wilderness boundaries. According to John Karel, "There were three cotton gins in operation within the area well before Hercules Glades was honored with official wilderness status."

Trough used by settlers to feed or water livestock, Hercules Glades
Wilderness. *Author's collection.*

Evidence of man's activities in the wilderness remain in the form of forty-one miles of roads, numerous house foundations, two spring houses, rock fences, concrete spring tanks, stock feed troughs built into the crotches of trees, ponds, and scattered bits of rusty wire fencing.

Despite these remnants of human habitation, Hercules Glades Wilderness is the only "Class 1" airshed on the Mark Twain Forest as defined by the 1977 Clean Air Act (CAA). The purpose of the Class 1 rating is the protection of regional air quality values according to the guidelines set by the Environmental Protection Agency (EPA). Managers of Class 1 areas, in this case the U.S. Forest Service, are given specific responsibilities to protect existing air quality. If, for instance, a facility like a power plant were proposed, and its emissions would have an adverse impact on air and water quality, and thus on vegetation, wildlife, and scenery, the manager and the EPA would intercede.

Henry Rowe Schoolcraft and Levi Pettibone were among the first to document Ozark wilderness, beginning in 1818. Their journals show that they traveled over prairies and to the tops of balds, or conical hills. It is quite likely that Schoolcraft and Pettibone savored the view from the top of Coy Bald, as well as from Upper and Lower Pilot Knob. Maybe they soaked their trail-weary feet is the cool waters of Long Creek.

There are times when I hike Hercules that I feel the presence of those who knew this land far better than I. I see Osage Indian encampments where Hercules Tower stands, and I can picture Osage warriors standing in the glades. They came to these sacred hills to discover themselves and seek visions of their future. We who follow do much the same. We live in a different time, but we still seek good medicine in the holy calm of nature.

6

Irish Wilderness

Solitary hikers report than powerful spirits inhabit the Irish Wilderness. It is claimed that these relate somehow to the moody water of the Eleven Point River on the west, to the shadows of furtive animals only barely sensed, to the glimpse of swaying ridgetop pines in a gray November bluster, or even the lingering wraiths of Indian and Irish hunters.

JOHN KAREL

THE IRISH, AT 16,500 acres, is the largest designated Wilderness in the state. It is a place where you can still get lost if you pay little or no heed to map and compass. I have been lost. On the occasion I'm recalling, I and my two hiking companions, both full-time Mark Twain National Forest employees, became temporarily "turned around." Lest you think I blamed them for our quandary, I'll settle the score now. There was no blame. We got "turned around" together. All of us were experienced hikers.

It was April 27, 1995. We had been trekking along the 18.6–mile Whites Creek Trail most of the day. We were running out of daylight, and to shorten our hike back to the trailhead, we decided to bushwhack a new route, using a straight-on compass and a map bearing from south to north. Somehow we missed connecting with the east-west trail that was within a mile of where our vehicles were parked. We were lucky. We just happened upon the trail. We finally made it to our destination at 9 P.M. Another Forest Service employee drove up about the same time. He had been looking for us. The wives of my companions had called him, worried because their husbands had been due home before dark.

To this day we don't know how we got off course. Just when you think you know the Irish, it will surprise you. We had been humbled by land that has never been easy on people. Irish is a treasure rich in history and steeped in folklore. Maybe something nudged us ever so slightly off course. Certainly we have not forgotten that adventure. If the hearts of my fellow hikers are in tune with mine, and I believe they are, all of us are pleased there is a place in Missouri that challenges the very survival skills of men and women.

Aldo Leopold knew this feeling well. He visited what is now the Irish Wilderness in 1927 and wrote a letter, to the Forest Service saying that it should be protected. The U.S. Forest Service has managed the area since 1930 in a special way. Leopold, an early wilderness advocate, is frequently called "the father of modern game management." He knew there are no guarantees in the wilderness, even when you are there for only a day. This is what he said about wilderness adventurers:

> No servant brought them meals; they got their meat out of the river or went without. No traffic cop whistled them off the hidden rock in the next rapids. No friendly roof kept them dry when they mis-guessed whether or not to pitch the tent. No guide showed them which camping spots offered a nightlong breeze, and which a nightlong misery of mosquitoes; which firewood made clean coals, and which only smoke. The elemental simplicities of wilderness travel were thrills not only because of their novelty, but because they represented complete freedom to make mistakes. The wilderness gave them their first taste of those rewards and penalties for wise and foolish acts which every woodsman faces daily, but against which civilization has built a thousand buffers.

Every Wilderness in Missouri offers the challenges Leopold describes. Those natural hurdles effectively separate true wilderness from the groomed, service-oriented city, state, and federal camping/hiking parks that do provide "cops" around every bend. I have camped, boated, and fished at those recreation areas and find most of them pleasant in a civilized sort of way. It is not my intention to denigrate them; they fill a need. The lasting value of wilderness is that it provides people with the option of seeking true adventure.

The late Dan Saults, a friend, a Missourian, and a fine writer who specialized in conservation issues, wrote eloquently of the Irish. So did state historic preservation official Booker H. Rucker. When testifying at a 1982 hearing in Washington, D.C., Rucker said, "[Wilderness is] a melancholy, but pleasant loneliness—miles and miles and miles. It gives richness and legendary lore to the state. If we were to run away from home, really run away, the place to head was the Irish." As early as 1949, Ozark conservation writer Leonard Hall proposed that the Irish be designated Wilderness.

I began hiking various sections of the Irish Wilderness in 1990. On one occasion I launched my canoe at Greer Crossing and Turner Mill North Access on the Eleven Point River and took out on the east bank near Whites Creek Float Camp. From there I backpacked the Whites Creek Trail to Whites Creek Cave and Fiddler Spring, where I spent an enjoyable clear, starry night on my first excursion.

My second time out, this time launching from Turner Mill, I elected not to camp on the trail but instead shouldered a light day-pack filled with snacks, water, and other essentials and walked to the Camp Five trailhead and picnic area. My goal that day was to do the entire 18.6-mile Whites Creek loop back to my boat, eliminating the Orchard Hollow loop in favor of a straighter, trailless route along the river. Unfortunately, by the time I reached the Camp Five trailhead I knew I would run out of April daylight before completing the loop. Not having had previous experience on that section of trail, I elected to double back. I don't like to return over my original route, but caution ruled, and as it turned out, I was rewarded. Halfway back to my boat, I rounded a bend in the trail and saw a flock of about forty wild turkeys twenty yards away. Apparently flock breakup and preparation for the mating season had not yet begun because there were both mature gobblers and juvenile jakes mixed in with a large congregation of hens. Some startled birds lumbered into the air. Others sounded shrill alarm putts and ran helter-skelter like miniature ostriches. I had never seen that many birds before.

I reached my canoe while there was still enough daylight to make camp on a level section of ridge about one hundred yards from the river. After I had built a small fire and grilled slices of summer sausage, I felt satisfied with my decision not to hike the entire Whites Creek loop that day. The next morning, with threatening gray clouds scudding by overhead, I paddled my seventeen-foot Old Town down to Riverton Access. From there I would be shuttled back to my truck, which was parked upstream at Turner Mill. I was thankful for the rain gear I had packed. Cold rain was pouring down before I reached my take-out point. Despite the downpour, I was comfortable. The exercise of paddling efficiently warms the upper torso. In two days of floating and hiking I had not seen another person. Paddling along in the rain, I felt like time had gone backward. I could have been a trapper heading for the nearest outpost. Just as the exertion had warmed my body, the feeling warmed my heart. I had spent the night on wild land. I was paddling my boat on one of Missouri's finest National Scenic Rivers—forty-four miles of which have been federally protected since 1968.

The Irish and her wild companion, the Eleven Point, offer the adventurer a multitude of options. They are never boring. There are several theories on how the river got its name. My favorite says that an early explorer stepped out his lean-to on the banks of the river early one morning and spotted an immense whitetail buck with eleven points on his thick-beamed rack. He bragged about the deer at the trading post a few days later, and Eleven Point stuck as the river's name. Another, less romantic story says a group of government surveyors so named it because the river is so crooked that compass points had to be changed eleven times in one mile.

The Irish's history mixes hauntingly well with the territory's natural splendor. It is difficult to hike or camp in the Irish without heeding its past. Most all the virgin timber was cut down in the early 1900s. The Irish is a forest of second-growth trees, but you would scarcely recognize that today. The topography itself has not changed, nor have the river, creeks, springs, seeps, caves, ridgetops, and bluffs. The heart of the land has remained intact. The land probably looks much as it did when the Osage Indians hunted there. Thanks to land purchase and protection by the U.S. Forest Service in the 1930s, the Irish was able to restore itself. The best-known history of the area began with a Catholic priest named Father John J. Hogan. Father Hogan and his Irish immigrants were the first recorded settlers in the wilderness area in 1859.

Several booklets and newspaper articles have documented the area's history and the short-lived Hogan settlement. Those brief histories include "History of White's Creek and the Irish Wilderness" by Ronald Wihenbrink, a Forest Service historian; "Father Hogan's 1859 Irish Wilderness Settlement" by Mike Crawford; "The Civil

War in Oregon County" by Jerry Ponder, "Irish Wilderness Site of Settlement for Immigrants" by Don Cullimore, in the *St. Louis Post-Dispatch*, and "Lost in the Mystery: Missouri's Irish Wilderness" by Roger Pryor, in the *Kansas City Star*. Of them all, Wihenbrink's history seems to me to best capture the tone of the period and the hardships settlers faced.

> "The quiet solitariness of the place seemed to inspire devotion. Nowhere could the human soul so profoundly worship as in the depths of that leafy forest, beneath the swaying branches of the lofty oaks and pines, where solitude and the heart of man united in praise and wonder of the Great Creator."
>
> FATHER JOHN HOGAN, 1892

Father Hogan and his Irish immigrants were the first recorded settlers in the wilderness area in 1859. It was there on a large tract of land that a one-story log house, 40 foot square, was erected and partitioned into two apartments—one for a chapel and the other for the priest's residence. The purpose of the settlement was to establish missions for the Irish working under poverty and separated family conditions on the railroads in St. Louis. What he hoped to provide for the immigrants and their families was the security of family life. In the spring of 1859 there were about 40 families on newly acquired government land. The settlers built modest log homes and cultivated crops with a sense of security.

They worked and reaped their crops in the fall of 1860. But shortly after, ominous clouds began to form which would bring devastation to the colony. The split of the Democratic Party over the free soil question resulted in the election of Abraham Lincoln. The new president was Republican and anti-slavery, sometimes called an abolitionist. The South rose in resentment and threatened succession.

In 1861, civil war rolled across the nation. In the border state of Missouri, the war was brutal, bloody and relentless. Father Hogan foresaw the civil war, yet felt secure that neither the North nor the South cared enough for the Irish Wilderness to occupy it. When in fact, the wilderness was completely surrounded, the Union armies to the north and northwest, and the Confederate armies to the south and southeast. The Irish settlement held little to attract an army. However, because of its terrain and isolation it did offer refuge for raiding parties of both armies.

The Irish Wilderness provided cover and protection for the murderous bands of bushwhackers who gave no allegiance to either the North or the South, and preyed on the helpless situation of the civilian population without regard for discrimination. Thus the Irish became a no-man's-land where civilized rules of warfare were discarded and blood-thirsty bands looted and murdered almost at will.

But what was the fate of the Irish Settlement? Records show only that there was a settlement there prior to the civil war and after the civil war, there was nothing. One legend claims that the Irish fled in the dark of the night. Another tells of murder by bushwhackers over a period of time.

Father Hogan went on to a distinguished career as bishop of Kansas City, and there is a high school there named for him. But he left no account of the fate of his Irish people in the wilderness. On May 17, 1879, the land where Father Hogan's church stood was sold for taxes.

I thought about the Irish and its mysterious history one morning as I drove to meet Darsan Wang and Ken Haberl for a "major assault" on the Whites Creek Trail. I thought about Civil War days and the Irish immigrants seeking a new way of life. I felt deeply moved by them. I envisioned family groups working their fields of corn or stacking wood for the winter ahead. I saw both joy and fear on their faces. Turning off the main highway and following the road that would take me to the settlement of Wilderness, I felt a chill. Those people seemed to be reaching out for help. Nothing about what happened at this mysterious place seems fair—at least in my mind.

I was looking forward to hiking the trail with Darsan and Ken. Both were recreation specialists for the Forest Service. Darsan was headquartered in Rolla, and Ken was at the Eleven Point Ranger District in Winona. Darsan was the primary contact within the Mark Twain Forest for information about Missouri Wilderness. We spoke often by phone. What he didn't already know about wilderness, he researched. His support was overwhelming.

I had never met Ken before. Like Darsan he was career Forest Service and was no doubt knowledgeable about every phase of Forest Service operations. There was little doubt we would have much in common. I soon discovered he was an avid hunter. That morning he went to the Wilderness two hours early so he could hunt turkeys before our hike. Unfortunately, he would later tell me, a strong breeze had prevailed through the night and well into the morning. He never heard a bird gobble. Turkeys are wary during windy conditions because they cannot detect predators, including man, as well as they can on a calm day. The birds simply do not move around much or respond to a hunter's hen calls.

Ken arrived at the designated meeting road a few minutes before Darsan. We were looking at a topographic map of the area and had begun tracing the route we would follow when our hiking partner pulled into the small turnoff where we had parked our trucks. Darsan apologized for being a few minutes late. He had not been able to resist taking an early drive to nearby Turner Mill, located on

District Recreation Specialist for Mark Twain Forest Ken Haberl (left) and former Wilderness Recreation Specialist for Mark Twain Forest Darwan Wang (right) refer to a topographic map of Irish Wilderness. *Author's collection.*

national forestland outside the Wilderness boundary. He had never seen the spot before and was impressed with its beauty.

Many such unique places, including Greer Spring, Greer Crossing Campground and River Access, Falling Spring, and McCormack Lake Recreation Area, are outside the Wilderness boundary but only short drives from the trailheads. The remains of the "New Liberty" Civilian Conservation Corps (CCC) Camp are just a short distance from the Irish. In the 1930s, the CCC's hardworking "tree armies" began restoring health to forestland. Standing on the site is eerie. You can almost hear the voices of the hardy young men as they set out with picks and shovels for a long day of planting trees to replace the ones cut down fifty years before.

Ken and I would leave our vehicles where they were. Darsan, who was driving an official Forest Service van, took us all to the Brawley Pond trailhead, our starting point, a few miles away. Ken and I loaded our daypacks with food, water, and rain suits before we left the turnoff. I added my small, point-and-shoot thirty-five–millimeter camera. Darsan readied his gear when we reached the trailhead.

We took a brief look at Brawley Pond, fringed with brown cattails from the summer before. The distance from the pond due south to Whites Creek Trail is 1.1 miles. The April morning was nearly perfect for hiking. A half-mile along the trail we saw the charcoal scars of a recent fire. Ken told me it had not been a large fire, and a team of firefighters, including him, had extinguished it without motorized machinery. He did not know how it started. When lives are at risk, aircraft and other machines are sometimes allowed in the Wilderness. That is the only exception to the "no motors" or "no wheeled conveyances" rule.

For the first mile, Ken and I talked about deer and turkey hunting in the Irish. He told me the area receives light to moderate hunting pressure because of its size. The long-distance walking necessary in Wilderness Areas tends to discourage some hunters. This dependence on legs and lungs, combined with the challenge of packing out a deer that may have been shot several miles from the trailhead, can be a deterrent to those not in good physical shape. Few modern-day sportsmen could have competed with the Indian and Irish hunters who once roamed this game-rich land.

Since the mating season for turkeys coincided with our hike, I kept looking for signs of scratching in the leaves but saw nothing fresh. Darsan was more interested in wildflowers and stopped often to photograph those we passed, such as wild sweet william and indian paintbrush.

The spur trail that connects with the Whites Creek Trail is relatively level, going through open woods without much in the way of distinguishing landmarks. Likewise, when we came to the junction with the main trail, the terrain was mostly level and basically nondescript. I did see some excellent locations to set up for turkeys and deer.

We had hiked a little over a mile of the Whites Creek Trail when the gentle terrain became more challenging near the bluffs overlooking the Eleven Point. From this point on, the handsome face of the Irish showed its unique scenery. Slightly north of Bliss Spring the contour lines on the topo map squeezed tightly together. We had been hiking along a half-mile of straight north-south trail and were approaching the east bank of the river. The steep limestone bluffs guarding the Eleven Point are stately defenders. And the view from above encourages contemplation and a pause to drink in the lofty beauty of wild land and wild river side by side.

We spent twenty 20 minutes snapping pictures before heading on to Bliss Spring. The Wilderness has a karst topography with features such as sinkholes, springs, and caves. Originally a seabed, it lies within the dolomitic Ozark "flint hill" region, where the bedrock consists of ancient deposits of carbonate sediments.

John Karel describes the karst terrain and its relationship to springs such as Bliss.

> In tracing drainages to the river, we begin to understand the uniqueness of the Irish and its limestone regions of abundant caves, sinkholes and springs. Up around the drainage heads, the topography is very gently rolling and pocked with numerous sinkholes. As the drainages gather volume, they gradually begin to develop signs of permanent flow. Just as the streams seem to be flowing well, we come to long stretches of dry gravel wash. Such "losing streams" are characteristic of karst country and indicate where water has descended underground to help feed subsurface water systems. Further down the valleys we discover the surface outlets for these pirated underground drainages. Small springs such as Fiddlers Spring and Bliss Spring emerge from dolomitic rock ledges in mossy grottoes. Like the water holding sinkholes, springs provide habitat for a specialized flora and water for many species of wildlife. Elevations range from 500 feet near the river to 900 feet at Camp Five Pond.

Bliss Spring and Bliss Hollow are truly blissful and served wonderfully well for our lunch stop. The noticeable difference between this spot and most other locations in the Wilderness is the shady, moist coolness and cold, gurgling spring water. Dwarf-crested iris (*Iris cristata*) are found nearby on shaded slopes in larger hollows as are a variety of moss and ferns. Close to the Eleven Point, black walnut, sycamore, and Ozark witch hazel can be seen. Occasionally springtime visitors come across brightly colored salamanders from the family *Ambystomatidae*. Called mole salamanders, these amphibians stay underground most of their lives. But they congregate in temporary pools and ponds (such as sinkhole ponds) after early spring rains for courtship and deposition of eggs.

Sandwiches and cookies, fruit and power bars tasted especially good in this most peaceful of outdoor dining spots. I carried two, thirty-two–ounce Nalgene water bottles in my pack. High-energy food and plenty of water are necessary for staying power on long-distance hikes. Forest Service brochures do not recommend drinking directly from a water source in any wilderness. Instead, the agency suggests filtering, boiling, or chemically treating the water.

Although the springs look pristine, there are too many unknown sources of pollution that enter the watershed. Many hikers and backpackers use small, lightweight water-purification devices.

My two filled thirty-two–ounce water bottles weighed four pounds, half the weight of a gallon of water, which would be impractical to carry under most hiking or backpacking situations. The secret to ample hydration, in cold or warm weather, is to drink plenty of water before the hike and continue to take in water during exercise.

It is easy to linger in a place like Bliss Spring, and we did just that. I was even considering a short siesta, when the other two got to their feet. Once on the trail, you want to see what's around the next bend. The upcoming four to five miles of hiking were sure to be the most invigorating of all. Temperatures were in the comfortable upper sixties.

We decided to take a short half-mile spur trail down to the river. There was a panoramic view from the bluffs, but the straight path down to the Eleven Point would take us to the bank for an up-close and personal encounter. Freshly chewed beaver sticks were strewn in abundance close to the bank. The river was running full and clear, just begging to be fished. The fishing is commonly good to excellent for smallmouth bass, rock bass, locally known as "goggle-eye," and trout.

The Missouri Department of Conservation's special trout-management area on the Eleven Point in Oregon County extends from its junction with Greer Spring Branch to Turner Mill, which was upstream from where we stood. In this river zone, trout under fifteen inches long can't be kept, and the limit is three trout of any species. The remainder of the river has a five-trout limit with no rules on length. A special permit is needed to fish for trout.

I would have given anything for a rod, reel, and some silver spinners or small jigs. Later in spring and summer, during prime insect hatches, fly fishermen ply the fertile waters of the Eleven Point. In terms of fly-fishing, it ranks as one of the best, if not *the* best, wild trout streams in the state. Actually, it would not be all that difficult to carry a multisectioned pack rod, reel, and small plastic lure box. Imagine an overnight camp down by the river complete with fresh trout fillets fried golden brown. The other option is float fishing from a canoe and camping on the bank. A boater could camp on the wilderness side and enjoy both fishing and hiking. Anglers can also hike in.

But that was enough daydreaming. It was a good thing we did not have fishing gear. We would have spent most of the day on the river. Instead of hiking back up the spur trail that had taken us to water's edge, we angled across a short stretch of bottomland to the main trail and climbed east away from the river. The trail followed river bluffs and heady scenery southeast until the abrupt horseshoe turn of Orchard Hollow. On the topo map, the horseshoe shows itself as the most obvious loop in the wilderness. We elected to walk the entire "thumb" rather than bushwhack downriver and meet up with the trail at Whites Creek Float Camp. About ninety minutes later, we had negotiated the horseshoe and found ourselves within a few hundred yards of Whites Creek Cave, one of the more significant natural features in the Irish.

As in most Wilderness Areas, unlike state parks, there are not many signs. The Irish and other wild lands are established as places where natural order rules. The fewer "signs" of man, the better. For those of us conditioned to being guided in the city, it takes some mental and physical adjustments to feel comfortable and confident with topo maps and compasses. There was, for instance, no sign that pointed to Whites Creek Cave. Ken and I had been there before, but even at that, it took close inspection to find the narrow spur trail that led to the cave entrance. Once there, the cave was obvious, because it had one of the few examples of man's intrusion into nature: iron bars were locked across its mouth. The cave is closed from September 15 through May 1 to protect its population of endangered Indiana bats. We missed the opening by five days, and the best we could do was peer between the bars and try to envision a spacious walk-in cavern about sixteen hundred feet long, with large black chambers containing crystalline formations such as stalactites, stalagmites, and columns.

From Whites Creek Cave we traveled east and then north to the Fiddler Spring area. To reach the spring, hikers follow a short, eighth-mile south-facing spur trail. If you have the time and energy, cozying up to Fiddler is worth the extra steps. This spring, like Bliss Spring, emerges from dolomitic rock ledges or grottoes. Looking at Fiddler and the narrow stream of clear, cold water flowing from its cavernous mouth, I visualized the grotto opening as the maw of a lunker largemouth bass. Fiddler, or "Largemouth," has a companion grotto slightly uphill and to the right. We took a break there, listening to a hypnotic gurgle of water, the source of which we couldn't see.

Shortly after resuming the main trail we came across a hillside that was painted red. At first the slope appeared to be on fire, but it turned out to be a wild garden of the reddest indian paintbrush I had ever seen. It has long been the state flower of Wyoming, and I have seen some beautiful stands of it there, but none came close to this one in the Irish. Darsan he spent the next fifteen minutes photographing "hillside fire" from every conceivable angle. When his mission was completed, he grinned and admitted he'd used up nearly all his film.

North of Fiddler Spring, Whites Creek proper shows itself in a most swampish mood. For close to a mile we walked along a shady trail adjacent to the creek. With dramatic limestone bluffs in the background and the sun shining on still, moody water and flooded trees, I was reminded of the Mingo Wilderness north of Missouri's bootheel.

Whites Creek runs fairly cool and fresh in the spring, but this part of it was flat and marshy. A network of small cave openings, just visible above the placid surface, formed a mysterious honeycomb at the base of the bluffs. The sun lit the limestone bluffs, submerged oaks, and sycamores with an eerie, shadowy light that lent a mysterious air to this secretive place. The signs of beaver were scattered in all directions along the bank and floating on the surface.

Darsan and I moved quickly along the creek bank, hoping to find just the right moody light and camera angles to capture the mystery and tranquility of this sanctuary. For a photographer at that moment, Whites Creek was irresistible. And it was there that my friend finally ran out of film. I offered him a roll of black-and-white, but he politely declined. We both realized that only living color could possibly do justice to this surreal niche of nature.

It was one of those days, one of those hikes, when nobody, at least not me, watches the time. The lengthening shadows cast by sixty-year-old white oak trees suddenly tipped me off that late afternoon was upon us. We had thought we could cover the entire loop without difficulty, and we probably could have if we had not lingered in one near-perfect diamond chip of nature after another. We had lost ourselves in the beauty of woods, river, springs, and creeks.

We continued on the main trail for another twenty minutes before Ken called for a meeting of the minds. There was absolutely no panic in his voice. He merely told us that before long we would run out of daylight, and we might want to consider a due-north bushwhack to cut off most of the trail's east loop. Darsan and I agreed. Ken and I took compass bearings. If our course was true, we would pass two or three woodland ponds or sinkholes en route to the east-west main trail, which was not far from where Darsan's van was parked.

The three of us still had spring in our legs, and the change of pace from walking a predictable trail to romping like deer through the woods was refreshing. We passed one of the ponds and felt confident we were on the right track. Then we came out on an east-west trail that, according to the topo map and our compass readings, was not supposed to be there. The path looked well used. I remembered something I had once read in a Forest Service pamphlet on Irish Wilderness. I did not remember the exact wording, but it had something to do with a confusing number of old woods roads in the Wilderness that do not appear on the map. The pamphlet cautioned hikers to watch where the main trail departs from the old roads. Could we have gotten turned around on one of them without noticing?

We walked east for a while and then doubled back for a quarter-mile, hoping to find something familiar. We discussed backtracking to the spot where we had originally left the main trail, but decided it was too risky. The northern east-west leg of the Whites Creek Trail extends almost completely across the top of the wilderness from boundary to boundary. By traveling due north, we knew we should eventually run into that trail. That's why we'd agreed to bushwhack in the first place.

We continued north, certain that we should find the trail that way. Instead we found another road that should not have been there. We eventually found a trail that led us back to where the van was parked, but it was not the trail we had started out on early that morning. I asked Ken and Darsan a few days later if they had solved the orienteering puzzle. The answer was no. We have since blamed it on the spirits who apparently roam the old woods roads. We meant them no harm of course, and perhaps they were just playing with us, seeing what we were made of. The next trip into the Irish may very well provide answers.

Given the size and habitat diversity of the Irish Wilderness, it is not surprising that this area is commonly called the last stronghold of the American black bear and the mountain lion in Missouri. There have been recent documented sightings of both. For this reason alone, the Irish has proven itself a most valuable preserve. Both species are elusive, naturally wary of man, and prefer dense and isolated habitat. For the patient hiker and informed tracker, there is always the possibility of cutting fresh paw prints on dirt trails, moist banks, spring seeps, or fresh snow. The observant naturalist may have the chance to see and photograph seldom-seen wildlife. Knowing that the Irish provides sufficient food, cover, and range for bears and cougars adds an element of mystery, suspense, and adventure to any hike or camp out.

For professional wildlife and ecosystem managers, the wilderness is a place where the natural variability of ecosystems can be measured. In this case, the Irish provides a barometer that forecasts the success or failure of bear and cougar populations in Missouri. Without protected wilderness, both species would probably disappear.

When the forest began regaining its health in the late 1930s, so did animals and birds native to the state. With the demise of market and subsistence hunting, and the enforcement of Missouri game laws, the whitetail deer and wild turkey made strong comebacks in the Irish Wilderness. Squirrels, coyotes, bobcats, raccoons, rabbits, and gray foxes are also common in the area, along with owls, turkey vultures, herons, pileated woodpeckers, and songbirds. Rattlesnakes, copperheads and the eastern cottonmouth are occasionally encountered in the Irish.

There is, according to John Karel, a special "honor roll" for the men and women who provided the legwork and inspiration in the fight to enroll the Irish Wilderness in the national wilderness preservation system. Without these grassroots workers and their allies in Congress, the bounty of the Irish could have been lost forever. It was officially designated by Public Law 98-289 on May 21, 1984, 125 years after Father Hogan and his Irish immigrants settled there. The best of the eight Wilderness Areas to be designated was saved for last in the first round of Missouri's fourteen-year campaign.

Karel credits Charlie Watson with a pivotal role in elevating the importance of eastern wilderness in 1967. Watson prefaced his national dialogue with the poignant question, "Is wilderness only a western idea?" His involvement stoked the belief that eastern wilderness, though relatively small in total size compared to that in the west and in Alaska, was just as vital to the nation and its people.

"If there was a pillar of emotional strength in the campaign for Irish Wilderness, it was Dorothy Ellis," John Karel said. "She was the Oregon County Court judge at the time and was quoted as saying,

'I don't see the Irish when I'm there, I feel it.' " Ellis hosted a barbecue reception at her Thayer ranchette to which she invited Representatives John Sieberling and Harold Volkmer. Among the festivities was the presentation of a scroll to Sieberling from the kids at Koshkonong School. The scroll said, "Save Our Wilderness!" How much influence the scroll had on Sieberling and Volkmer nobody knew for sure, but both men became staunch supporters of Irish Wilderness designation.

The story does not end there. The cookout and reception hosted by Dorothy Ellis were well timed. Opponents of wilderness designation, including Missouri Congressman Bill Emerson from Cape Girardeau, were holding a barbecue and reception that same day. Apparently the antiwilderness group, including Emerson, who favored lead and zinc mining on the proposed area, saw the Ellis pasture filled with the cars of those supporting wilderness. According to observers, Congressman Emerson was surprised and baffled at the size of the crowd.

"There were a lot of people in Oregon County who were pushing for wilderness," according to John Karel, "but what they needed was a strong person like Dorothy Ellis. She was southern in her demeanor—a gentle woman made out of steel. She was, like many supporters in Oregon Country, one of 'Hogan's Heros.' "

Oregon County judge Louis Simpson and Senator John Danforth were also instrumental in supporting Irish Wilderness designation, as were Dan Saults and Don Cullimore. Ernie Dickerman of the Sierra Club contributed some timely advice on how to deal with opponents: "Bend the tree a little but don't try to cut it down." John Karel is lavish in his praise of other supporters, but he had as much to do with securing wilderness protection as anybody. "The Irish promotes dreams and fantasies," he said. "The place is a mental refuge. It exhibited poor tree production and is basically devoid of mineral potential. What it has, better than anything else, is wilderness production. Wilderness casts a sense of power—the Irish has it—even when compared to wilderness areas out west."

Greg Iffrig was a graduate student who became an employee of the Department of Natural Resources. He served as co-chairman of the Missouri Wilderness Coalition. Iffrig had a special and vital role in the coordination of grassroots affiliates across Missouri and donated countless hours for travel, meetings, and telephone work. His role was crucial to the success of the campaign.

As hikers, backpackers, campers, paddlers, hunters, fishermen, naturalists, and dreamers, we may never fully understand the moods of Irish Wilderness past and present, but we should be grateful to the many good people who devoted their hearts and minds to keeping the Irish alive for us and for those who follow us.

NOTE: Because of the prominence and recreational advantages of the Eleven Point National Wild and Scenic River in relation to the adjoining Irish Wilderness, a brief float and canoe guide accompanies this chapter.

Eleven Point River–Irish Wilderness Float Guide

One of the blessings the Irish Wilderness enjoys is having the Eleven Point National Wild and Scenic River as a major part of its western boundary. This idyllic partnership of natural treasures permits visitors to access the Wilderness by canoe, kayak, johnboat, or inflatable raft. No motors are allowed on the forty-four–mile stretch of protected water.

With alternating stretches of Class 2 rapids and deep clear pools, the river offers a good float for canoeists of intermediate skill. Fishing is commonly good to excellent. Several routes lie along the stretch from Thomasville to Highway 142, forty-four miles downstream.

Thomasville to Cane Bluff (9.3 Miles)

The initial section of the river offers the best opportunity for solitude but is floatable only when water levels are above normal, usually in the spring or after significant rainfall. The deep pools in this stretch offer good fishing for smallmouth bass. The average gradient or streambed drop is 6.5 feet/mile.

Cane Bluff to Greer (7.3 Miles)

This section also offers plenty of solitude and fine scenery. The towering bluff on the left at 14.3 mile was used around 1900 to launch virgin pine logs into the river. From there they floated downstream to a holding dam, where they were taken out and sent by train to the mill. Remnant logs can still be seen on the river bottom at Boom Hole. At 16 miles, Greer Spring Branch, now managed by the U.S. Forest Service enters the river and more than doubles the Eleven

Point's volume with its clear, cold (sixty-six degrees) water. Good trout fishing, managed by the Missouri Department of Conservation, is enjoyed below the spring; special regulations apply. The average gradient is 6.5 feet/mile.

Greer Crossing to Turner's Mill (4.9 Miles)
Greer Crossing is one of the more popular access areas, with moderate to heavy float traffic in late spring and summer. This section features the Blue Hole at Graveyard Hollow and Mary Decker Shoal, a river "chute" with fast water and large boulders in the stream. This is an excellent trout-fishing stretch and is managed by the Missouri Department of Conservation, and special regulations apply. The average gradient is 5.6 feet/mile.

Turner's Mill to Riverton (14.2 Miles)
This trip gives floaters an opportunity to see the Turner's Mill site, where the town of Surprise was once located. Other points of interest include McDowell Cave, Horseshoe Bend, and Boze Mill Spring. Whites Creek Float Camp and access to the Whites Creek Trail in the Irish Wilderness are found along this section. Turner's Mill access is in the special trout management area; again, special regulations apply. Below Boze Spring is a chute or rapid called Halls Bay. This can be a tricky spot for inexperienced floaters. When in doubt about running the rapid, it may be best to line canoes or boats around it. The average gradient is 5.6 feet/mile.

Greer Crossing to Riverton (19.1 Miles)
This is a popular two-day float that receives moderate to heavy use on weekends during late spring and summer. At Greer Crossing access there is a nineteen-unit campground, picnic area, and hiking trails to McCormack Lake. Take caution when camping this area during heavy rains as overflow water tends to flood the campground. The average gradient is 5.6 feet/mile.

Riverton to Highway 142 (8.6 Miles)
This portion of the river is slow and free of hazards. It receives light use, and floaters can expect peace and solitude. Because there is less river traffic and most of the land on either side is privately owned (under scenic easement), the prospects for observing wildlife are good. Blue, Jones, and Sullivan Springs are just a short

distance downriver. These springs make up an area called the "Narrows," which gets its name from a narrow ridge of land between the river and Frederick Creek. The average gradient is 4.3 feet/mile.

Missouri Ozark Waterways by Oz Hawksley is an excellent float guide and the bible for paddlers in the Ozarks. The book is inexpensive and available at bookstores, canoe liveries, specialty outdoor equipment shops, and libraries throughout Missouri. A trip that combines floating, fishing, hiking, and camping in the Irish Wilderness and Eleven Point River territory is a total outdoor adventure experience that satisfies the craving we have for truly wild lands and untamed waters.

7

Mingo Wilderness

Woe unto them that join house to house,
That lay field to field,
Till there be no place
That they may be placed alone
In the midst of the earth.

ISAIAH

MINGO AND HERCULES Glades became Missouri's first congressionally designated Wilderness Areas on October 19, 1976. Even
among the extraordinary Wilderness Areas Missouri has to offer,
Mingo stands out. It is the last original tupelo-and-cypress swamp
of significant size in the once-swampy Bootheel of the state.

In the late 1930s, interest began to develop in purchasing the
Mingo area as a National Wildlife Refuge. Even though the area had
many scars from improper land use and most of the wildlife was
gone, its capacity to produce timber and sustain wildlife was remembered. In 1945, the purchase of refuge lands began, and through
careful management, most of the productivity of the swamp was restored. The 21,676–acre refuge, managed by the U.S. Fish and
Wildlife Service, under the Department of the Interior, is now able to
accomplish its primary objective—provide food and shelter for migratory waterfowl. Waterfowl hunters from across the nation de-

serve much of the credit for Mingo's salvation. The Migratory Bird Hunting Stamp Act of 1934 requires hunters to purchase annually a migratory bird or "duck stamp." Funds collected from stamp sales have been used to purchase numerous refuges, including Mingo.

Within the refuge, 8,000 acres, consisting mostly of Monopoly Marsh, sometimes called Missouri's largest natural lake, and the Mingo River, are protected under the national wilderness preservation system. The use or possession of gasoline-powered boat motors is prohibited on all refuge waters. Electric trolling motors are permitted outside the Wilderness Area. No motors of any kind are allowed in the Wilderness itself. Paddle boats, including canoes, kayaks, pirogues, Poke boats, and kick boats, are best for fishing and exploring the Wilderness in peace and quiet.

Unlike many of areas that eventually became designated Wilderness in Missouri, Mingo had been well managed. The Fish and Wildlife Service had overseen it since 1945. There was no threat of heavy management practices, such as the logging and mineral prospecting that were commonly proposed for Forest Service lands that qualified as potential Wilderness Areas. Still, there were a significant number of concerned Missourians who felt that Mingo needed even greater protection than the national refuge system could give it. The Fish and Wildlife Service initially opposed designating the area a Wilderness, believing that some of their waterfowl management techniques, which had proved overwhelmingly successful at Mingo, would be altered or forbidden by regulations. For instance, water levels at the refuge are manipulated through the use of water control structures, ditches, and dikes, helping produce an annual crop of natural food. A six-hundred–acre farm provides more food for wildlife. Most of this land is tilled by neighboring farmers, who then receive part of the crop. The refuge's share of the crop is left standing in the fields for wildlife. Waterfowl management also concentrates on the construction and placement of man-made nesting habitat for wood ducks. Many predator-proof nest boxes have been installed. These boxes, combined with food and cover on the refuge, have resulted in a dramatic increase in numbers of the strikingly beautiful "woody."

The differences between wilderness proponents and the Fish and Wildlife Service were ironed out. Because the water table of southeast Missouri had been so altered by extensive drainage and channelization outside the refuge, the agency found it necessary to actively

A paddler in a Poke boat admires a wood duck box on a cypress tree in Mingo Swamp. *Author's collection.*

support the natural water levels in the wilderness. Fortunately, according to John Karel, this was being accomplished by facilities outside the Wilderness Area, and there was no conflict with the provisions of the Wilderness Act.

There is little doubt that the refuge and Wilderness Area complement each other. You can hike or take a self-guided auto tour around the area, but the only way to see the real Mingo is by boat. Only that way will you have a genuine Wilderness adventure. At one time, the Mississippi River flowed through the area where the refuge is now located. About 18,000 years ago, the river shifted east, and a dense swamp began to form in the abandoned channel. From the very beginning, Mingo Swamp was a haven for wildlife. Indian tribes were attracted to the area by the plentiful game. Numerous Indian artifacts and archeological remains of old Indian camps and village sites have been discovered on the refuge.

The area may have been named for the Mingo Indians, who, along with the Mohican, Delaware, Huron, Mohawk, and Iroquois tribes, originally lived along the northeast coast. In James Fenimore Cooper's *The Deerslayer*, Natty Bumppo, Hurry Harry, and old Tom Hutter have no respect for the Mingos. As Natty puts it, "I saw the Mingos, and know that they are out on the trail of mortal men, and not for beaver or deer." The Mingos were commonly called blackguards. They roamed the area, robbing and killing colonists as well as other Indians. They, like the French, were accused of being bloodthirsty when it came to their warring tactics.

So much of early Indian history has been lost to white colonization and the displacement of Indians from their native lands. When the area now known as New England was settled, some Indian tribes fled west. Others fought until they were virtually wiped out. The Mingos, despite their ferocity, may have recognized the superior force of the white enemy and fled into the Bootheel's swamps. They were well versed in traveling by canoe. Abundant wildlife provided food, and the deep forest hid them. As settlers pushed westward, the Mingos were forced from their sanctuary and probably fell prey to the government's eradication plan.

By 1890, Mingo's vast forest of cypress and tupelo was supporting a thriving lumber industry. After the timber was removed, large ditches were dug through the swamp to drain the area for farming. Over a million dollars were spent in an effort that was only partially successful. By the time of the Great Depression, the bad economy, failed drainage attempts, poor farming practices, and numerous fires had caused economic and ecological bankruptcy in Mingo. Now, the only sizeable remnant of the original swamp is in the Mingo National Wildlife Refuge in Wayne and Stoddard Counties near the town of Puxico.

My most vivid recollection of Mingo is from late March 1995. I had been hiking and camping in two other Wilderness Areas in the eastern Ozarks. Since it had been several years since I had last visited the refuge, I brought along a Poke boat, hoping I would have time to paddle the Mingo River, Stanley Creek, and Monopoly Marsh. I finished shooting the photos I needed at Bell Mountain and Rockpile by mid-morning Friday, leaving me the rest of the afternoon to explore Mingo. Before putting the boat in at Flat Banks, I stopped at the Mingo Visitor Center, a handsome structure that blends well with woodland scenery. I picked up a free Mingo guide that included a map of the area. The center gift shop also offered a generous supply of books for sale, such as identification guides, histories, and trail and hiking guides.

Fish and Wildlife Service staff are on hand to answer specific questions. For instance, although there is no charge for using the Mingo Visitor Center, a $3 daily entrance permit, Federal duck stamp, or Golden Passport is required for each vehicle. The center, located on Highway 51, one and a half miles north of Puxico, is open weekdays 8 A.M. to 4 P.M. year-round and weekends 9 A.M. to 4 P.M. from April 15 through June 15 and September 15 through November 15.

Visitors are permitted on the refuge from one hour before sunrise until a half hour after sunset. The refuge is closed from October 1 through March 14 with the following exceptions: the Boardwalk Nature Trail and Bluff Road Observation Tower are open all year, and the auto tour is open on Sundays in October and November. The refuge hunting area is open to properly registered hunters, and the area west of Ditch 5 is open to fishing and photography all year. There is limited hunting for deer, turkey, squirrel, and waterfowl during appropriate seasons. Hunters should contact the Mingo Visitor Center for current regulations. An area within a quarter mile of the Monopoly Lake Bald Eagle Nest is closed to all entry. There are picnic areas within the refuge but overnight camping is prohibited. As refuge Superintendent Gerald Clawson, whose office is located in the Mingo Visitor Center told me, "For most people, that kind of

camping with all the 'creepy crawlers' is probably not in big demand." He had a point.

According to John Karel,

> Mingo is probably the most important single stronghold for the unusual
> southern coastal plain species of reptiles and amphibians left in Mis-
> souri. Such species as the western chicken turtle, western mud snake,
> and canebrake rattlesnake occur in the swamp but are threatened else-
> where in the state by habitat destruction. One major factor in the abun-
> dance of reptiles in the swamp, besides the favorable climate, is the
> presence of Ozark bluffs, such as Fry Bluff, adjacent to the lowland
> swamps where reptiles, especially snakes, can seek refuge and hibernate
> in the winter months. Elsewhere in the Bootheel these crucial denning
> areas have either been destroyed outright or else pillaged by commercial
> animal collectors.

Biologist Archie Carr observes, "Reptiles are a part of the old wilderness of earth—If we let the reptiles go it is a sign we are ready to
let all wilderness go."

I don't enjoy camping with snakes, but I could visualize late-fall,
winter, and early-spring camping on the dry banks when the
"creepy crawlers" are snug in their dens. I feel shortchanged when I
cannot camp in wilderness. Like I said before, you have to sleep
with wilderness in order to fully understand it. I could however,
understand the reasoning of refuge managers.

The trappings of civilization within the Mingo Refuge certainly
set it apart from the seven other Wilderness Areas in the state,
which are managed by the U.S. Forest Service. There are more regulations, more "managed" options like the Boardwalk Nature Trail
and the auto tour. These in no way diminish the unique splendor of
Mingo's inner heart, the part where walking is impossible, where it
is necessary to wield paddles or oars to see and understand the vital
organs of the real swamp, and where you can see whitetail deer, otters, gaudy male wood ducks, and water moccasins as thick as a
man's arm. There is no other Wilderness in Missouri where you can
glide along over flat, black water to the inner sanctum.

I launched my boat at Flat Bank on that warm, breezy March afternoon. No one else was around. Packed in a small cooler that fit
under the pointed nose of the Poke boat's deck were water bottles,
sandwiches, granola bars, and a cigar. I also carried binoculars and
a compact, water-resistant thirty-five–millimeter camera. I stripped
off my T-shirt and allowed the sun's soothing rays a chance to share

their special verve. I watched small bluegill speed from the sides of the boat as I worked the double paddle for the first time.

The course was straight and narrow without any discernible current. Both banks accommodated stately stands of oak and hickory trees. The left bank had picnic tables interspersed along the route. There was also a simple crushed limestone road that followed the bank downstream. I would never have discovered the road if a car had not driven by. Ten or fifteen minutes later I reached a Wilderness marker buoy and a concrete boat launch. A pair of anglers were fishing a short distance away, and I asked them if they'd had any luck. "Nothing to brag about," they said. They were using small minnows for bait fish under plastic bobbers. I had left a light spinning rod and five-weight fly rod in the truck.

I could have eliminated fifteen minutes' worth of paddling if I had known about the downstream launch. But at the time it did not make much difference. The paddling was easy and I continued the journey on the Mingo. My plan was to cut west at the mouth of Stanley Creek and explore as far as I could upstream, then, time permitting, get back on Mingo and head onto Monopoly Marsh. Not long after entering Wilderness waters, the scenery changed dramatically from four-foot–high banks on either side of the river to scarcely any banks at all. Land and water flattened out and spread in all directions. At first it was relatively easy to define primary banks and the main river channel. But the farther I went into the Wilderness, the more land and water spread. The correct route became less obvious, and I took greater care in watching where I was going. I carried a compass and map so I was not particularly worried about getting lost. The map showed that the Mingo coursed northeast and ended up in Monopoly Marsh. Stanley Creek lay due west, and I figured its mouth would be easy to recognize. Stanley was about a mile up from the Wilderness marker buoy.

There were a lot of fallen trees at the mouth of the creek, but the Poke boat was nimble and narrow enough to work around the snags. I watched carefully for snakes sunning themselves on logs. The last thing I wanted to do was bump into a limb and cause a snake to drop into my boat. I have seen this happen to other paddlers on occasion. If panic sets in, the paddlers may turn their boats over. Veteran paddlers are alert and usually able to avoid snakes.

I worked around the tangles cautiously and then broke out of the woody maze into a large open pool of water. About halfway across the pool, fifteen yards away, I spotted a charcoal-colored snake swimming. At first all I could see was its head and a small portion of the body. When the snake turned around to see what had caused the disturbance in the water, a larger portion of its thick body was visible. It was a water moccasin, sometimes called a cottonmouth. Suddenly I had the urge to get close enough to take a picture of the snake. My camera was within easy reach.

As I readied the camera, the snake began swimming away. I followed with stronger paddle strokes, hoping the reptile would stop again and present me with a good angle. When I was within ten yards of it, the snake stopped abruptly, turned, and lifted itself higher off the water for a better look at me. I was just about to put the viewfinder to my eye when the moccasin began to move closer to me. For a moment I was mesmerized at how swiftly it closed the distance between us. Apparently I had angered this Mingo resident by encroaching on its space. Moccasins rarely swim away from a threat.

I dropped the camera in my lap, grabbed the paddle that was balanced on the boat's deck, and began a hasty retreat. I was headed back to the tangles of downed trees I had earlier negotiated when it dawned on me that if I got into that mess the snake could be on me in no time. I circled away from the wood pile and stroked on a diagonal course away from the moccasin as fast as I could.

Why the snake gave up I'll never know. He was twenty feet away and closing when he disappeared under the water. The vanishing act scared me because I figured he might surface close to me and easily slither up on the "moving log" I was paddling. I paddled as fast as I could, bull dogging awkwardly and precariously through the maze of annoying downfall that separated me from the mouth of Stanley Creek. When I finally reached the Mingo, I took several deep breaths, trying to coax my heart into resuming normal beats. I still think of what might have happened if the cottonmouth had gotten onto the boat.

With the exception of one other episode that afternoon, the paddle into Monopoly Marsh was as peaceful and satisfying as any flatwater float I've taken. The farther I pushed into the marsh, the more wood ducks I encountered. Their shrill squeals alerted me to their presence before I saw them. They flew through thick stands of trees swiftly and easily, with no apparent fear. Some flew over open marsh in pairs or groups of fours. These birds were probably early arrivals for the spring mating season.

Most of the wood duck population is found in the Mississippi and Atlantic Flyways. Mingo marsh provides perfect cover for them. Natural and man-made nesting cavities and boxes are abundant. Such sites are vital to the well-being of this species. Unlike ground-nesting ducks, downy "woody" ducklings, with prodding from their mother, drop from their rearing trees or boxes into the water shortly after they hatch. From that point, the adult female tends to the brood with a continuous regimen of swimming, flying, and self-defense lessons. Wood ducks eat a variety of foods found on the forest floor and in the water, including acorns, berries, grapes, seeds, and duckweed.

As I neared the main marsh, dense cover gave way to open canopies that permitted sunlight through. Carpets of emerald green duckweed, small floating plants the size of BBs, grew profusely in sunny pools. The boat's hull skimming over this lid of green produced an eerie sound, like some hidden creature's labored breathing. At first, I was confused by the sound and I kept looking around to see where it was coming from. It took me several minutes to discover the source. Every time I stroked the paddle and propelled the boat forward, the sound of "heavy breathing" rose from the surface. I managed a laugh about it, but a solitary swamp ride in Mingo can be eerie enough without conjuring up "the creature from the black lagoon."

Mingo is unique in many ways, but nothing is more special to the eyes of visitors than two species of trees found there—bald cypress and water tupelo. Both trees are traditionally found in southeastern wetlands. The entire Missouri Bootheel was once covered with swamps, bald cypress, and water tupelo. Now, there are just a few locations in the region where they can be found. Mingo has the largest population. For a northerner like myself, the initial sight of those "southern" trees in Missouri is a rare and unforgettable treat to the senses. Both species grow no farther north than thirty-eight degrees latitude, and the western fringe of their range is in western Louisiana and eastern Texas. Within that range, there is more bald cypress than water tupelo.

The first time I paddled Mingo, I could not keep my eyes off those trees. For me, they represented another world. The cypress lacked the curtains of Spanish moss prevalent in the deep South, but I envisioned it anyway. Like the redwood, bald cypress has an ancient lineage. There are only two species, found in southern United States and Mexico. The trees grow up to 125 feet tall and reach 3 to 5 feet in diameter. The trunk flares out at the base into a swollen, deeply lobed buttresslike structure. Woody "knees," from a few inches to several feet tall, protrude above the water from shallow, wide-spreading root systems. The exact function of these characteristic "knees" is not known. The light-green lustrous leaves and small round cones are unique among trees. Flowers appear in March and April. Some of the seeds provide food for gray squirrels and wood ducks. Cypress was once one of the most plentiful trees along drainage ditches in the Southeast, but its value as a source of rot-resistant wood has caused serious depletion.

Water tupelo is a companion species to the bald cypress, and its lower trunk is often swollen, deeply lobed, and buttressed like that of the cypress. Water tupelo is similar to the more populous and wide-ranging black tupelo but has larger leaves, 5 to 7 inches long and 2 to 4 inches wide. The fruit, borne on slender, drooping stalks 3 to 4 inches long, is about 1 inch long, dark purple in color with a tough skin and a thin layer of flesh over the seed. Trees may reach 110 feet in height and 3 to 4 feet in diameter. In a forest stand, the water tupelo develops a long, clean trunk above its buttressed base.

Monopoly Marsh is essentially the heart of the Mingo Wilderness. Broad and shallow, perfect for accommodating thousands of waterfowl during peak northern and southern migrations, the lake has open water intermittently spiced with stands of bald cypress, water tupelo, and a rich variety of other wetland vegetation. I have paddled part of the lake's perimeter and enjoyed close encounters with ducks, geese, herons, and shorebirds, as well as raccoons, beavers, swamp rabbits, river otters, turkey, and whitetail deer. Other species that inhabit Mingo, although I haven't seen them myself, are long-tailed weasels, bobcats, and black bears. For me, the open expanses of the marsh are not as exciting as the Mingo River, Stanley Creek, and miles of ditches within the refuge. The ecological diversity of the interior swamp is what this unique Wilderness is all about.

It was on my return trip from Monopoly Marsh that afternoon that the "second episode" occurred. I had spent about three hours, and I had to answer the call of nature. The Poke boat is a stable craft but not quite steady enough for standing up and relieving oneself on board. There are very few banks on the river that are level with

Mingo Wilderness is the last stronghold of cypress and tupelo swamps in Missouri. The "elephant foot" of the cypress is just one of the natural attractions of the swampland. *Author's collection.*

the water. That means a paddler cannot glide the boat onto the bank to beach it.

I did however find a spot not far from the mouth of Stanley Creek where I thought I could land the boat. So I "parallel parked" along the low bank, swung one leg over the cockpit, and put my foot down. It sank about four inches even before I'd put my weight on it. I tried to pull it out of the mud, which could more accurately be described as quicksand, but couldn't. I remained calm. Rather than tip the boat over, I swung my other foot over the hull and clawed my fingers into the top of the bank. Now both feet were stuck, and I was barely clinging to the bank, while the boat did its best to float away. Fortunately, I had wrapped part of the nylon bow rope around my wrist.

I forgot to mention that my footgear for the float consisted of nylon-strapped "river sandals," which are fine for conventional paddling, rafting, and wading but not well suited to quicksand. The sandals seemed to be coming unhooked from my feet. Things were getting serious. Panic more than clear thinking forced me to lunge toward the bank in hopes of reaching the top and, at the same time, freeing my feet. I was prepared to lose my sandals. I was a little more concerned about losing the boat. If I let the boat drift away I would have to hike out on foot, shoeless perhaps, and would probably experience firsthand many of the "creepy crawlers" that Gerry Clawson had talked about.

I am happy to report that the lunge, by no means acrobatic, worked. The hook-and-loop fasteners on the sandals held firm, and the boat, with no appreciable weight in it, followed me up onto the bank without knocking me out. Once up and standing on firm ground, I nearly forgot the reason for what should have been a simple boat landing. Then I remembered.

I would have lingered on land, maybe even taken a short walk to limber up, had it not been for the remaining challenge of getting back into the boat. The mud on my feet, legs, and chest was nearly impossible to remove. I honestly believe that Mingo's bottom is quicksand, or at least very deep mud, and floaters should be aware of it. Getting stuck in Mingo's muck could lead to serious consequences.

Getting from the bank back into the boat was slightly less anxiety-provoking than the exit. I used the double paddle as a brace, crouched down holding the cockpit with the other hand, and swung first one leg, then the other into the boat. Once inside the Poke boat, the body becomes ballast because of the hull's design and its low center of gravity. But now I had no leverage, and pulling the paddle blade out of the mud was a problem. I yanked so hard that when it came loose the backlash nearly ejected me out the other side of the boat.

That experience proved that some of the simplest pursuits—those taken for granted in everyday life—may not be so simple in the realm of Wilderness and certainly not in Mingo. The place shows many faces.

The sun, which had felt so wonderful on my back early in the day, had dipped deep into the western sky. Now the shade was lengthening, and the temperature reminded me it was March. I dug into the dry box and pulled out my T-shirt and a nylon windbreaker. Suddenly, the swamp changed faces; it showed a more mysterious side than it had in the bright sun. The transition made me paddle faster and harder. The upper Mingo River held no defined banks or boundaries—navigating back to the boat launch would be difficult on a moonless night. But there was still some light, and I wanted to see any creatures that had come out since my trip upstream.

I paddled past the tallest, thickest water tupelo I had seen all day. There was a large, well-aged wood duck nesting box about fifteen feet above the water. The unique duck nursery was made of sawed-off hollow logs. I wondered how many mother ducks had coaxed their hatchlings to drop from that tupelo castle. How many had survived the teeth or talons, or shotguns, of predators? When would the new wood duck family move into the big box?

Loud splashing off the right bank startled me. I saw a blur of buckskin, and at least four deer bounded away through the wet forest. From the trail of water and mud they had created, the whitetails were probably standing near the bank when they saw and heard me coming. I was dead even with them and didn't even know it when they decided to bolt. Deer are fond of swamps because of the food and cover they provide. There is limited hunting for deer at Mingo. Given the terrain and vegetation there, I would assume smart bucks have the edge when it comes to dealing with hunters.

Earlier that afternoon, I had spotted two fresh otter slides from the bank down into the water. Not long after the encounter with the deer, I spotted my very first Missouri otter. He was running along the bank not ten yards away, and when I paddled closer, the otter literally dove into the river without the aid of a slide. I never saw the animal surface. The Missouri Department of Conservation began reintroducing otters in the state in the early 1990s, and re-stocking has been so successful that limited trapping is allowed.

One thing became obvious on the return trip. Feeding swirls were now common in the shadowy river. Some of them were accompanied by loud splashes that I was sure were made by bass, and that revved my adrenaline. It was unlikely that carp would be splashing this late in the day. I had left my fishing rods behind because I planned to explore and take pictures. Now I wished I had them. A small topwater plug on the spinning rod or a cork or hair bug tied to fly rod leader would quite likely draw the attention of surface-feeding bass. There were no other fishermen in sight. There's no excuse for leaving rods in the truck.

The sun was setting when I reached the Wilderness marker buoy. Just for the heck of it I decided to count the number of paddle strokes it took from that point to the boat launch; it took 486. The next visit to Mingo I would use the concrete ramp at the Wilderness marker.

By the time I reached the take out, unloaded the boat, and strapped it to the roof carrier, darkness had settled over Mingo refuge. On my way out, I saw at least thirty deer feeding in a field not far from Flat Banks. Since camping was not allowed on the refuge, I headed to the Duck Creek Conservation Area a few miles away. Duck hunting is allowed on Pool 8, a wade-in area on the Mingo Refuge, and on three pools with blinds at Duck Creek. The Missouri Department of Conservation provides sites for primitive camping. It was there, under the glow of a Coleman lantern, that I pitched a tent and grilled hot dogs over a wood fire.

Before falling asleep that night, I thought of what it would have been like to camp on the banks of the Mingo River. It was a cool night, in the low fifties, and I doubted the "creepy crawlers" would be out in force. Then again, I remembered the determined water moccasin who had seemed out to get me. In what patch of swampy darkness was that snake lurking? And there were others for sure. The last thing I needed was a cottonmouth in my sleeping bag. Maybe Gerry Clawson was right after all.

The next day I broke camp early and headed back to Mingo. Gerry Clawson loaned me the key that would unlock several gates along the auto tour route. A dry spell had rendered the route drivable, and I wanted to see Mingo from a different perspective. The morning tour would also permit me to walk the Boardwalk Nature Trail and climb the observation tower for a wide-open view of Rockhouse Marsh. If time permitted, I would put the boat in and cast plugs and poppers to the bass that had teased me yesterday.

Beginning on Bluff Road below the Mingo Visitor Center, the twenty-five self-guided auto tour ends three miles north of the Mingo Visitor Center on Highway 51. Numbered stations along the winding route designate various points of interest. The drive takes about two hours to complete and includes Rockhouse Cypress Pool, which is one of the two major water impounds on the refuge. The large cypress trees have buttress roots that anchor them to the soft soil and play a role in getting air to submerged parts.

The next station is Limestone Bluffs. The Mississippi River flowed through the Mingo area over ten thousand years ago, and the bluffs are a visible reminder of ancient days. The striking limestone cliffs are similar to those found along the Mississippi River today. The Bluff Archeology Site is a two thousand-year–old Indian hunting camp. It was excavated by archaeologists from Southeast Missouri State University. The evidence found there indicates that the abundance of fish and game in the area was the main reason Indians used the area for thousands of years. Down the road from the bluff is a black gum tree that is the largest known tree of its kind in Missouri. In all, there are ten trees on Mingo that hold state or national records. Other areas of interest are the Mingo Job Corps Conservation Center and the water-control structures that are the heart of waterfowl management for the refuge. The Wilderness Area extends to the right of the tour road for seven miles.

Station 8 is called Bluff Lookout, and it marks the eastern ridge of the Missouri Ozarks. The Mingo area is often described as the point where the Ozark highlands meets the lowlands of the of the Mississippi River embayment in southeast Missouri. The hills to the east are Crowley's Ridge, which separates the old channel of the Mississippi River below the bluff from its present channel forty miles to the east.

Stanley Creek is a tributary of the old Mingo River. It's a popular fishing spot for catfish, bass, crappie, and bluegill. On the auto tour there is a two-mile round-trip walk that leads to a settler's old cabin. The Sweet family constructed it in 1933. Next stop is the Fry Bluff overlook that is known as a primary hibernation area for snakes. A mile to the east, on top of a large cypress tree, is a bald eagle's nest. While the numbers of bald eagles wintering in Mingo have risen significantly in recent years, nesting sights are not that common in Missouri.

The view of Monopoly Lake from a bluff offered a dramatic overview of prime waterfowl habitat. To encourage the regrowth of cypress and tupelo, the marsh is periodically drained by refuge personnel. This allows seeds to sprout and encourages the growth of waterfowl plants such as smartweed and sedges.

The autumn auto tour provides a "big picture" of Mingo, and I recommend that Wilderness users take time to cover the twenty-five–mile course. While it lacks the up-close and personal touch of boat touring, the overhead view highlights the significance of a unique natural area in the state. The contrast of bluffs and rolling hardwood timber on the top fringe of land with the tupelo-cypress swamp below makes for a stunning contrast in nature. When I visited Mingo two weeks later, I drove the road again, trying to absorb the best of both worlds. Up in the hills I was in the Ozarks, and the dogwoods and redbuds flowering. Down on the water, I could have been on a Louisiana bayou.

Hardcore hikers could describe the Mingo Boardwalk Nature

Trail as touristy and too easy. I thought the same thing when I pulled into the convenient, roomy, paved parking lot. But I walked it nonetheless and packed my camera and telephoto lens with me. The boardwalk path is a one-mile loop trail through bottomland hardwood swamp. Numbered stops along the way tell the swamp's story. Practically speaking, there is no other way you could hike this trail. Without boards under your boots, you'd sink to your chin, maybe further. The hike experience is a well-done nature and history lesson that complements a full-fledged Wilderness boat tour later on.

Mingo has many natural cycles in addition to those imposed by man. The water level in the swamp fluctuates with the seasons. Shallow water floods the swamp during the winter and spring, creating an excellent resting and feeding area for birds. The water recedes in late spring, and the swamp resembles a dry forest through the summer growing season and into autumn. The cycle varies from year to year, depending on rainfall and management.

In addition to water tupelo and cypress, pin oak, sycamore, and water locust trees thrive in the swamp because they tolerate short-term flooding. Buttonbush and black willow grow profusely. Common spring flowers you are likely to see at Mingo include spring beauty, mayapple, Dutchman's breeches, red buckeye, wild ginger, jack-in-the-pulpit, yellow violet, yellow rocket, swamp buttercup, bellwort, bluebells, blue violet, blue phlox or wild sweet william, and johnny-jump-ups. White oak, redbud, dogwood, and hickory trees prosper in the hills at a slightly higher elevation. The tall bottomland timber attracts numerous songbirds, including warblers, finches, wrens, gnat catchers, and thrashers. At least 207 species of birds have been reported on the refuge.

A tornado struck the boardwalk site in the spring of 1993 and took the tops out of trees that once shaded the area. The spot was exposed to direct sunlight for the first time in decades, and hundreds of seeds that had been dormant germinated and began to grow. Grasses, forbs, and trees sprouted up, competing with one another for nutrients, water, and sunlight. Over time the new trees will outgrow the grasses and forbs that are pioneering the disturbed area, and bushy undergrowth will gradually develop into a mature forest. In natural resource management, this takeover is called ecological succession.

The signs posted on the boardwalk trail are educational, but the best discoveries occur spontaneously. I have walked the trail many times. Early morning and late afternoon are the best times. On my first time through, it was like being at a zoo. I came upon a white-tail fawn, who stood and stared at me for several minutes. Then a doe also appeared, probably the fawn's mother. Neither animal showed any fear, and I snapped several pictures. The wildlife along the boardwalk tend to appear without the slightest sound because the moist soil muffles any noise. In addition to the doe and fawn, before darkness set in, I saw three raccoons, a dozen or so male wood ducks, several great blue herons, and an otter. For the photographer or naturalist, it pays to walk the boardwalk.

After driving the auto tour and hiking the boardwalk, it was close to noon by the time I got back to Flat Banks and launched the Poke boat. Visions of the feeding swirls I had seen and heard the evening before made it impossible for me to head home without making a few casts with spinning and fly rods. I figured if nothing else I could catch bluegills on the small cork popping bug I had tied to a six-foot leader. And sure enough that happened without much fanfare. I caught four- to six-inch bluegills on nearly every cast.

After an hour or so of catching scrappy panfish, I paddled to the Wilderness marker buoy and switched to a spinning rod and three-inch Rebel Pop-R floaters. I caught a mix of bluegill and eight- to ten-inch bass. I had hoped for larger bass, but I wasn't complaining. The fact that I was catching plenty of fish out of the Mingo River was reward enough. I might have caught larger bass in the early morning or late afternoon, but I had to be back home that evening. I would definitely fish Mingo and Stanley Creek on my next visit.

Gerald Clawson had told me at our first meeting that entering Mingo was like taking a step back in time. But it wasn't until I had paddled, photographed, hiked, and fished Mingo for several seasons that I truly understood what he meant. Within the boundaries of refuge and Wilderness, I felt the long-ago surge of the Mississippi. I savored the wonderful absence of growling machines and city stench. Only the cry of geese and the squeals of "painted" wood ducks echoed over dark brooding water. The bouquet of damp swamp is rich, addictive perfume. The crash of thunder over Rockhouse Marsh is the sound of the drumbeats and death songs of Indians long gone. The world changes. But the past clings to Mingo.

Turkey hunters walk a dogwood-lined trail, Piney Creek Wilderness.
Author's collection.

Flowering dogwood against a blue sky. *Author's collection.*

Bent trees in slough on White's Creek, Irish Wilderness. *Author's collection.*

Raccoon hunts for
snails and crayfish in
Little Paddy Creek,
Paddy Creek
Wilderness.
Author's collection.

Old wagon wheel, one of the remnants of human habitation found in
Wilderness Areas. *Author's collection.*

Spider in web. *Author's collection.*

Persimmons, a favorite
treat of many animals and
some humans.
Author's collection.

View of Table Rock Lake, Piney Creek Wilderness. *Author's collection.*

A hunter waits, camouflaged in the forest. *Author's collection.*

Wild turkey, Piney Creek Wilderness. *Author's collection.*

Two whitetail does and a fawn watch the photographer. *Author's collection.*

View of Piney Creek Wilderness from Piney Lookout Tower.
Author's collection.

Hiker's pack and boots, note
lug soles for better traction.
Author's collection.

8

Paddy Creek Wilderness

It is the marriage of the soul with Nature that makes the intellect fruitful, and gives birth to imagination.

HENRY DAVID THOREAU

PADDY CREEK became a federally designated Wilderness when President Ronald Reagan signed Public Law #409 on January 3, 1983. The 7,020–acre area is located in northwestern Texas County. It is within the Houston-Rolla Ranger District, thirty-five miles southwest of Rolla and sixteen miles west of Licking. It is named for Sylvester Paddy, who, in the early 1800s, began logging the area. The timber was transported by river to St. Louis, where it was used extensively in the construction of that city. From the mid–1800s until the 1930s, the area was homesteaded, and once the marketable trees were gone, it was used as open range.

The transformation of one of the finest wooded and riparian natural areas in the state into erosion-prone range was typical of that era; lumbermen and settlers sacrificed beauty for commerce. It wasn't until the late 1930s, when the U.S. Forest Service took control of the land, that recovery began. The beauty of Paddy Creek Wilderness is the result of "modern" conservation methods and nature's ability to heal itself when given the chance. It's sometimes difficult to believe that Paddy's beautiful stands of trees are mostly second growth and that rivers like the Big Piney and creeks like Big and Little Paddy ran muddy due to erosion just one hundred years ago.

A hiker can still see the lines of a few old fields near the drainage ditches; however, nature has very efficiently reclaimed the land. The fields that remain are reminders of history and do have merit as potentially good spots to stalk deer and turkey with rifle, bow, or camera.

The brightest stars of this Wilderness are Big Paddy and Little Paddy Creeks. Some parts of the creeks feature steep cliffs and rock outcroppings; other sections have lush meadows on either side. The setting is idyllic, especially in the spring when water is flush and a multitude of wildflowers line the banks. The bottomland scenes are reminiscent, although on a smaller scale, of the riparian meadows in the Rocky Mountain West, most notably those in Yellowstone Park.

The uniqueness of this Wilderness, aside from its uncommon Roubidoux sandstone geology and dramatic vistas, is the creeks themselves. They both run a long, winding course through the heart of the area's 7,020 acres until they join near the northeast boundary not far from Paddy Creek Campground. The Wilderness is the watershed for both creeks, which, in turn, feed into the Big Piney River outside the Wilderness, just southwest of the Slabtown Bluff Trail. Little and Big Paddy, fed by fifty-three small springs, have deep, permanent pools and falls that maintain flow continuously throughout the year. Elevation drops from 1480 feet at a point near the Roby Tower, which is outside the western edge of the area, to 980 feet where Paddy Creek meets the eastern boundary of the Wilderness.

The first time I visited Paddy Creek Wilderness I found myself "lost" thirty yards from my truck. I knew where I was, but I could not find the Big Piney Trailhead at Roby Lake Recreation Area. Roby Lake is one of three trailheads for the Big Piney Trail. Facilities there include year-round drinking water, a picnic area, and toilets. The road to Roby Lake is simple enough to find. It is one mile north of the town of Roby on Highway 17, then about a half mile southeast on Forest Road 274. There is a large parking lot for cars and trucks as well as trailer parking for boats. The lake itself is a five-acre gem stocked with bass, bluegill, and catfish. There's a simple launch there for carrying nonmotorized boats down to the water.

Roby Lake is a pleasant spot from which to access the Wilderness for hiking and backpacking because of the area's facilities. But, as I was later told by ranger Dean Dickens, someone had stolen the Wilderness trailhead sign that had been posted on a gate across just north of the lake and picnic tables. I saw the gate and barbed wire fence when I arrived, but the barrier looked very much like it was protecting private land. Yet the Paddy Creek Wilderness pamphlet I referred to showed the trail beginning on a northeasterly diagonal before making an obvious fork separating the north loop and south loop of the Big Piney Trail.

It wasn't until I drove the short distance to the Roby Lookout Tower and talked with a Forest Service employee there that the location of the trailhead was confirmed. When I returned to Roby Lake I took a closer look at the gate and the pasture on the other side. Apparently, few people had been using the access because there was little evidence of a path. Nevertheless, I was satisfied that cutting across the pasture would eventually put me on the main trail. I retrieved my pack from the truck and began my hike. Halfway across the pasture, the trail became more obvious. It led to the forest fringe. From there, a well-defined path headed straight to a Wilderness registration desk that lacked both sign-in sheets and pencils to record my overnight stay. There was no mistaking the trail from that point on, even though some of the Wilderness signposts were without directional signs. As in all Wilderness Areas, hikers and campers should rely on maps and compasses, and, to a lesser degree, pedometers, for staying on a true course. Wilderness signs have a habit of disappearing.

I decided to hike the north loop, which would take me to a pair of springs and a pond near the military road. Instead of hiking all the way to Big Piney Trail Camp on the northeastern corner of the Big Piney Trail, I would take a shortcut to the lesser loop midway through the center of the Wilderness and camp where the trail crossed Little Paddy Creek. The next day I would complete the trail on the south loop. I was packing about forty pounds and opted for the shorter loop mainly because it was my first visit and I wanted to take my time learning the trails and admiring the vistas, creeks, and springs.

Missouri's seven Forest Service Wilderness Areas have many similarities, but each one also has special characteristics. Paddy Creek's uniqueness was obvious from the very beginning of my hike. For instance, once I had completed the 1½–mile section from

Dean Dickens, Mark Twain
Forest's only Wilderness ranger,
at Roby Lake Trailhead, Paddy
Creek Wilderness.
Author's collection.

Roby Lake to the north loop of the Big Piney Trail, I saw more spur
trails, old roads, and bridle paths than I had at any other Wilderness
Area. The alternate trails are confusing, and a hiker needs to stay
alert and regularly check both topo map and compass.

One reason for the abundance of side trails is the Wilderness's location in the central portion of the Ozarks. The area was, and still is,
readily accessible. As part of the Salem Plateau, much of which is
rolling uplands, the area was used and modified by lumbermen and
ranchers. Virgin logs were hewn into railroad ties at a mill located at
the junction of Big Paddy and Little Paddy Creeks. From there they
were hauled by wagon to the Big Piney River, bound into large
rafts, and floated down to auction sites. The presence of the military
at Fort Leonard Wood, north of the Wilderness near Waynesville,
also had an impact on the area. Military Road, which crosses the
area, was originally built as an access route for army training. While
maneuvers no longer take place in Paddy Creek Wilderness, it is
common to hear artillery fire from the base thirty miles to the north.
Intrusive activity in the area largely stopped when the boundaries
were drawn, but about twenty-eight miles of old woods roads still
exist. They can be confusing, but they do not spoil the character of
Paddy Creek.

Roubidoux sandstone forms the thinner top ledges of the bluffs, and Gasconade dolomite, the thicker layers beneath. Characteristically, dolomite in the Ozarks is vulnerable to water penetration, and the Wilderness is blessed with caves, springs, a natural bridge, and an arch. The Forest Service has identified twenty small caves and unusual rock formations and more than fifty springs. The springs, many of them small, emerge from the ground in shaded, fern-bordered rock grottoes.

It didn't surprise me when I came across a spring at the 1.4 mile mark on the north loop. The first five miles of the trail are characterized by a network of five intermittent streams that eventually flow into Little Paddy Creek. The springs make ideal stopping points for resting, having snacks, and taking photos. I was sitting against my pack, hiking boots off, eating a granola bar and taking in the solitude and sunshine when I heard a thumping noise about twenty yards above me. A few minutes later a doe materialized from behind a cluster of cedar trees. What little breeze there was must have been in my favor because she had no idea I was so close to her. She would take a step or two, the source of the thumping noise I had heard earlier, stop and lower her head to feed. Then she would jerk her head up quickly and look around. The deer stared directly at me, trying to decode my presence. I expected her to bolt. If nothing else, my bright clothing and backpack should have caused her alarm. I have hunted deer many times with bow and arrow and rifle. Deer quickly sense danger. This one apparently could not figure out the "lump" on the ground. She never did spook but moved slowly down the hill, continuing her pattern of feeding and checking for danger. I gave her plenty of time to eat in peace before I pulled on my boots and returned to the trail.

A half hour later, I reached a spacious open flat with a large pond. In fact, the pond may be the one of the biggest in the Wilderness system. The sign just off the trail read "Pond and food plot." (This location is listed in the Forest Service pamphlet and trail map as "Pond by Military Road.") Conspicuous to the eye were disturbed leaves in all directions. The feeding sign was fresh, possibly from that morning or the previous afternoon. The spring turkey season was two weeks away. Unseasonably cool weather could have delayed flock breakup into smaller mating groups and individual gobblers.

Just then a loud, throaty gobble rang out below the flat. It was repeated, and I knew for sure that one mature tom had staked out a mating territory. Perhaps the boss gobblers had broken away from the main flock, leaving the hens on their own to disperse when the time was right. There were still plenty of acorns on the ground, and the possibility existed that the mature females were taking in extra food for the egg-laying and incubation period that would follow mating. On the other hand, gobblers eat little or nothing during the mating season, relying instead on a built-in "breast sponge" for nutrition.

The Paddy Creek Wilderness, because of its food and water supplies, as well as ample hiding and escape cover, is known for its good deer and turkey hunting. There was little doubt in my mind that the very flat I was on would be an excellent spot for a stand during the November deer season or the April gobbler hunt. As I would find out later, this wasn't the only prime spot on the north loop. At least six other areas showed plenty of turkey and deer sign. I could picture a cozy camp, with a crackling fire before each tent. Wilderness hunting is not for everybody, but few places in the state can match these areas in terms of quality hunting experiences.

The lovesick tom was still gobbling when I resumed the northeast trail toward the east loop that would take me down into the valley of Little Paddy Creek. After a morning of traveling the ridges, I was ready for the lower elevations and looking forward to my first chance to camp creekside. I took the right fork of the shortcut loop and found that portions of the trail down to the creek contained chunks of Roubidoux sandstone. Some of the sandstone had tumbled off the bluff ledges and created a maze of boulders. Surrounded by its beauty, I took a ten-minute granola-and-water break. In no other Missouri Wilderness had I seen these boulder monuments.

From that point, I followed a small stream that ran parallel to the trail down into the valley. I broke out into a splendid fringe of shortleaf pine trees before spotting Little Paddy Creek. The valley was perhaps three hundred yards wide in places, dotted with pines and cedar trees. An old woods road followed the creek upstream for a short distance. The road could have been used by the early logging industry to get lumber to market since the juncture of Little and Big Paddy Creeks was less than a mile from that spot.

Rather than camping on the bank of the creek, where the vegetation was thick and tended to be thorny, I opted for a wooded shelf of land immediately above the creek. A mixture of stately pines and mature oak and hickory trees grew there. The elevated position gave me a pleasant overview of the creek and its valley, and the site offered protection in case of rain. A small fire ring was already in place. There was plenty of flat ground to accommodate my two-person pack tent. After setting up camp, I took a short nap outside the tent on the camp mat I ordinarily use underneath my sleeping bag. The temperature was in the high sixties with a slight breeze, perfect for a siesta under the sun. I feel asleep quickly and woke up twenty minutes later, groggy but anxious to walk Little Paddy's bank in search of fish and animal life as well as spring flowers.

There was a deep, clear hole, about half the size of a basketball court, forty yards downstream from camp. The elevated bank was grassy and cropped short there, so I decided to sit and watch the water. Clarity was excellent; I could see small fish hovering near a submerged log. I recognized longeared sunfish by their rounded bodies. The pool also contained smallmouth bass from five to six inches long. As their names suggest, Little Paddy does not have the water volume of Big Paddy. Some parts of the stream dry up in late spring and summer, but there are enough deep pools like the one I observed to sustain moderate populations of game fish throughout the year. Fishing pressure is light on both creeks, and the fish populations are no longer hazarded by the uncontrolled logging and cattle operations that polluted the water.

Signs of beaver were plentiful. There were segments of both creeks dammed from bank to bank. The pools created usually hold good populations of bass and sunfish. A slow, quiet low-profile approach, like standing or kneeling several feet back from the edge of the bank, is required for successful fishing. Aquatic residents are wary of shadows on the water—especially those that could be made by great blue herons, ospreys, eagles, or humans. Trapping pressure is also light, especially in the remote parts of the Wilderness. By the late 1800s, the beaver had been, for the most part, wiped out. Today, under regulated trapping seasons and methods, the animal has made a successful comeback. Thanks to Wilderness designation, natural life cycles for wildlife and fish are protected from most forms of pollution. In Paddy Creek, even otters and mink are making a comeback.

After hiking a half mile downstream from camp, then doubling back and hiking another half mile upstream, I felt adequately familiar with the creek and some of its moods. Tomorrow morning I would leave the creek and head south to the loop of the Big Piney

Trail that would take me back to the Roby Lake Trailhead. The only thing I regretted was not carrying a light pack rod and small spinners and jigs with me. Observing fish in a stream is fine. Catching them is better. I would have released the fish. To this day, I have not caught a fish from Little Paddy.

The sun was setting as I gathered deadfall for a fire. I had packed in a small grill specifically for two thick pork chops that were in a plastic bag inside the pack. I also had one prebaked, prebuttered potato wrapped in foil. There is a time and place for dehydrated food and a time for genuine protein. Grilling chops in the Wilderness has special appeal. Vegetables included raw carrot sticks and broccoli crowns that would be dipped into a mixture of extra virgin olive oil and white balsamic vinegar. The zesty concoction was in a slim, four-inch-high leakproof Nalgene bottle that weighed next to nothing.

Darkness was upon me by the time a suitable bed of coals was glowing. Rocks at each corner held the grill about five inches above the heat. The only cooking light I had was my trusty headlamp—a no-hands camp tool that I find indispensable. I placed the potato near the edge of the coals for frequent turning, then lowered the chops onto the grill, where they began sizzling almost immediately.

There are those who may ask why a person would backpack into a Wilderness alone and eat alone under the stars. There are those who need not ask those questions because they already know the answer: there is great satisfaction in doing both alone. And there is great enjoyment in doing the same thing in the company of others. It is the choice that makes Wilderness life so delectable for both men and women. Anyone with the desire and confidence can enjoy such an adventure. When you're alone, it is easier to find who you really are.

I ate the food on a paper plate supported by a wicker one. My camp knife cut easily into the generously peppered chops. My vegetables provided a crisp counterpoint. And I finished my meal with tea and Fig Newtons. My Wilderness feast capped off a delightful day of exploration. But it was not the day's crowning glory. As I sat sipping my tea, a large dog appeared near the fire. Its appearance startled me. The dog sniffed the air. It took a step toward the cook fire that I had built into a flaming beacon, and I realized that the dog was actually a coyote. In the glow of the fire, I could see his hungry eyes and pointed nose. The animal's head bobbed up and down, as he tried to figure out the mysterious scent, a mixture of the grilled meat, sweet wood smoke, and man. Perhaps he had never smelled the odor of humans before. I thought the coyote would come closer to investigate, but he bounded off with a stiff-legged gait. I stayed with the fire, the stars, and the half-moon for another hour before settling into the tent and bed. After mentally reviewing my day's journey, I was on the brink of sleep when I heard a coyote howl in the distance, down in the creek valley.

In my dreams, I heard a turkey gobble loud and often. The sound disturbed me because the bird rambled over and over, so close I could hear the "tic and hum" of his rigid wing feathers dragging the ground. It was one of those dreams, either annoying or scary, that lifts a person from sleep before he or she is ready to wake. I felt myself trying to claw free of the dream. When I finally did I was staring at the powder blue roof of my tent. It was far brighter than I expected. Daylight was at least an hour old. My hands clutched both sides of the sleeping bag as though I had been fighting to escape it or the turkey of my dreams. I watched my fingers relax and open. Then the dream attacked again, louder than before.

A turkey bellowed uphill from the tent. I bailed out of the sleeping bag, crawled speedily to the zippered tent flap, opened it noisily and scurried out, shoeless, practically crawling to last night's fire ring. The lone gobbler was thirty to forty yards uphill in open timber and in full strut. I saw him perfectly, especially the head, neck, and wattles of red, white and blue. He circled slowly during his passion dance. His barred black-and-white wings flashed like checkered flags. I stood still, decked out in dark blue polypropylene long underwear that apparently gave me a nonhuman look, or else the amorous male simply didn't care who was watching.

The display lasted about ten minutes. I would have given anything to have had my camera and telephoto lens in hand. A soft ray of early sun lit the bird as though he were on stage. I have heard that strutting turkeys, wishing to capture the attention of hens, will seek out "lighted" display zones for better visibility. In fact, I had seen such a show before while hunting spring turkeys in Pennsylvania. That bird displayed well out of shooting range for an hour. He finally quit when a hen entered the arena, and the two of them walked away.

The Paddy Creek gobbler was not as fortunate. He must have finally recognized me for what I was. Turning downhill, he stared from the strut for a few seconds, and then in a flash transformed from gaudy puffiness to a sleek black tom with multicolored head and neck. He putted the alarm call loudly as though just recognizing the danger of the bright blue tent and the dark blue man. He walked, ran, and then went airborne in an attempt to escape the scene as quickly as possible. The whole show was fascinating. I would take the "annoying" gobbler of my dreams in lieu of an alarm clock any day.

It was then that I realized there was frost on the tent fly, and my bare feet felt like blocks of ice. Shivering, I scrambled into the tent and dressed quickly. I lit a small fire for warmth and began to prepare coffee and oatmeal. An hour later, I broke camp, left the creek, and headed south on the spur trail that would connect with the south loop of the Big Piney Trail. I was looking forward to the remainder of the hike. I had heard many enticing descriptions of the scenic overlook southeast of where the trail crosses again over Little Paddy. I expected I was about four miles away.

After leaving bottomland, the terrain became much steeper. My map showed the trail cutting through crowded contour lines. Yesterday I had hiked easy, level trails. But my after-breakfast walk had me leaning into the mountain for twenty minutes or more. Actually, the uphill climb felt pretty good. A hiker can almost feel his thighs and calves building strength and his lungs gaining capacity and efficiency. If my legs made the choice between steep uphill or steep downhill, they would choose uphill every time, due in part to some old sports injuries from high school and college days.

The descent from the mountain was smooth. The only excitement occurred when I was almost to the trail junction, and I flushed a hen turkey crossing the trail. The directional trail sign at the fork was missing. The pole was still standing. Heading south like I was, the Piney Trail was obvious. But for hikers headed northeast out of Roby Lake Trailhead to the Paddy Creek Trailhead and Campground, the junction could prove confusing. I've never quite understood the likes of Wilderness users who take signs. While compass and map should override markers, fledgling hikers and those who depend on signs could find the situation disconcerting.

I crossed Little Paddy Creek, stopping on the opposite bank to eat a granola bar and examine upstream and downstream. Upstream I saw a mink scurry from one side of the creek to the other. Once on the other side, the furbearer stopped and stood erect, fifteen yards away, for a better look at me. Again, a camera and long lens would have been perfect. Both were nestled in my pack, which I slipped off in hopes I could get to the equipment before this member of the weasel family fled to safety. I had no sooner zipped open a side compartment than the mink vanished through a stand of hackberry trees. I removed the camera and lens from the pack anyway. From that point, I carried the equipment around my neck.

Downstream I saw a beaver swimming across the tail end of a large pool of water that had been dammed with willow, cedar, and hackberry sticks. Before I could raise the camera, the animal slapped his tail and submerged. I shed the pack, sat down on the bank, and waited ten minutes in hopes the beaver would reappear. Finally, disappointed, I buckled back into my equipment and headed for the scenic overlook.

There was no mistaking this spot. It is unique among Wilderness vistas. I saw it as a long, flat-topped ridge laden with bluffs and boulders that look down upon Little Paddy Creek, shortleaf pine stands, and hardwood trees of all sizes and descriptions. The boulder "seats" on the ridge beckon hikers, campers, and photographers. Obviously others find this rock and wooded Eden an attraction worth getting to know. Of all the places I've hiked and camped in Paddy Creek Wilderness, this is the one with the most fire rings and perfectly level spots for tents. It's difficult to leave this overlook because the desire to pitch a tent and live here for several days is strong. I felt it the first time I visited the spot, but family commitments urged me on. I could feel the same urge now. The place is a natural jewel.

As a deer hunter, I could not help but picture myself planted on one of those rock chairs, which I would have cushioned with a foam pad, waiting for a buck to show on the network of game trails below. Packing a deer out of that setting would require strong legs and help from a partner, but the privilege of taking game in this spectacular setting would be worth the effort. No other venison would ever taste as good.

It is a little over a mile from the scenic overlook to the Big Piney north and south loop trail junction to the west. Most of the trail skirts bottomland. It was in that vicinity that I flushed a woodcock. I didn't see the bird as I was approaching and was startled when it went airborne like a miniature helicopter close to my feet. Then it leveled off and disappeared in the maze of saplings that characterized the area.

Close to the trail junction, an unusual stand of pines caught my

Grove of shortleaf pine trees that were planted in rows forty or fifty years ago in Paddy Creek Wilderness. *Author's collection.*

attention. Something was different. They seemed too perfect. It wasn't until I attained the proper angle along the trail that I saw they had been planted in straight lines like rows of corn. From every angle, these fifty- to sixty-year-old trees presented a geometric masterpiece of straight trunks and perfectly needled crowns.

I reached the south trail juncture that would take me back to Roby Lake. My truck was still the only vehicle in the parking lot. After stowing my camera and pack, I opened the cooler that held sandwiches and soft drinks. I sat at one of the picnic tables and ate while the sun was setting over the lake. Nature's show was not over yet. A beaver swam across the lake. A flock of blue-winged teal darted and circled over the water. And somewhere across Roby Lake, back in the woods, a barred owl asked, "Who cooks for you . . . who cooks for you all?" Before I drove away, I thought once more about how wonderful it would be to camp on top of the scenic overlook. There would be a next time.

Paddy Creek Wilderness is forested with black, white, scarlet, and post oaks, as well as hickories, but the star of the show is shortleaf pine. Many visitors, including John Karel, believe this area has the finest stands of pine in the state's Wilderness system, due primarily to the sandy soils that develop over the Roubidoux sandstone formation, creating excellent growing conditions for Missouri's only native pine tree. Catching sight of these majestic trees on the sandstone ledges of the upper bluffs overlooking Big and Little Paddy Creeks nearly always provides a reason to pause and take in the area's unique beauty. Even in midwinter, with deciduous trees bare, the forest remains alive and vibrant thanks to evergreens.

For those who appreciate trees of all sizes and descriptions, Paddy Creek bottomland produces box elder, maple, sycamore, ash, elm, and river birch, which are especially beautiful from mid-October until the first or second week in November. I was hiking down along Big Paddy in late October two years ago. At dusk, on a crisp autumn day, the sun's waning light literally lit up the hollow below me. The yellow maples in particular were glowing as though bathed in stage lighting. Everything else was dull and nearly indistinguishable. It was one of the most dramatically beautiful scenes I had ever witnessed.

It is the wide variety of trees and vegetation, undisturbed by man, that lend uniqueness to all Wilderness Areas, including Paddy Creek. Trumpet creeper adorns many of those bottomland trees. Sassafras, redbud, and flowering dogwood favor the shade. And in the wet soil near the creeks, an observer can find arrowhead and wild rye. Blackgum, Virginia creeper, blackberry, and fragrant and shining sumac add to the color show in fall. Even poison ivy adds a splash of crimson to nature's palette.

Wildflowers in the Wilderness include Queen Anne's lace, black-eyed susan, yellow St.-John's-wort, fleabane daisies, tick trefoil, jewelweed, white avens, horsemint, wild rose, and deptford pink. Coralberry fruits are dark red in clusters of four. Blue lobelia's elongated blue flowers have white stripes on the outside. Dittany has tiny purple flowers. In the fall, the prevailing wildflowers are goldenrod and several species of white, blue, and purple asters. *Missouri Wildflowers* by Edgar Denison is an immense help in iden-tifying the flowers found in Wilderness Areas.

I hiked the Wilderness with Dean Dickens, the Mark Twain For-est's only Wilderness ranger, on April 14, 1995. We had planned an earlier trip, but unusually dry weather conditions for late winter and early spring in Missouri had kept him busy monitoring and fighting small fires throughout the state. Fortunately, a three-day period of heavy rainfall the second week in April put an end to the threat of fire. We planned our trip. I met him at Forest Service head-quarters in Ava, also the base of the Ava/Cassville/Willow Springs Ranger District.

At the time, the forty-three-year-old ranger had been with the Forest Service sixteen and a half years. He once shared Missouri Wilderness duties with another ranger, but congressional cutbacks have seriously reduced Forest Service staff and programs. We drove to the Military Road access, off of Forest Service 220, which serves as the eastern boundary of Paddy Creek Wilderness. The road is more of a wide trail now and is being reclaimed by nature. It leads down to Big Paddy Creek and is a popular spot for turkey and deer hunters. On this morning, about a week ahead of spring turkey sea-son, we would not see any other vehicles parked at the unofficial trailhead.

It was all downhill for about a mile. The walking was easy, and soon we broke out into lush bottomland already carpeted with thick grass. Shortleaf pine and cedar trees bordered the bank of the creek. I was amazed at Paddy Creek's width, depth, and clarity. We stood in front of a large crystal pool hoping to catch a glimpse of a trophy smallmouth bass when a turkey gobbled forty yards behind us. The bird was in the woods, not far from the path we had just walked down. He gobbled six times. I asked Dean if he had ever hunted this area and he said no. It certainly looked like a perfect spot for hunting and fishing.

At the end of the pool, near the side of a bluff, a large boulder had fallen into the water. I evaluated the spot as perfect habitat for smallmouth and goggle-eye (rock bass). But again I hadn't packed a fishing rod. Dean had planned to hike south along the creek to a ford nearly two miles downstream that had been used in early set-tlement days. But there were problems. Recent rains had swollen the creek, filling it flush to the banks. We were able to leap across narrow side streams, but fording the main creek was impossible unless we wanted to get thoroughly drenched. The downstream route was blocked so we headed upstream a quarter mile. Beaver sign was everywhere. Huge pine and sycamore trees had been chewed. The comeback of the beaver is a fine testimony to modern wildlife management, but without regulated trapping in the area, it was obvious that mature stands of magnificent streamside trees were falling to industrious beavers.

Not wanting to get wet on a chilly morning, we left the stream and hiked back up the road. We would explore several other "unof-ficial" trailheads that led down to the creek. I had never seen the Paddy Creek campground and picnic area, immediately outside the northeast boundary of Wilderness, so we drove there. For Wilder-ness users arriving or departing the area, the camp area and north-east trailhead is a fine spot to start or finish an adventure. There are several points of interest just inside or outside the Wilderness.

The Paddy Creek campground has twenty-three units with tables and fireplaces. The adjacent picnic facilities include tables, grills, and rest rooms. The campground is closed from December 1 to March 15. However, during this period a person can camp in the picnic area.

Paddy Creek Trail is a one-mile loop that begins at the picnic area and runs southwest into the Wilderness along the creek, climbing the steep bluffs on the south side of the creek. These bluffs provide a scenic overlook above the creek. The loop trail descends the hill-side and crosses the creek. Through the woods, it turns northeast and back to the picnic area.

Slabtown Bluff Trail and scenic overlook are well worth the hike. The two-mile path begins near the boat ramp on the east bank of the Big Piney River. It runs south along the river, winding below

Shortleaf pine tree chewed by
beaver in Paddy Creek
Wilderness.
Author's collection.

picturesque bluffs. The trail climbs to the top of the bluffs and returns to Slabtown River Access.

While Dean and I did not cover a lot of hiking miles that day, my
time with him was well spent. He showed me various access areas
around the perimeter of Paddy Creek that I probably would not
have visited on my own. We talked about wilderness principles and
the value of those special lands.

Of major concern were wilderness abuses, and the one that concerned him most was illegal all-terrain vehicle (ATV) use on lands
where motorized equipment is prohibited. He was proud of the fact
that the fine for illegal ATV entry in Wilderness Areas had risen
from 50 to 150 dollars. Of course, to stop people from using ATVs,
he has to catch them, and he has a lot of ground to cover. I'm hoping
that Dean Dickens gets some help in the near future, that the Forest
Service can hire more Wilderness rangers to patrol the finest natural
areas in the state on a regular basis. The presence of these men and
women goes a long way in teaching wilderness manners, educating
the public and preventing abuses.

Not long ago I returned to the spot that Dean had showed me off
the Military Road Trail. Once I saw the place, I could never get it out
of my mind. It was early May. This time I was equipped with back-

pack, tent, and all the gear needed for a two-day stay. There was not other vehicle at the trailhead.

The downhill hike was familiar, and when I broke out of the timber, the valley was as beautiful as ever. The true value of wild lands is that they are never changed by the hand, or the whim, of man. But I did discover something drastically different as I walked to the edge of Paddy Creek. The pool of bass water that Dean Dickens had showed me seemed to have doubled in size. I quickly saw the reason why. Beavers had built an immense stick- and-earth dam. Apparently, the previous dam had been washed out by heavy rain. Wildlife experts claim that beavers replace old dams with bigger ones in order to reach new sources of food and building material without leaving the protection of water. These animals could obviously reach new trees; many pines, cedars, and sycamores had already been felled by sharp yellow teeth. I felt bad for the monarch trees and their fate as dam-building material. But this was unimpeded nature at work. Minutes later I discovered another positive twist to the new construction. While inspecting the new dam, I glimpsed a bass in the cloudy water. If my eyes served me right, the fish would measure over twelve inches—a lunker for Paddy Creek. The water was dingier than when I first saw it with Dean. I was disappointed; it had lost its pristine clarity. Recent beaver work had caused some temporary erosion.

After setting the tent and organizing my camp kitchen, I tied on a two-inch, brown curltail, segmented, soft plastic bait, appropriately called a spring grub. The lure was a proven performer on the smallmouth streams near my home in Ozark. I fished the deep, stained water near the dam, and on my fourth cast I felt a hard strike. The fish turned out to be a goggle-eye of seven or eight inches. I kept it for a fresh-fish supplement to the macaroni and cheese I planned to have that evening. About ten minutes later, fishing the same spot, I caught a smallmouth bass that I estimated to be twelve inches. The season for bass in streams does not open in Missouri until the Saturday of Memorial Day weekend. I admired the bronze fish and quickly released it.

For the next two hours I walked up and down one side of the big pool. I added four more keeper goggle-eye, a bluegill, and seven bass much smaller than the first one I had landed. I have caught fish in Devil's Backbone, Mingo, Irish, and Piney Creek Wilderness Areas, but none of those experiences were as satisfying as the fish caught in Paddy Creek—a true wilderness creek that lies in the bosom of forever-preserved land. For many anglers, it is not how many fish are caught or the size of those fish that counts, but where and how they were caught. In this case, I was on trophy land, and they were trophy fish!

The pan-fried goggle-eye reduced the macaroni to side-dish status. As at so many camp meals, the food tasted delicious, and for conversation, I had barred owls bantering back and forth. When they finally made peace, the valley turned quiet until I entered the tent and burrowed into the sleeping bag. Then I heard shots, or what I thought were shots, several of them in unison. At first I thought they were coming from the forest road above me. But the volleys sounded too close. Then, recognizing the source, I laughed, although I could still feel the leftover fear.

Leathery beaver tails when slapped hard on the surface of water in protest or warning sound like gunshots. Canoe paddlers can duplicate the sound to perfection by taking a paddle and slapping it directly on the surface. I had not seen any beavers while fishing earlier, only their sign. There is little doubt that they saw, heard, or sensed my presence. The nighttime serenade of "shots" fired by the beaver gang was a warning. I was infringing on their water. They had first claim. And in the wilderness nature takes precedence, as well it should.

9

Piney Creek Wilderness

The American public wanted two distinct environments on their national forests: The comfortable and the modern and the peaceful timelessness where vast forests germinate, flourish, and die; and rot and grow again without any relationship to the ambitions and interferences of man.

BOB MARSHALL

PINEY CREEK Wilderness is forty-seven miles from my home. I visit this familiar treasure in all seasons. It is there that I hunt, fish, backpack, cross-country ski, and meditate. It is where I go to escape the hectic trappings of modern life. I first visited Piney Creek in 1978, shortly after moving to Ozark, Missouri, and if I had to move away, it is the place I would miss the most.

Piney Creek was not enrolled into the national wilderness preservation system until December 22, 1980. Before that cars and trucks, driven mostly by hunters and campers, motored along Piney's old ridgetop logging roads. Both the Forest Service and the Missouri Department of Conservation recognized the forest's potential for high-quality nonmotorized recreation. Even as a study site, the facets of this precious wilderness jewel were evident.

A walk-in-only spring turkey hunt was inaugurated in 1978. At first, it seemed strange to leave the vehicle at the trailhead and walk into Piney. But after one or two outings, that "strangeness" felt good to me and to most other hunters. Largely eliminated was the crowding and interference among hunters brought about by easy access to popular spots. Hunters like myself who didn't mind walking a few miles down the trail had a better chance of finding gobblers and longer to work the tough ol' longbeards that sometimes take their own sweet time coming to the call. Gone were the noise and pollution of cars, trucks, and chain saws as well as the litter discarded by their owners.

After twenty years of turkey hunting in Piney, in the last eighteen, with no motors allowed, I've seen the quality of the hunt improve dramatically. I'm glad I had the opportunity to experience the area both ways. The comparison makes clear the positive transformation of Piney Creek from managed drive-in recreational area to a Wilderness Area that gets better with age. I did not have this opportunity with the other six Wilderness Area managed by the Forest Service. This is one of the reasons the 8,142–acre Piney Creek is so special to me.

I was elated when President Jimmy Carter signed Public Law 96-550, giving Piney Creek Wilderness status. The area had been gutted in the late 1800s when several railroad companies wiped out its timber. Cattlemen and homesteaders settled in, and erosion followed. The upper ridges of the area were used to grow strawberry and tomato crops for a few years in the early 1900s. But Piney Creek is at its best as forestland. Like the state's other Wilderness Areas, it had been disfigured, but its heart and soul remained. The Forest Service, conservation groups, and private citizens rallied for forest restoration in the late 1930s and won. Nature took care of the rest. Reclaimed was a rugged mountain paradise like no other in the state.

I first traveled into Piney by houseboat. A neighbor had invited me to hunt deer with him and his son. Instead of driving into the forest and camping, we boated five miles from the Cape Fair boat dock to where Piney Creek enters Table Rock Lake. Ed and his son, Alan, moored the sixty-foot boat off a scenic point that separated Piney Creek proper from South Piney Creek, a tributary. We arrived at the spot on a gray, blustery Friday in November. I remember seeing scaup, more commonly called bluebills, flying in swift, compact flocks back and forth over the lake's backwater, which afforded both food and cover. That area of the lake hadn't been developed, and the view from the boat was breathtaking. The mountaintops

were shrouded by low-lying clouds and their sides were fully carpeted with oak, hickory, and shortleaf pine trees. The area was
named for the thick stands of ridgetop pines.

I was to find out later from Ed that the U.S. Army Corps of Engineers controls this forty-three–acre parcel of land along Piney
Creek within the Table Rock Lake's flood zone. The rest of the land
is managed by the Forest Service.

Despite the cold, windy day, we were snug and warm inside the
boat's heated cabin. We stowed gear in preparation for the next
day's season opener, hoping that the wind, a negative factor in deer
hunting, would subside. The cold was not a problem, since whitetails are more apt to feed and travel during daylight hours in cold
weather. After lunch, we decided to scout the mountain directly
above the houseboat. An old logging road ran from the lake to the
highway trailhead five miles away. Little did I know at the time
that my first step on the Piney Creek Trail would mark the beginning of twenty years of adventures in this rugged forest. I would
return many times to the trail that Ed, Alan, and I hiked that day.

The first half mile of path leading from the lake was steep. The
terrain at lower elevations was brushy, filled mostly with eastern
red cedar and understory shrubs and trees like dogwood, redbud,
serviceberry, hackberry, and sumac. As we climbed higher, the forest opened into magnificent stands of white oak, hickory, and
maple. It was the beauty of this very first hike with friends and
neighbors, a father and son who shared their favorite spot with me,
that solidly hooked me on Piney.

Ed had three spots in mind that he thought would be good
stands for ambushing deer. He and Alan had any-deer permits,
which meant they could shoot a buck or doe. My permit limited me
to shooting a buck. We looked at each location and found they had
all the ingredients that make for a good stand, such as nearby game
trails, buck scrapes, and rubs in forest saddles that deer like to use
when crossing from one ridge to another or escaping danger. The
closest stand was mine; Alan's was three quarters of the way up the
mountain; and Ed's was in between ours. I was anxious to hike to
the top of the mountain, but Ed was concerned we would spook the
deer. So we returned to the boat for the night.

We woke at 4:30 A.M., and after a quick breakfast of oatmeal and
coffee, we readied our hunting gear. Once outside, we tiptoed to
minimize the noise created by the leaves crunching under our

boots. It was still pitch black. The chances of deer seeing us were slight, but whitetails are primarily nocturnal feeders, and they could very well be listening close to the trail. We had seen plenty of deer sign in the area and wanted to move to our spots as quietly as possible. I was the first to peel off from the group. The place I would sit, made comfortable with a boat cushion, was only ten feet off the trail. I was well hidden in front of a wide oak tree, but I also had good visibility down the trail.

Slowly, the blackness gave way to the misty gray of false dawn. I stared at a fuzzy landscape of trees, searching for, but not finding, the sharp focus I needed. I scanned the mist for a deer's form but saw only the dreamlike picture of the woods around me. The day eventually dawned bright and clear. An hour after legal shooting light, the woods came alive with yelps, lost bird whistles, and clucks of turkeys close by. I expected the flock to break out onto the trail. They were within thirty yards of where I sat, but I never saw them, nor did I see or hear a deer that morning.

We were all back at the boat by noon as planned. None of us had seen anything. Ed especially seemed surprised by the lack of deer movement. Generally, opening morning means enough hunters roaming the woods to stir deer out of hiding. But none of us were panicking. We would be hunting through Monday; there was plenty of time to try a variety of potential hot spots.

On board Ed's houseboat, the main meal was served midday on the back deck, weather permitting. This eliminated a lot of night-time cleanup when everybody was tired. At 1 P.M. the temperature was fifty-four degrees, and the day was gorgeous, sunny with a light breeze. The surprise at lunch was prebarbecued raccoon served with hot sweet potato pie. I had never eaten racoon before. It was somewhat stringy but had a good porklike taste. Once I got over the realization of what I was eating, I enjoyed it. The sweet potato pie complemented the meat.

After lunch, Ed and Alan decided to take naps. They looked at me funny when I opted for a hike up the mountain to see for myself what it looked like. Ed told me he never did much good hunting in the after-noon. Before leaving, I boiled water for hot chocolate and filled a quart-size vacuum bottle. I stowed the bottle in a daypack along with a game saw, rope, matches, compass, gloves, candy bars, and hard candy. By the time I got my gear ready and jumped off the boat, Ed and Alan were already asleep in their bunks, "sawing logs" in dreamland.

I took my time climbing the mountain, searching on either side of the trail for sights or sounds of deer. The spot where I had hunted that morning looked tempting, but I passed it up. At a slow, deliberate pace, the climb to the top took about twenty minutes. I liked what I saw there. A flat thicket with mature white oak trees and sporadic stands of cedar, certainly appeared to have potential as good deer cover. I left the trail and walked about forty yards into the timber. A massive oak tree stood in a partial clearing. The thick trunk would make a good backrest and would break my silhouette.

I settled into the spot, 30.06 rifle resting on my thighs and the small pack on the ground off to one side. It was 3:30 and already the sun was dipping low in the west. There was still a hint of warmth in the golden rays. It felt good to sit there, relaxed and at peace with the world. About twenty minutes later, I reached for the thermos of hot chocolate in my pack. I had been watching a chipmunk scurry in and out of the leaf litter. The animal paid no attention to me as I poured the steaming chocolate into the cup and took a sip, then another. I was about to drink again when I sensed a presence off to my left. Shifting only my eyes, I caught a flicker of movement. The movement advanced and a hide of grayish brown appeared bigger than life. A deer, forty feet away, was moving slowly forward, lowering her head to feed and then raising her head and taking one or two deliberate steps ahead.

The doe continued this slow, methodical pace until she was quartered to the right, about thirty yards in front of me. It was then that the sinking sun illuminated the shiny glow of an antler. The "doe" was a buck. With cup still in hand and rifle across my legs, I could feel my heart begin to pound. I set the half-filled cup down in slow motion. Getting the rifle into shooting position presented a more formidable challenge. Every time the buck dropped his head to feed, I hoisted the rifle a few inches. My arms were shaking. Deer have excellent peripheral vision, and I honestly thought he would bolt before I had a chance to bring the stock to my shoulder. To compound the situation, the animal was close to moving over the lip of the ridge and downhill into the valley below. When I finally shouldered the rifle, the deer was nearly over the ridge. I flipped the safety off, sighted, centered the crosshairs behind the right front leg, and fired.

The shot was true and it dispatched the animal quickly, but when I reached the deer I panicked. The antler I thought I had seen in the sun's glow had vanished. Had I mistaken part of an ear for an antler in the low light?

I lifted the deer's head and found the answer. A single eight-inch antler was buried in leaves and soil, still attached to the skull, when the deer fell. The buck had only one antler. I had assumed he had two and that I just didn't see the other one. It was a relief to discover that I had indeed killed a legal buck, my first one in Piney Creek. When I dragged the animal out to the trail, another hunter appeared a few yards away. He told me he had heard the shot. When he saw the buck's single antler, he told me that he was sure the same deer had run by him twice, once in the morning and again about an hour ago. But neither time was he able to get his rifle up to make a shot.

After tagging the buck, I attached a rope to the animal's neck and secured the front legs in order to drag it down the mountain. The trail to the houseboat, on a carpet of leaves, made the chore relatively easy. When I reached the boat, darkness had fully descended over the lake. The cozy cabin was bright and cheerful with lights. My partners inside were probably wondering if I had gotten lost. I left the deer on the bank and entered the cabin. Ed and Alan were sitting at the table drinking coffee. Alan asked me if I had seen any deer. I nodded and told them to come out and take a look. They stared at each other and simultaneously blurted, "You got one?" "Sure did," I responded. They followed me out the door.

The buck with one antler would never go to the taxidermist. But the antler does hang on a rawhide thong in my living room—a reminder of my first successful Piney Creek hunt. As Ed commented, the deer didn't have much of a rack but he was a large-bodied deer and would make good eating. We hung the buck from a railing on the houseboat. It was cold enough to age the meat without risk of spoilage. Ed had brought a bottle of homemade wine for just such an occasion. We toasted my success, friendship, and the beauties of Piney Creek. The memories of that hunt and my introduction to the Wilderness have never faded.

There is an excellent view of Piney Creek Wilderness from the Piney Tower, a half mile off Highway 76, on Lake Road 76-6, southwest of Cape Fair. From the top of the tower, a visitor can easily understand why wilderness expert John Karel describes the face of Piney "as a sea of rolling waves of tree covered hills." It is also obvious why Piney Creek was enrolled in the national wilderness preservation system. The Wilderness stands as a protected 8,400–acre island of natural beauty amidst the rapid and sometimes haphazard development on Table Rock Lake and popular southwest Missouri tourist destinations such as Branson, Hollister, and Kimberling City. Compared to Hercules Glades Wilderness to the east, Piney is more uniformly forested. It is impossible to hike in Piney Creek without being touched by the grandeur of its magnificent trees.

The Wilderness is located in the Ava/Cassville/Willow Springs Ranger District in Stone and Barry Counties near the west end of Table Rock Lake. It is the only Wilderness in the state with access to a major water impoundment, Table Rock, with its 52,300 surface acres and 857 shoreline miles. The Wilderness is accessible by boat from the north, approximately five miles from the Corps of Engineer's Cape Fair public-use area and boat ramp or from the Aunts Creek area.

Like Paddy Creek Wilderness, Piney has a significant free-flowing stream, five miles long, entirely within the Wilderness boundary. Unlike Big Paddy Creek, Piney Creek is an intermittent stream fed by small springs. Although the stream contains minnows, crayfish, and other aquatic life, the only sport fishing opportunities in Piney are at its mouth, where it empties into Table Rock Lake. By midsummer, some parts of the creek are dry. I have followed the length of Piney Creek from its beginning at a series of small, ledge-rock springs near Highway 76. The stream is initially a foot wide until it meets a network of tributary hollows that add water to Piney from springs and runoff. The creek descends into forest bottomland and gradually picks up more water on its eastern course to the lake. Piney Creek, crystal clear and shimmering over multicolored beds of chert and slab rock, splits the heart of the Wilderness almost perfectly into two equal halves. Ridgetop trails from the north near Piney Tower and ridge paths from the south converge in Piney Creek valley. The five-mile hike from the Highway 76 trailhead, near the forest warden's house, down into Piney's heart, is the highlight of bottomland trekking adventure. My family and I have made this hike several times. Compared to the ridgetop trails, the creek trail is not as well defined, but it is simple to follow. I can still picture my kids, Brittany and Scotty, scampering like deer through the woods and creek bottoms. Down in the bottoms there is more freedom to roam and bushwhack up numerous side hollows. On the bottomland hike, you cannot hear noise from the highway. Allow most of the day for this hike. Take time to explore the area where the creek meets the lake.

In the spring, if the lake is at normal power pool (915 feet) or above, carp gather in this area to spawn. It's also a good spot to catch black and white bass and crappie. In the fall, the brushy bottomland where creek meets lake offers good deer-hunting locations. There are plenty of scenic camping spots in this area with views of both the creek and the lake. In fact, the very first time I camped in Piney Creek, I set my tent on a bench of high land with just such a view. I hiked in from the Piney Tower Trail by myself. My Brittany spaniel, my favorite quail- and pheasant-hunting partner, had been killed by a car on the highway near my home the day before. The dog was special, and I needed to get away to grieve and think about our adventures together.

Two things stand out in my mind from that trip. The beauty of land and water in that location was spectacular. It had a powerful soothing effect, helping me get over the hurt of losing a special dog. I camped for two days. I took my family with me the next time, and the location became very special to us. We returned there for fishing and hunting many times in the spring and fall. The good memories shared with family and friends eventually purged the sadness of losing a good dog.

That first night I camped there, something strange happened that will forever stick in my mind. After sitting by the campfire and reflecting on life in general until 10 P.M. or so, I was ready for sleep. I crawled into the sleeping bag minutes later and dozed off. I don't know how long I had been sleeping when I awoke suddenly to bright light illuminating the tent. It was coming from the area outside. I stuck my head out of the tent flap and saw what looked like a moon rover.

The space-age contraption seemed to be hovering over the water. Four bright lights, like auto beams on high, cut through the mist rising over the water. I couldn't hear the sound of an engine, but this thing was headed right for my camp. I ducked back behind the tent flap. Only when this craft had made an abrupt turn, veering away from the shallow creek, did I see the two shadowy figures in the boat. They were holding spears and said not a word, or if they did, I couldn't hear them.

It wasn't until I talked to my friend Ed Fears several days later that I fully understood what I had witnessed that night. My neighbor laughed when I told him I had had every reason to believe I would be plucked from earth by aliens driving some kind of space craft. Being new to the Ozarks, I was not even remotely aware that people ventured out at night in lighted boats to spear, or gig, suckers. "Why didn't I hear a motor noise or these people talking?" I asked Ed. He told me they were probably in a johnboat with car lights mounted on the bow to shine into the water. He informed me that serious giggers don't talk much, and when they do, they speak in whispers so as not to spook the suckers below their boats. They were no doubt using an electric trolling motor to propel them silently in their search for fish. And they probably chose Piney Creek for its superb water clarity and the fact that suckers, highly prized as food when filleted and scored, spawn in April. The mystery was solved. I've camped at that same location there many times since then, but I have never seen another gigger "moon ride" into Piney Creek.

For hikers traversing the full length of Piney Creek Trail, there is an option to returning along the stream uphill to the highway. Leaving a second vehicle at the Tar Kiln Trailhead along the southern Wilderness boundary opens up a new and different route. That trail meets Piney Creek close to where it enters Table Rock Lake. The return trip on Tar Kiln features a challenging uphill switchback climb out of the Piney Creek valley onto a fairly level ridge trail bordered with shortleaf pine trees and magnificent stands of oak, hickory, maple, and dogwood trees. Side ridges off the main trail offer superb views of east-west valleys.

Because of its preserve designation and exclusive claim to Piney Creek proper, the Wilderness has considerable scientific value as an outdoor laboratory. Professors from local colleges and universities, in Springfield, Missouri, as well as some from far away, have studied and compiled information about the area, much of it centered on the stream, its purity, and the influence of possible outside pollution sources on the surface or underground. Piney Creek itself is a barometer of true water quality, past, present, and future.

John Karel once described the Piney Creek Wilderness as "family wilderness," and I couldn't agree more. Ridgetop trails, most old logging and settlement roads, are relatively easy to negotiate. Since 1980, nature's hand has been whittling former auto routes down to size, making them less-obvious, slimmer versions that support wildflowers, shrub borders, grass, weeds, and blackberry brambles. Forest Service maintenance is minimal. Horse use causes the most obvious wear, especially on steep grades. The lugged soles of hunters and hikers, though sometimes criticized by smooth-sole purists, do not contribute to trail wear in Missouri Wilderness.

Nearly all trails in Piney lead down to the creek. A few minor ones peter out on short ridgetops. For family groups that include novice hikers, there is little chance of getting lost. There is only one modified loop trail in the area. And there are few bogus spur paths to lead hikers off the main route. Prominent are twelve forest trail-heads, some signed, others not posted but obvious. A family can tai-lor the length of a hike, whether it's to a camping destination or for the pleasure of the exercise, to the competence and endurance level of its members. As in all Wilderness Areas, there are magnificent primitive campsites to be found in every direction.

My own children, who are twenty-two and twenty, may well have camped, hiked, hunted, and fished in Piney Creek more than any other young adults their age. They know Piney's beauty and solitude as well as I do, and we all treasure the memories of fishing, hunting, and family outings there. With both of them away at col-lege now, I am the primary keeper of our Piney Wilderness tradi-tion. I hike, camp, and hunt the same spots that we enjoyed together. Always when I visit these special places, fond memories of the past spring up through old campfire rings and "secret places" where gobblers and buck deer materialized out of nowhere.

One of our favorite camps was near Wildcat Hollow. We loved it for its seclusion, and we nicknamed it "basin" because of its shape. I found it deer hunting one year and told my wife and kids about it. The following spring we camped there during turkey season. The small fire ring we built rests undisturbed to this day. Others may have used the camp over the years, but if so, they left no obvious signs. The beauty of wilderness is that it rarely changes, except when hard winds, ice storms, and tornadoes topple trees and branches. Unlike in the "outside world," familiar places and things remain intact. By remaining whole and recognizable in the Wilder-ness vault, these nuggets of permanence become more valuable as the years go by. Because they can always be revisited, they are eas-ily and joyously recalled.

In 1985, I, my wife, Kathy, and the kids backpacked a deer-hunt-ing camp into the basin site. Brittany was ten and Scotty was eight at the time. They each had their own scaled-down Coleman back-packs in which they carried sleeping bags and pads, as well as clothing, water, and a portion of the food supply. My wife and I hauled the rest. We set up two, two-person backpack tents, one pitched by the kids for their use and the other for Kathy and me. We set camp on Friday in preparation for the Saturday opening of firearms deer season. Brittany was not a hunter, but she wanted to accompany her mother, who was, the next morning. Scotty, who was two years away from carrying his own deer rifle, would accompany me. Having been to this spot many times, my wife chose her location for the morning hunt, and I picked mine. We would hunt about six hundred yards apart off different ridges.

Next morning we woke an hour before dawn and dressed hurriedly in the cold tents. A hard frost had powdered the tent flies crystal white. I lit a single-burner pack stove and heated water for instant oatmeal and hot chocolate. In our daypacks we would take granola bars, candy bars, and hot chocolate in four-cup vacuum bottles. Neither Kathy nor I had far to walk to our hunting spots. After breakfast we bid each other good luck and headed in opposite directions. It was still dark, but we didn't use flashlights.

My son and I hunted about sixty yards off a ridge that I had never hunted before. I had a premonition about the spot. It was close to an area I had hunted before. We found a pair of trees, about six feet apart, to use as backrests. We each had camouflage boat cushions under our rumps to make the waiting more comfortable. Although only eight years old, Scott had hunted with me before for deer, duck, and turkey. He was always enthusiastic and never complained about the cold or about not being able to carry the gun. That day we waited nearly three hours without seeing or hearing deer.

In November, when it's cold on the deer stand, dawn comes grudgingly. The warming effects of oatmeal and hot drinks had worn off. When it was light enough to see down into the hollow, I spotted an old, dilapidated, homemade wooden tree stand about forty yards downhill from where we sat. There was little doubt in my mind that the hunter who set it in the tree had built the stand and used it before Piney Creek became a Wilderness. I pointed it out to Scott and whispered to him that the stand's location probably confirmed that we'd picked ourselves a pretty good spot to sit and wait.

Dawn arrived with a tiny, star-shaped beam of sunlight. It was 7 A.M. and the sun was offering no warmth; we could only hope that solar energy would warm us up soon. I knew my son had to be cold, I was. By 8 A.M., nothing had occurred to spur the adrenaline. Sometimes scampering squirrels can quicken the heartbeat. But they were not to be seen or heard. It was about this time I began questioning my decision to hunt this spot in favor of other areas I knew better. But the presence of the rickety old tree stand stuck in my mind as a positive sign that some hunter before me had thought the place worthy of stand. I didn't tell Scott, but I decided to wait another hour. Then we would head to another area close by.

Eventually, the sun's warmth reached us, and that made sitting and waiting easier. But there was still no sign of deer. At five minutes to nine, I almost whispered to Scott that we had had enough of our current location. I glanced down at the old tree stand, its weathered planks now illuminated by streaks of sunshine, and decided to stay put for another five minutes.

A minute passed, and I heard something running in the leaves. It sounded like a horse. I stared at the gully below in hopes of seeing a deer. The thumping of hooves grew louder. I wondered if my son heard them as well. I would have expected a deer to flee by running through the bottom of the hollow, but when I looked up at the opposite ridge, I saw a buck appear over the lip. Without hesitating, he bolted straight down into the hollow.

The gully was full of saplings and weeds. The heavy-antlered buck came to an abrupt halt in the bottom, surveying both the route that led down to the lake and the uphill saddle crossing where we sat. I figured this was my only chance for a standing shot, and I readied the 30.06 Winchester. The deer looked hazy through the scope, indicating the saplings were probably thicker than they appeared. The deer could have been one hundred yards away. For some reason, I didn't feel comfortable trying this shot. I felt certain that my son was wondering why I didn't shoot.

Suddenly the buck started climbing the ridge where we sat. This was a huge break. I was surprised that he would take the uphill route. He obviously had no idea we were there. He was coming up the hill off to my left. As a left-handed shooter, I rotated my rump to the left in an attempt to compensate for the awkward angle I would have when he drew level with me. The buck moved swiftly upward as though somebody or something was following close behind. I panicked for a moment, thinking another hunter might appear over the ridge and shoot the deer. When the animal was even with our position, he stopped abruptly and looked directly at me from seventy yards away. I squeezed the trigger, and he bolted five yards, running full tilt into a tree. He never moved again.

My son and I hurried to the spot and admired the buck's antlers. Then Scott walked a foot or so downhill and picked up the left-side antlers. In looking through the scope and making the shot, I hadn't been aware, as Scotty had, that the animal broke off one side of the rack when he lunged into the tree trunk. The break was about five inches from the brow point. A taxidermist would have no trouble mending the antlers.

I field dressed the deer on the steep incline and began the arduous job of dragging the big buck up the hill. Scott helped as best he could. The distance to the trail on top was not great, but even so, hauling the buck up to level ground took twenty minutes. I was drenched with sweat when we reached the top. From that point, dragging the deer back to camp was relatively simple. My son kept asking me if he could drag the deer. He would pull it a foot or so and then give the rope back to me. I was pretty well assured that he had deer hunting in his blood from that point on. He had spotted the buck when I did and held perfectly still while I waited for a clean shot.

Kathy and Brittany had not made it back to camp yet. When I hoisted the deer as well as I could onto a tree limb, the buck looked more impressive than ever. My wife and daughter walked into camp an hour later. They did not immediately spot the trophy. Kathy asked me if we had heard a close shot. I told her it had probably been mine. Scotty pointed to the tree where the deer was hanging.

The whitetail was the largest I had ever shot. And it just happened to be on my birthday. I had celebrated November birthdays several times in Piney Creek with my family. This one was extra special. Scott and I told the story of the big buck's demise at least four times. We sat around a warm fire as the western sky glowed yellow and crimson. It was then that Scotty got up and danced around the campfire. He told me it was to celebrate my deer. Then it was Brittany's turn, her mother's, and finally mine. I caught several pictures of the kids' ceremonial dancing. But even if the camera had failed I would always recall the images of that day and night in my mind. I visited the spot in November 1997, as I do every year, during a deer hunt. I stared into the same fire ring and visualized the kids doing their dance with an acrylic western sky as a backdrop. I sat on a log and wished in the worst way we were all there to recreate the scene.

Piney Creek is packed with a variety of real and emotional treasures. Some of the treasures are private and guarded by the heart; some are universally shared as relatives and friends build lasting memories in a special place where nothing really changes.

James Fenimore Cooper in his classic *The Deerslayer* described the wilderness of upper New York State in the 1840s as "solemn solitude and sweet repose." For me and my family, Fenimore's words describe our feelings for Piney Creek. I have celebrated fifteen birthdays in Piney, complete with cakes, presents, and occasional bottles of champagne or wine packed in from the trailhead. That day, November 12, always finds me there for deer hunting. For me it is the perfect place for such an occasion because when I am there with loved ones, my senses are alive and my outlook on life is consistently positive. Much of the inspiration for these feelings is the "solemn solitude and sweet repose" I always find in the wilderness. There is time to think and reflect, time to formulate new goals and change what needs to be changed, and time to realize that pure and simple wilderness replenishes body and soul like no other place. This same philosophy was important in biblical times when the Lord himself, as well as his prophets, trekked into mountains or desert to find renewal and understanding. It is just as important now.

Wilderness is both a place and a feeling. I believe it is the finest medicine for healing ailments of mind and body. It is especially valuable in defining and curing the complications of modern life, when we are brought to bay by computers, telephones, television, automobiles, crime, crowding, indoor living, lack of exercise, and last but worst of all, nonstop product advertising and rampant consumerism. It is in Piney Creek, because of its proximity to where I live, that I regularly shed the lead weights of life. I suppose if everybody knew what I know, and felt as I do, there would be no room left in Missouri Wilderness Areas. And maybe this could happen. To prevent that, we should enlist more areas in the state and nation for those prescribing to wilderness therapy.

My Piney Creek memories are plentiful. No amount of history, scientific ecology, or windy dissertations on the value of wilderness can compare to adventures shared in the past and those planned for the future. Yes, Piney Creek is a family wilderness, but it is also a place for solitary hikers, friends, scout and church groups, people young and old. The door to Missouri Wilderness is open to everyone.

Before Piney Creek became a Wilderness, District Ranger Paul Martin and Wilderness Ranger Dean Dickens, whom I have mentioned before, called my home in Ozark and made an appointment to talk to me. They knew I wrote regular weekly outdoor columns for the *Springfield News-Leader*. I had an idea what they wanted to discuss and was happy meet with them. The two Forest Service representatives were drumming up support for Piney Creek's Wilderness designation. I suspected they already knew my feelings about public lands and their value. And when they asked how I felt about Piney Creek, I told them I had already hunted, fished, hiked, and camped there. I agreed that Wilderness designation was the best thing for Piney. I assured Paul and Dean that it would be a privilege to get the word out through my column and my daily radio program, "Our Great Outdoors," which was syndicated on the Missouri Network.

Piney Creek and all designated Wilderness are special. Everyone who has enjoyed them and taken away a memory of them has profited. Land, water, and traditions are preserved. Adventures can be created and recreated without the lingering fear that today's spectacular forest is tomorrow's planned community or enormous shopping mall. Removed are the frustrations and political tradeoffs that result in under-the-table deals, privatization, and the "No Trespassing—Violators Will Be Prosecuted" signs that follow. For today in Missouri, as in other states, practically nothing is safe from the developer's hand. Nothing is too remote for the growling bulldozer. And Piney Creek could have, without the likes of John Karel, Dan Saults, Bill Bates, and others who fought for preservation, been some millionaire's 8,142–acre hunting preserve, complete with wrap-around security fence.

My daughter learned to pitch her own tent in Piney Creek. She learned that her leg muscles, lung capacity, and hiking endurance were equal to, even a little better than, that of boys her same age. It was there that she was given the opportunity to hunt, and to this day she is a defender of the sport, although she has decided shooting birds and animals is not for her. She is a camper, hiker, backpacker, and canoeist. And her savvy and toughness outdoors come primarily from her forest skills, learned from her parents and her own heart in Piney Creek.

Scott Farmer, the author's son, with wild turkeys shot in Piney Creek
Wilderness. *Author's collection.*

Scott shot his first buck and his first spring gobbler in Piney. The head of the eight-point is mounted on the wall. He is not the purist hiker or paddler that his sister is. He uses his legs and a canoe paddle as necessary tools for reaching good hunting and fishing spots. His favorite place in Piney is the water camp when it can be reached by boat. Then, regardless of whether it's fall, winter, or spring he will combine fishing with hunting. He loves to do both.

One time in April, when we were camped at the mouth of Piney Creek with another father and son, Scott was fishing for bass from the bank. He happened to look down between his feet. Laying in a bed of cherty gravel and sand below him was a perfect arrowhead with a heartlike pattern plainly visible on one side. It was the most dramatically beautiful artifact that either one of us had ever found. We knew the area had been part of an Osage Indian hunting ground as late as the 1700s. My son's arrowhead made that knowledge more personal and meaningful. When hunting or fishing in Piney, it is easy to visualize the native people, the original and most respectful residents, utilizing the area's bounty of game, fish, furbearers, and wood.

The water camp has afforded my son and me fine fishing for black and white bass and crappie. The best fishing is in April, May, and November. A Wilderness marker buoy signals the "No motor" zone on that portion of the lake. Most every fisherman I have encountered there shuts down the main outboard when in the area. Some still use electric motors for propulsion, which is technically illegal in the Wilderness. The noise factor is pretty much eliminated, and that's what maintains the integrity of the Wilderness. Not all of the Wilderness bordering the lake is in the "No motor" zone. The area has received more fishing pressure in recent years from March through November, and it is difficult, if not impossible, to avoid motor noise on the lake-facing front range of Piney's hills. To escape boat noise and highway din, it is necessary to seek middle ground on the ridges or low ground between them. Those hideaways tucked along Piney Creek proper, well away from the lake, are nicely soundproofed. There are many such spots in Piney that provide sufficient insulation from civilization, where sweet music emanates from whippoorwills, spring peepers, barred owls, migrating geese, crackling fires, and if the mood is right, camp singing.

For me, Piney Creek Wilderness has spawned uncommon and unexpected adventures, signposts along the road of life that put the passing years in perspective. It is not that Piney is unique among Missouri Wilderness in shaping these fascinating occurrences. I am convinced that all designated Wilderness is so blessed. But I have spent more time in Piney than the others and have been privileged to see many of its wild moods, moods that reject man's tempering.

I have yet to tell you about the time when my son and I were turkey hunting and camping there, and a tornado struck. And the time in October 1995 when I was bow hunting, and I heard a commotion on the hill behind me. Thinking I'd find deer, I turned slowly, my arrow nocked, and faced three enormous wild hogs. And I need to share with you the legend of Dave Sample, full-blooded Native American and highly decorated Vietnam veteran who knew Piney Creek, its moods, powers, and bounties better than anybody else. And I have to tell you that bobwhite quail hunting can be good in certain Piney Creek habitats. And when it snows in southwestern Missouri, there is no better place to cross-country ski than Piney.

I mentioned that Scott shot his first spring gobbler in Piney, but before that was accomplished we came eyeball to eyeball with the longest, fattest timber rattler we had ever laid eyes on. And because of that snake and our stupidity, we did something crazy and illegal.

Eye contact with a wild animal can be a scary thing. It was in Piney that I looked into the eyes of that wariest of wild animals— the coyote. A partner and I walked along a main Piney trail accompanied by a lone coyote, who stayed ten feet away for nearly one hundred yards before scampering off. Why the animal stayed with us, we'll never know.

And then there was the big snow during firearms deer season in 1995 when Piney looked like Alaska, and all the ghostly whitetails of the Wilderness showed themselves as if frolicking in two-foot–high drifts for the pure fun of it.

The mystery of phantom gobblers across the lake from our beloved water camp is yet unsolved. They gobble in the morning; they gobble at noon, at sunset, and on moonlit nights. We have learned to ignore them, for when we attempt to pursue these "loud-mouth" romeos by paddling our canoe across the lake, they are nowhere to be found.

Scott and I can laugh now about the April morning in 1995 when the tornado hovered above our turkey camp at a place we call "camp ridge." But that morning the pleasurable pursuits of turkey hunting nearly turned into a nightmare.

Storms had been in the area throughout the night, and we had been wakened several times by high winds and pelting rain. That was not out of the ordinary for southern Missouri in April. The ridge was ordinarily an ideal place to pitch a tent. Few people frequented the area off the main trail, and the location gave us easy access to several other spots that spring turkeys seemed to favor. The high spine itself served as an excellent listening post for hearing the passionate pleas of spring gobblers. Because the ridge was in the middle of the Wilderness and heavily guarded by rich stands of pines and oaks, we rarely heard boat or car noise. The place just had a comfortable feel to it.

When the alarm clock woke me at 4:30 A.M. that morning, I could tell that the wind had died and the rain had stopped. I figured things were going our way. After dressing, I lit the stove and heated water for instant oatmeal. Scott and I were excited about the lucky break in the weather. As still as it was, we would be able to accurately pinpoint the location of any birds that gobbled. Things were not exactly normal though. It was almost too still and the dawn sky had a pale yellow cast. We could smell more rain to come. We'd packed our rain suits, and we stood a few minutes, wasting precious time, trying to decide if we should slip into them just in case. We decided to carry them. We had made a poor decision. Five minutes later, while we were walking down the familiar ridge, the sky opened. By the time I unpacked the rain suit from my daypack I was soaked. My son, being more nimble, avoided a major soaking by shimmying into rain pants and jacket in record time.

Just as quickly as the rain had started, it changed from hard vertical to stinging horizontal drops. Thunder roared and lightning crackled all around us. We were still walking down ridge when large shortleaf pine trees suddenly took on the look of palm trees battling the surge of a Florida hurricane. We realized our bodies were being pushed by the wind in the wrong direction. Without hesitation, both of us wrapped our arms around pine trees and held on. The storm, sounding like a freight train, was upon us. We heard the rifle crack of a tree splitting apart not far away. I realized that every pine tree on the ridge could suffer the same fate. And then I didn't think anymore, I just held on.

Five minutes later, the wind, or whatever you want to call that dark bully, retreated or dissipated. We never did see a funnel cloud. We were too busy hugging trees. Afterward, a calmer rain fell vertically.

We thought about going back to camp to see if the tent was still standing, but then a turkey gobbled loud and clear off the point of the ridge. We grinned at each other and headed the bird's way, trying our best to ignore the spongy camouflage clothing under our rain suits. For an hour, we tried to call the turkey in, but more hard rain and renegade lightning snuffed the hunt. When we got back to camp, we found the tent still standing and still dry inside. It took us an hour to get a fire going. And eventually we quit shivering.

The weather extremes in Piney Creek may not be worse than in any other location, but sometimes they seem that way. We have seen our share of snow in the Wilderness. Snow and Piney Creek go good together, like frosting on a cake. Several years ago the Ozarks was blessed or cursed, depending on your point of view, with a generous supply of snow. In the city, the white stuff turned slushy, dirty, and sometimes hazardous. In Piney it lay soft and seductive, just begging to be skied on. Having lived in Wyoming, my family already had cross-country skis. It was a simple matter of loading up gear, food, and drink and driving to the Wilderness.

If there is a more perfect place for ski touring in the Ozarks, I have not yet found it. The main trails into the heart of Piney are made up of straightaways, moderate hills, and scenery that rivals the ski-touring trails out west. There is flat skiing and downhill runs through timber that challenge the most daring of snow lovers. And there's a solid guarantee that only an act of nature can wipe the snow away. Since cars and trucks are prohibited, no snow plows are allowed. The snow lays on the ground longer because it's protected by tall trees. A good snow that falls sixty miles north, in Springfield, Missouri, may provide one or two days's worth of skiing. In the Wilderness, that same snow can last for two weeks or more.

There are no crowded slopes or trails? I have never seen another cross-country skier, outside our own party, taking advantage of Piney's winter ski trails. We ski a while. Then we take a break for hot food, drink, and robust conversation centered on the joys of snowy nature and its rewards. Because no one can harvest wood in the Wilderness for commercial or home use, there are always plenty of deadfall trees to choose from, more than enough wood for a generous winter fire. The fare usually consists of hot dogs, brats, or Italian sausage, baked beans, and hot cider, coffee, or tea, all of which easily can be carried by several skiers in daypacks or stored in the vehicle at the trailhead until needed. Now that winter's best secret is out of the bag, there should be no more poking fun at the "Show-Me" state with cynical "Ski Missouri" posters. Wilderness cross-country skiing is for real.

Wild hogs are for real too. For several years, Mark Twain National Forest personnel had acknowledged the existence of feral swine at Piney Creek and other Wilderness Areas throughout the state. I believed the Forest Service, but in eighteen years of roaming Piney Creek during all seasons, I had never crossed paths with a hog. Then, in 1996, it happened.

Scott and I were bow hunting for deer and turkey on two different ridges in mid-October. We had pitched a tent camp near the trailhead. After lunch on Saturday, we headed to our stands. The maples and oaks were changing colors, even though the weather had been unseasonably balmy. Earlier that morning I had missed a twenty-five–yard shot at a large doe that was framed between two oak trees. All I had to do was put the arrow between the trees, a space about two feet wide, for a good chance at a clean shot. But when I released the arrow, the shaft veered far to the right and glanced off the tree. The deer bolted away. My poor arrow release had deprived me of venison.

I spent the rest of the afternoon waiting at the same spot I had hunted that morning. About 3:30, I heard a commotion up the hill behind me. It sounded like two or three deer scurrying down the hill. I dared not turn around. The only chance I had was to keep still and hope they would not scent me. If they passed by within a reasonable distance, I might have another chance at putting away some meat for the winter. Instead of descending into the draw below me, the animals stopped above me and began feeding. They were noisy. Too noisy for deer. The shuffling sounds could very well have been coming from a flock of turkeys. Another few minutes passed, and my curiosity got the better of me. I turned slowly, holding my bow at full draw. Expecting to see birds or deer, I was shocked to see three large pigs. One, the biggest and most aggressive feeder, was completely black. Another hog had black-and-white spots, and the third one was mostly white with a few saucer-size light brown spots.

There are no hunting seasons or limits on feral hogs, and neither the Forest Service or the Missouri Department of Conservation are opposed to hunters shooting them. I came to full draw in a very awkward position, so painfully awkward that I elected not to release an arrow. If they had been ten yards closer, about twenty yards away, I might have tried a shot at the black boar. I have never hunted wild boar, but hunters who have say that when they are wounded, they are very unpredictable and capable of charging the hunter who fired the bullet or arrow. If I had been carrying a rifle, I would have stood a chance of tasting Piney Creek pork chops. I elected to put down the bow.

I watched the pigs for the next ten minutes. The black boar seemed edgy, and although these creatures are supposed to have poor eyesight, he seemed to sense my presence. Gradually, the three animals moved slowly up the hill, still feeding, and disappeared over the top. I could hear them chewing and snorting for the next ten minutes. I couldn't help but think that this was the first time I had came face to face with a potentially dangerous adversary in Piney Creek Wilderness. The thought of it produced a case of the shivers. I have not seen a wild hog in Piney since that day.

I have a theory about designated Wilderness Areas. My opinion is that all forms of wildlife in protected areas are far more wary than those in civilized places, where they become used to the sounds of people and their vehicles. This notion has proven itself time after time with Piney Creek's whitetail deer and wild turkey population, and with other, less commonly seen animals like mountain lions, bobcats, black bears, and wild hogs.

Two major disturbances in Piney Creek include the opening of firearms deer season and the start of spring turkey season. Although Piney receives relatively little hunting pressure compared to drive-in areas, what disruption it gets from humans is no doubt "heard" or "felt" in every foot of forest and glade. Compared to wild creatures bent on survival, man is loud, clumsy, and easily detected.

Wild creatures that live in solitude most of the year are well tuned to the annual invasions of their turf. A hiker who walks several miles through the Wilderness without seeing a deer, turkey, pileated woodpecker, squirrel, or chipmunk is bound to believe that few animals and birds exist there. Nothing could be further from the truth. Some hunters, myself included, hunt Wilderness Areas because of this challenge. In our hearts we know that the birds and mammals that live there have the upper hand. Our occasional successes are never taken for granted. The Wilderness takes care of its own, and those who hunt there are at peace with that covenant.

There was one notable exception to my theory. Several years ago, a friend and I were walking down one of Piney's main trails a week before the opening of spring turkey season. We were scouting for sign and looking for morel mushrooms. We weren't talking, just watching out. I saw nothing unusual until I looked right. There, ten feet away, matching us step for step, was a full-grown coyote just off the trail. The animal watched me with pale green eyes. I poked my partner gently in the side, but we never spoke and never broke stride. Neither did the coyote. We stared at each other again. Finally I came to an abrupt halt. The coyote stopped too, backed off two or three feet, and sat down like a dog who was ready to accept a bone.

We stood there silently for about thirty seconds. Then we resumed walking. The coyote followed, striding even with us. We stopped again. Our wild companion did the same but did not sit this time; instead he raised his head skyward and sniffed the air. He took one more look at me, turned to his right, and walked slowly away through cedar and sapling oaks. We watched him until he disappeared from sight.

I wanted to call him back like a dog, but thought better of it. There had been no mark from a collar, no hint that he was seeking food or attention, no air of domestication at all. For a few moments, we had seemed to understand each other; we were both curious and both amazed that there could be peace and trust between us. At least that's what I thought. I don't know what he thought. I did wonder if he would be able to communicate his encounter with humans to others of his pack. Had I been given the kind of sign that Native Americans speak of receiving from animals? The encounter will always be treasured as good medicine.

I have told you of a one-time successful quail hunt in Hercules Glades Wilderness. I found even better, more consistent bobwhite quail hunting in Piney Creek where numerous bottomland fields produce native grasses, wild rose and blackberry thickets, and enough cover and food to support healthy coveys of quail. I don't hunt them as much as I did when everything about Piney was new and wondrous to me, but I see and hear them all the time, from ground blind or tree stand in November and in late spring and early summer, when their shrill mating whistles echo off the ridges. It feels good knowing they are there and holding their own.

And now, let me tell you about the rattlesnake. It made its home in Piney Creek. I had taken my son, age ten, on his first hunt for spring gobblers. We did not see the snake at first, but instead heard a hissing sound like air leaking from a tire. Then we saw him coiled on a sunlit bed of small rocks, a timber rattler as thick as my wrist. The tail, with a prominent string of slowly rattling buttons, was erect. Scott dispatched the snake with one shot to the head from his twenty-gauge shotgun. I skinned it, cleaned it, and put the skin and meat in a plastic bag that I carried in my turkey vest. I told the boy the rattler was just as much a trophy as a long-bearded tom. I promised I would tan the skin for him and mount it on a fancy wooden board.

About twenty minutes later we were set up on another ridge when a turkey gobbled. We moved twice to get into a good position for calling. Scotty sat in front of a tree. I called from another tree fifteen feet behind him. A second gobbler joined the duel, and the two birds double- and triple-gobbled to each other and in answer to my call. But they were in no hurry to advance.

The fifteen-minute flurry of gobbling was followed by sudden silence. I wondered if another hunter had heard the commotion and moved in on the birds. Twenty minutes had passed when I saw Scott come to attention and brace his cheek against the gun stock. He moved the barrel slowly to the right, and it was then I saw the bobbing red, white, and blue head. The turkey stopped twenty-five yards away and stared into the woods beyond us, searching no doubt for the seductive hen he thought he'd heard. "Shoot, Scotty, shoot," I whispered. A second later his shotgun roared and the bird's head dropped from sight. The gobbler chortled in his death throes. The boy ran to his first turkey. "Be careful of the spurs!" I yelled.

We tagged the turkey with the required yellow band around the leg and then just stood and admired it for a long time. My son carried his bird as long as he could. It was three miles back to the truck. About halfway there, I took over. Later, at the check station at Cape Fair, the tom tipped the scale at 21 pounds. His beard was 9½ inches long and the spurs were a full inch. The owner of the gas station took a picture of the boy and his trophy and gave it to him. I've kept that Polaroid snapshot all these years on my office desk under glass, but when the time is right, I'll pass it on to him.

I found out a few weeks later that it is illegal to kill snakes in Missouri, whether they be harmless garter snakes or venomous rattlers. Snakes do play a significant role in the balance of nature. The timber rattler that Scott dispatched was fully utilized. Fried rattlesnake made a unique meal, and to this day, the tanned skin of the five-foot snake hangs on a fancy cedar board in Scott's bedroom as testimony to one of our wild adventures at Piney Creek.

Because of its wilderness character, and the fact that many people would rather drive than walk, Piney Creek does not attract enough visitors to ever become crowded. In fact, I rarely see anyone when I am there. The few chance meetings are generally acknowledged with a wave and brief greeting. Sometimes those verbal exchanges are whispered so as not to disturb the tranquility, even sanctity, of the place. There was one exception.

The first time I met Dave Sample in Piney Creek I knew he was an extraordinary individual. It took no special perception to recognize he was one of a kind, and from that day on, I thought of him as a hero. We had a lot in common. We both loved Piney Creek. I always saw him there during deer and turkey seasons. It was impossible to miss his trailhead camp; it had the big tepee adorned with Indian symbols and the outdoor kitchen equipped with cast-iron kettles. He cooked over a crackling hickory fire, and whatever was bubbling always smelled wonderful. He invited me into his cozy tepee on several occasions. A small wood fire inside kept it warm on cold November days. Elk and deer hides served as carpets.

More often than not, there was a thick-beamed whitetail buck hanging from a game pole close by. I never asked Dave exactly where he shot those bucks, and he never volunteered the information. But I have an idea he hiked down into those deep Wilderness creek bottoms that most hunters avoided. While everyone else was hunting above, Dave slipped into the jungle cover where the bucks hid from the hunters on the ridgetop trails. He told me once it wasn't that hard hiking to where the bucks were, but it was tough packing them out. Considering that Dave had lost his right leg to a land mine in the Vietnam War, it was amazing how well he walked and climbed on rugged terrain. If he was in pain, he never showed it.

One hunting season, I saw a fine buck hanging from a game pole near his camp. I stopped and congratulated him, but he only grinned. He told me that his son, Frankie, had shot the deer—his first. Dave strutted with pride over his son's accomplishment. No doubt he also was proud as a strutting boss gobbler when Frankie played varsity baseball at College of the Ozarks. Dave had been a good baseball player in his day.

I told Dave I wanted to make my own tepee with a hunting design smaller that his full-size lodge, and he volunteered to help me. On a trip to Wyoming I cut lodge poles the size he recommended and then purchased enough canvas locally for the hunting tepee pattern. I still have the poles and canvas. The materials never have been crafted into a livable lodge. Dave had repeatedly invited me to his shop in Crane, Missouri, but for one reason or another I never made it down there.

I saw Dave again when we were both hunting gobblers in Piney Creek. We talked about how poor the hunting was that spring, and he hinted to me that he might try to find a new place to hunt. We were both unsuccessful that day. But the beauty of the Wilderness more than made up for any disappointment. Talk turned to plans for finally making my tepee. He gave me his business card and told me to call him.

That was the last time I saw Dave Sample. He quit pitching his lodge at the trailhead. Yet, every time I hunt, hike, or camp Piney, I think of him, his family, and friends, who brightened the forest with their deep respect for the outdoors, their Native American traditions, and their joyful approach to hunting. Dave passed away on October 8, 1997. I read his obituary in the Springfield paper two days later. The article described him as an outdoorsman, buckskinner, highly decorated war veteran, scoutmaster, husband, father, and friend to man. He was a true hero.

Not long after his death, I hunted fall turkeys in Piney Creek. My favorite spot is near where Dave used to pitch his tepee. I parked close to the trailhead where I first met him. Standing there, I could envision his lodge, smoke curling from its peak. I told Dave he would be missed. Piney Creek never has been quite the same without his presence. A few hours later, following a ridgetop trail, I found a flock of turkeys and scattered them in all directions. Not long afterward, I called in two birds from that group who were eager to reassemble. One of them made a fine Thanksgiving meal. Dave would have been happy to know the hunting was good that day. I could not help but think he might have been responsible for that.

Now, sitting at the computer, I have this burning desire to dig out my tepee poles and try to locate the place where I stored a bundle of canvas designed to pattern nicely into a conical hunting lodge. Deer season is a month off, and the hunting lodge would be perfect for camping. Thank you, Dave.

I've described many memorable days in Piney Creek. Even now, after going there for twenty years, I find that almost every outing has its share of special moments. But some are extraordinary, like a Friday and Saturday in November 1995.

Scott and I boated into Piney shortly after noon on Friday. The firearms deer season would open Saturday, and we wanted to arrive in plenty of time to set up a tent camp and still get in a few hours of bass fishing. The day was unseasonably warm, in the mid-sixties, and it felt more like spring than mid-November. It didn't take long to pitch the tent and ready the camp kitchen under a nylon tarp. Some of the best fishing of the year occurs on Table Rock Lake in November; that's when shad, the primary bait fish in the lake, are moving into coves and feeder-stream areas like Piney Creek, in search of plankton.

The significance of the food chain in late autumn, when fish are stoking up on food in preparation for winter, makes itself known in the area where Piney Creek meets the lake. Surface plugs and spinnerbaits are effective lures for black and white bass. On this calm, sunny day, however, the fish were uncooperative. We fished for two hours without getting a bite. Meanwhile, the sky was turning a sullen yellow color. We had no sooner beached and tied the boat than the first heavy drops of rain began falling. I complimented my son on the rain tarp he had erected over the kitchen area. Instead of huddling in the tent, we set a pair of lawn chairs under the tarp and watched the once-bright sky turn from yellow to dark gray to black.

The rain fell hard for an hour and the temperature dropped a dramatic twenty degrees, according to a thermometer we'd attached to the outside of the tent. The rain turned to hail—first pea-size, then grape-size, then, finally, the size of hickory nuts. As the wind intensity picked up, some of those hail stones began slicing diagonally, hitting the sides of the tent and occasionally pelting the lawn chairs and table under the tarp.

We ate cold sandwiches and sipped hot chocolate and tea, which we'd heated on a single-burner stove. We had planned a more elaborate meal for our first night in camp, but as the weather soured and the wind side-armed stinging hail stones, we decided to hole up in the tent until the nasty storm subsided. Unfortunately, the hail kept falling, and the temperature dropped another ten degrees. We played blackjack for an hour; then it grew too cold inside the tent to play, and we climbed into our sleeping bags.

I woke up at 3 A.M., shivering despite a good sleeping bag with a comfort range for temperatures down to ten below zero. There was an ever-so-faint drumming on the roof. I zipped open the entry flaps to find snow on the ground. The only positive aspect of the situation was that we'd have a good tracking snow in Piney Creek for the very first time. Scott turned over in his bag and asked if we had a window open. I told him about the snow and the twenty-degree–temperature reading on the gauge. Although we were equipped for cold weather, the frigid moisture within the nylon tent made our sleeping quarters feel like a walk-in freezer. I slept in five-minute spurts until the alarm finally sounded at 4:30.

Dressing was torturous. I layered on clothing as fast as I could, then I stepped out into the crackling cold. There were at least five inches of snow on the ground, but the stars were shining bright, and most important, the wind had stopped. I heated water for oatmeal and hot chocolate, then I refilled the pot and heated more water to make enough hot chocolate to fill two, one-pint vacuum bottles. We would carry them, along with sandwiches and granola bars, in our daypacks. The forty-degree temperature difference from the afternoon before slowed us down. We seemed to be doing everything in slow motion. By the time we had our packs and rifles ready, it was light enough to see. Ordinarily we are on stand at least thirty minutes before the sun comes up.

I had hunted in the snow a lot in Wyoming and always enjoyed the tracking conditions. My son, on the other hand, did not realize the advantages that a fresh snow bestows on the hunter. A quarter mile out of camp, we saw the footprints of other hunters. We veered off that trail and headed a different direction.

Scott and I split up at a familiar junction. He had his own game plan, and I had mine. As it turned out, we saw more deer that day in Piney Creek than we ever had before. The snow might have made the whitetails more visible, or maybe on that particular day the deer were roaming more in search of food and cover. Whatever it was, I bagged my deer at 2 P.M. and dragged it back to camp. On my way back to the tent, I heard shooting from the direction that Scott had gone. I hoped that he was successful. My son made it back to camp by dusk. He had taken a shot at a six-point buck at eighty yards but missed it. After that, he saw another seven deer but never was in the right position for a clean shot. I told him that the snow was moving the animals and that tomorrow would probably offer another good chance to add more venison to the freezer.

Sunday turned mild, and most of the snow melted. When we broke camp it was close to fifty degrees. Scott saw two deer that morning, but they eluded him. And while we were both disappointed about not getting a second deer, we knew we would never forget this trip. The dramatic shift in the weather had made hunting in Piney Creek even more exciting than usual.

Understanding and accepting Piney Creek is not always easy. This is a place that can confuse hunters. No story shows this as clearly as the mystery of the "water camp" gobblers. Many seasons the gobblers have led us a merry chase across the bay. We'd hear them calling, and across we would go in paddle or motor boats. Often, once we reached the shoreline, we could no longer hear the turkeys. Sometimes we would hear the deep yodeling of turkeys, but it was coming from somewhere above us. We would try to get in position on the same level as the bird in order to call it into shotgun range.

Only once have we been able to work one of these elusive toms into the call. That time was about seven years ago. It was midmorning, and Scott and I heard a gobbler sounding off every few minutes from across the lake. We paddled a canoe over to the spot, got quietly out of the boat, and began our ascent. When we reached the elevation that we thought would put us on even track with the gobbler, we set up for calling. Scott was twenty yards out in front of me. I was doing the calling. As usual the turkey had stopped gobbling when we first reached the shore. I called for thirty minutes without getting a response. It was the same old confusion until I saw my son raise his shotgun ever so slightly.

I expected to hear the thunder of the twelve-gauge three-inch magnum shotshell. There was nothing but quiet. A half hour later Scott arose and slowly walked back to the spot where I sat. He told me that when he raised his gun he thought he saw the bright blue head and red wattles of a male turkey. But by the time he saw the bird clearly, it was thirty-five to forty yards away. Having completed a hunter education and safety class when he was ten years old, my son was hesitant to shoot at "turkey colors" without positively identifying the turkey itself. I told him I was proud of him for making the right decision. That's the closest either one of us ever came to shooting what we now call one of the "phantom gobblers of mystery ridge."

That Sunday we were breaking camp in the midafternoon when

two gobblers began proclaiming their masculinity from midway up mystery ridge. They gobbled constantly for thirty minutes. Legal shooting hours end at noon or one each day, depending on whether daylight savings time is in effect. There was no way we could legally boat across the bay and work those birds. Even if we had been able to, we would probably have never found them. We have heard gobbling birds over there in the morning, at noon, and in the black of night, when they shouldn't be gobbling at all. Maybe the gobblers across from the water camp are nothing but ghosts of turkeys past. If they are, they're not the only spirits in Piney. There are deer that roam behind camp in the middle of the night—some blowing, some grunting loud enough to wake us up—but are never seen in the light of day.

There is wildlife in Piney that is uncommon elsewhere in Missouri. Chance upon the busy great blue heron rookery near the lake, and you are apt to see long, bony, prehistoric-looking birds and hear them squawking mightily to protest your uninvited presence. The Piney Creek area features one of the largest wintering population of bald eagles in the state. It is also home to roadrunners, armadillos, collared lizards, scorpions, copperheads, and western pygmy and eastern timber rattlers.

The secrets of Piney Creek only increase its fascination.

10

Rockpile Wilderness

In Missouri we have created refuges for animals, to protect them from man.
Now we need refuges for man, to protect him from the machines he created.

DAN SAULTS

ROCKPILE WILDERNESS is in Madison County, southwest of
Fredericktown. It has three features that distinguish it from all other
Wilderness Areas. First, the 4,131–acre area is by far the smallest
wilderness in the state; second, it takes its name from an ancient circle of igneous rocks on Rockpile Mountain arranged before the
coming of European men. Third, the Wilderness features a dramatically beautiful bend in the St. Francis River that touches the southwest corner of Rockpile—a magnificent place to pitch a tent and
savor the river, its bluffs and caves, and the hidden treasure of unspoiled nature.

Elevations range from 1,305 feet at Little Grass Mountain Trailhead to 520 feet in the bottoms. Wilderness land along the St. Francis features a majestic north-facing bluff of sandstone and dolomite.
The bluff is pocked with caves. Lush vegetation grows from the
wall's cracks and ledges and lends it a soft tropical appearance.

One of the clefts in the bluff forms a narrow, deep-soiled ravine
which harbors a stand of trees similar to those found in the forests
of Appalachia. Large specimens of basswood, butternut, Kentucky

177

coffee, walnut, sugar maple, white oak, butternut hickory, and red oak thrive. Due to their inaccessibility, they were spared from the saw and are now the crown jewels of Rockpile.

The Wilderness is located within the St. Francois Mountains, one of the oldest landforms in North America. The mountains are made up of rounded granite knobs over dolomitic limestone. Ridges are steep with rocky, wide slopes. Rockpile Mountain itself is primarily a broken ridge running from Little Grass Mountain and its one and only trailhead on the north to the national forest boundary four miles to the south.

The only public access is by the Faro Tower Road on the north. The trailhead is located at the west end of the small parking area. A granite boulder carved with the words "Rock Pile Mtn. Wilderness" serves as a trailhead marker. There has been some debate about whether Rockpile is correctly spelled as one or two words, and Forest Service literature and signing reflect that inconsistency. The current and correct spelling is Rockpile.

The Wilderness is almost entirely surrounded by private land. On my first visit to Rockpile four years ago, I was saddened by the amount of litter that had been dumped along the gravel road that leads to Little Grass Mountain Trailhead parking. Several empty motor oil containers, two gallon jugs for antifreeze, and other assorted trash had been dumped just underneath the trailhead marker. Of all the Wilderness Areas in the state, Rockpile looked as though its trailhead and parking area had suffered the most abuse; however, there was no evidence of neglect on the trail.

It was March of 1995, and I was on a week-long trip to explore both Rockpile and Mingo Wilderness Areas. I spent two days at Mingo then drove north and west to Rockpile. I stocked up on supplies in Fredericktown and then took Highway 67 south to County Road C, drove ten miles on C to County Road 406, and followed it to Forest Road 2124. Actually, I had to do a little backtracking that first time. As is so often the case in Wilderness Areas, one of the metal signs along the highway had been removed. It took me an extra forty-five minutes to find the trailhead.

In my opinion Rockpile is the Wilderness Area most difficult for first-time users to locate. A few more signs, left in place of course, and a more detailed description of the route in the Rockpile Forest Service brochure would help. The trailhead itself is understated compared to those of other Wilderness Areas. Visitors should keep the difficulty in mind and arrive at the area with plenty of daylight left. Good camping spots enroute to the area are few and far between.

The day I was there, it was cloudy, breezy, and cool. A perfect day to hike. I set out. I knew from the map that after making a sharp loop west and east from Little Grass Mountain, initially negotiating steep downhill switchbacks, the route would straighten out and proceed due south to Rockpile Mountain. From that point, ridges and saddles, rather than steep up-and-down trails, would make easy and enjoyable hiking. The open forest, strewn with granite boulders, gave the Wilderness an appearance that was different from others I'd visited.

I saw plenty of evidence that the area was popular with hunters. I counted six or seven tree stands, most of them old, along the trail to Rockpile Mountain. Wildlife was scarce the day I hiked, and fresh sign of deer or turkeys on either side of the trail was nonexistent.

Although small in size, with only two miles of maintained trail, Rockpile is easily accessed by walking old woods roads or cross-country hiking, bushwhacking, with topographic map and compass. Ironically, I found myself temporarily "turned around" in this area more than once. And though I don't like to admit it, my first search for Rockpile Mountain and the ancient circle of rocks took a lot longer than it should have. I simply veered off course several different times, believing I was headed in the right direction. There are enough roads and spur trails that even experienced hikers should be alert to staying on course. Numerous forks in the trail demand attention with map and compass.

In mistakenly heading west for a mile or more on my first visit, I became enamored with the miniature beauty of intermittent Cave Branch. When I checked the topo map and realized my mistake, I decided to follow the branch all the way to the St. Francis River. The miscalculation turned out to be a blessing. I enjoyed the natural beauty along the river and then a tour of Turkey Pen Hollow and the hidden treasure of the virgin trees that I had read about. It was among them that the seed for a future overnight camp was planted. The ultimate camp in Rockpile is near the river, with its bluffs, caves, and springs, and the ravine of special trees. A southern loop trail passes through the ancient rock site then veers northwest to Cave Branch and east to the main north-south route back to the trailhead.

There was still plenty of time to visit the ancient site. I back-tracked along Cave Branch and saw the remnants of a hunting camp a few yards from the water. A large piece of clear plastic tarp, possibly used as a shelter for cooking during the deer season, was flapping in the wind. In this valley of beauty, the plastic was grossly out of place. I folded the tarp into as small a piece as possible and tied it to my daypack.

About twenty minutes later I made it back to the fork where I had taken the turn that led me to the river. It was a tricky spot that appeared to course due east, instead of south, the direction I needed to go to reach the rocks. However, after sixty yards or so, the trail swung to the right or south. If I had taken a compass bearing at that junction, the mystery would have been easily solved. But sometimes, "mistakes" happen for the best.

I eventually found the trail to Rockpile Mountain. However, there were so many "false" hills or crests before I made the final assault, I was beginning to think that the mountain climbed forever. It then became clear why Rockpile Mountain was more accurately described as a series of broken ridges. For at least three different climbs, there was a "hill behind a hill" as though the final summit kept retreating. The higher I climbed, the larger and more crowded the granite boulders on the forest floor became.

When I finally made it to the top, the trail veered west. I followed it for a while, but it started to descend, which didn't make sense. I believed the ancient rocks would be on the mountain's highest point. I retraced my steps and ascended without any kind of trail to follow. I stayed on a straight north-south bearing and eventually came to a large irregular circle that could also be described at some connecting points as rectangular.

The rocks were laid out on a bare granite slab with one red cedar tree protruding conspicuously. The rockpile had four directional spokes and a three-foot–high granite rockpile in the center. At first, I was excited that I had found the ancient rocks, but a few minutes later, I began to think that this strange circle of rocks was modern. The location of the pile pretty well fit the description I had read, but it was just too neat and well preserved. Still, the circle was interesting, and I wondered who would have taken the time to build it. Was the counterfeit a ploy to keep others from finding the real rocks, or was it modern man's way of honoring the ancients whose traditions and ceremonies brought them to the mountain?

I photographed the stone work and then spent some time soaking in the sunshine of a March day that had turned summerlike. Whether it was the six or seven miles I had hiked or a strong sense of power from the modern circle, I felt wonderfully at ease reclining on a smooth slab of granite just outside the circle of rocks. Afterward, I thought it strange that I did not immediately rush in all directions trying to find the authentic rocks.

I dozed there for about forty-five minutes and then quickly rose to my feet as though awakened by an alarm. I took a north-south bearing down the crest of the mountain. I ran smack into the real circle of ancient rocks just south of the trail that veered west on my initial approach. I had actually walked within three feet of the spot on two occasions without knowing it.

The rock wall and circle was two to three feet high in places and three or four feet in diameter. Some of the rocks had fallen to the weedy ground. They may have been knocked over. How much tampering and vandalism had been done to this ancient monument I'll never know, and its quite likely nobody really knows. I did talk with one local resident and his family who assured me the circle of rocks had stood at least five feet high at one time. The man explained that "four wheelers" removed some of the rocks for souvenirs shortly before the area was designated Wilderness.

There were several small trees growing within the circle of rocks—a miniature circle compared to the modern one already mentioned. A squared-off boulder resembling a stone seat stood neatly in the middle of the circle. Cedar trees and high weeds encircled the rocks. I stood there amazed for several minutes that I had not seen this landmark when I first passed by it. I walked around the rocks but not inside the circle. It was then that I discovered that the pattern was not obvious at certain angles and positions. Yet when I stood facing directly north, there was no mistaking their presence. Perhaps the pile was built that way on purpose—revealed and concealed at the same time. Then too the direction north could have special significance. This was pure speculation.

John Karel describes his meeting of the rocks before the area became designated Wilderness:

> Near the top of Rockpile, in a scraggly growth of twisted oaks and adjacent to one of the scarce barrens, broods the source of the mountain's name, a circular pile of igneous boulders constructed before the advent

Rockpile Mountain Wilderness was named for an ancient mound of rocks. Before Wilderness designation, many of the rocks were removed as souvenirs. *Author's collection.*

of European explorers. Despite the fact that through the years curious but careless people have reduced the height of the rock enclosure, this structure is still easily discerned and continues to provoke questions for which hard answers are unknown.

Most people wonder if the rocks mark a burial site or a sentinel post, or perhaps a ceremonial site where rituals were performed. When was it constructed, and by what group of people? Has the environment around the rockpile changed since its construction? Is it likely that in the past the open barrens were more extensive and that more commanding vistas marked this peak as a logical center of activity? Other peaks in the region are higher, others can be found with broader, more commanding views. Why was this knob chosen over the others?

Much of the pilfering of the rocks seems to be associated lately with use of four wheel drive vehicles that presently have access to the old logging trails in the area. Wilderness designation will close these old trails to mechanized vehicles and help to protect the rockpile from further deterioration. In the future, others should have the opportunity to pause on this igneous hill and wonder about the earlier people who used the place long ago for their own purposes.

Ironically, the U.S. Forest Service has done nothing to shed light on the mystery of the ancient rockpile. No research appears to have been conducted, but one thing is known: Rockpile Mountain is in close proximity to ancient groups of mounds and village sites in Madison County and other numerous sites in the Missouri Bootheel. It is logical to assume that the circle of boulders could be connected to ancient tribes who lived, hunted, and fished on the edge of Missouri's mountainous and flat land transition zone. Indigenous peoples have historically sought out high places for spiritual guidance, vision quests, and rituals, as well as for sources of wood and game. For a better understanding of the relationship between ancient peoples and the land, you can read *Paradigms of the Past: The Story of Missouri Archaeology* by Michael J. O'Brien.

West and then due north of Rockpile Mountain there's a spur trail that follows the intermittent Cave Branch as it meanders northwest through a splendid miniature gorge, complete with narrow shut-ins. While they are not on the scale of Johnson's Shut-Ins, they are significant nevertheless and well worth a look. During the spring, the narrow gorges produce cascades that tumble over granite rocks covered with a lacy network of lichen, moss, and ferns. The opportunities for spectacular photos, despite the scaled-down size of the waterway, are numerous. This is my favorite time of year to visit and photograph this area.

At times, due to the rapid flow of water from steep areas of

Close by the real mound of rocks on Rockpile is another circle on a level slab of granite. The counterfeit creation is interesting but definitely modern. The creator is unknown. *Author's collection.*

exposed rock, runoff becomes a torrent following heavy rain. In other words, there's not enough soil for saturation into the ground and no place for the water to go but down. Like the rest of the St. Francois Mountains area, the uplands are covered with oak, hickory, and short-leaf pine. Found beneath the mixed hardwood old-growth trees in the ravine is understory, consisting of American hornbeam, papaw (sometimes spelled paw paw), spicebush, and a variety of ferns and herbs such as hepatica, wild ginger and ginseng. Rose azaleas, considered by many to be Missouri's most beautiful native shrub, bloom in late April and May on rocky hillsides and in scattered granite glades.

Wildlife includes whitetail deer, wild turkey, squirrels, rabbits, raccoons, a variety of turtles, lizards, and snakes, including timber rattlers and copperheads. Bird life includes pileated woodpeckers, hawks, barred and great horned owls, turkey vultures, and a variety of songbirds. In four different trips, including two campovers at Rockpile Wilderness, I have yet to spot a deer or turkey. However, my first night camping in Rockpile, a deer woke me up in the middle of the night with its loud snorting. I'll never know for sure if the deer was retaliating for my snoring.

Existing signs of man's activities in the area before it became a Wilderness, besides the rock arrangement, include fifteen miles of woods roads, wildlife ponds and food plots and the remains of a stone and concrete spring house.

Because of the relatively small size of Rockpile Wilderness, some outdoor adventurers take advantage of other natural areas close by. These include Crane Lake Recreation Area, Marble Creek Recreation Area, and the spectacular Silver Mines Recreation Area, where canoe and kayak races are held each March. Other nearby areas include Sam A. Baker State Park, Coldwater State Forest, Hawn State Park, St. Joe State Park, Elephant Rocks State Park, Taum Sauk Mountain State Park, Johnson's Shut-Ins State Park, and Fort Davidson State Historic Site.

The ancient rockpile and Rockpile Mountain certainly attract their share of hikers to the Wilderness. The unknown exerts a significant and mysterious attraction, and the rock circle can in some ways be compared to England's Stonehenge or the ancient geology of Wyoming's Bighorn Medicine Wheel. But Rockpile is more than the past, more than an unknown circle of granite boulders. This Wilderness Area provides some of the finest "open forest" camping and backpacking in Missouri. The two overnight camps I enjoyed, the first one alone and the most recent with two friends, were spectacular for their unique location, diverse scenery, and unparalleled grandeur and solitude.

I returned to Rockpile the third week in March with a backpack that weighed forty-five pounds when loaded with enough food and gear for an overnight camp. I knew that backpacking and camping by myself would produce personal insights into the character of this land and its wildlife, as they had at all the other Wilderness Areas in the state. It's not that these things elude me when I'm with a partner or a group or that several day hikes cannot garner similar nuggets of discovery; rather, it's a wilderness test that forces introspection. There is nothing said except what I say to myself.

It's certainly not as much fun to hike and camp a new spot alone. An agreeable partner who shares a love for wilderness and its unique gifts adds immensely to the adventure and its memory. Alone, I assume a more scientific spirit as an observer whose mission is to take the time to identify trees, plants, animal tracks, birds, geology, and artifacts. I leave no leaf unturned. And there is pleasure in doing this slow, quiet investigation of a certain Wilderness like Rockpile, at a snail's pace, with few or no distractions.

And at night, in the black stillness of a world without artificial light, noise, or images, one meets the face of wilderness that many day hikers miss. Without a partner to highlight and recap the day, the lone camper converses within the mind. The solitary traveler, me, thinks of the world outside the tent flap. Barred owls become restless with their own thoughts so they hoot for company under cover of darkness.

A lone coyote wails somewhere across the St. Francis River. And just outside the tent walls, a four-legged creature, maybe opossum, raccoon, or skunk, is shuffling in the leaves, possibly on the track of a few spilled noodles from my dehydrated instant cup-of-soup. More goes on in the Wilderness at night than during the day. Somewhere out there, deer get up from their beds, stretch, and roam. Wild turkeys curl their large leathery toes around safe, high roosting tree limbs that protect them from the jaws of predatory coyotes and fox.

My favorite camping spot in Rockpile lies in the southwestern portion of the Wilderness bordering the St. Francis River, Turkey Pen Hollow, and Cave Branch. When I first saw this place there was little doubt I would be back to set stakes here. It is a destination within itself, an area that rivals the best to be found in all other Wilderness in the state.

Close by is the narrow, deep-soiled ravine that harbors trees reminiscent of lush Appalachian forests. American basswood has the largest leaves of the native basswoods. On the large specimens found in the ravine, the gray bark is ridged and furrowed. These trees grow from sixty to eighty feet tall and two to three feet in diameter. The wood of the tree is light and strong. Another tree in this narrow oasis is a member of the walnut family. The butternut grows up to sixty feet tall and reaches one to two feet in diameter. The oval fruit has a greenish-brown husk with a sticky surface. The husk contains a yellow or orange dye. Its wood is a lighter brown than that of the black walnut.

The Kentucky coffeetree is a member of the legume family. This tree has bipinnately compound leaves, one to three feet long. Purplish-brown pods, four to ten inches long and one to two inches wide, have sixty to eighty round flattened, reddish brown seeds imbedded in the pulp. The tree grows seventy-five to one hundred feet tall and two to three feet in diameter. Furrowed bark is dark gray to brown, and the branches, unlike other members of the legume family, lack spines.

Large, healthy specimens of black walnut, sugar maple, butternut hickory, and white and red oak escaped timber cutting due to the inaccessibility of the gorge. Understory there includes papaw, hornbeam, and spicebush. Papaw are part of the custard-apple family. They produce fruit irregularly oblong to five inches with rind ranging from yellow to dark brown enclosing flesh that is white to yellow and flat, dark brown seeds. The fruit is edible when ripe. It is sometimes called the Ozark banana by locals. The papaw is a large shrub or small tree, twenty to thirty feet tall and six to fifteen inches in diameter. The American hornbeam is a small tree with birchlike leaves. Staminate catkins to 1.5 inches long in spring are not preformed. These trees are recognized by their many pendant clusters of loose, leafy, three-pointed bracts, each bearing a small, nutlike seed attached to the base. American hornbeam has a short, fluted or "muscular" trunk and smooth blue-gray bark. It grows to forty feet tall and one to two feet in diameter. It is most common in moist, rich soil bordering streams, like the St. Francis or swamps.

Spicebush is a shrub that can be abundant in moist, rich soil near streams or swampy forests. Spicebush has smooth, shiny leaves that emit a pungent, pleasant aroma when broken. Small yellowish flowers along the branches become red berries in fall. Spicebush fruits are sought by migrating songbirds. They are also a favorite fall food of wild turkeys.

Following Cave Branch below the shut-ins, down to the where the St Francis flows, and then about another a half mile south, the hiker meets the large westward bend of the river. There is a monumental north-facing bluff carved from sandstone and dolomite at this location. The bluff is pocked with caves.

There are countless photo opportunities along and in the vicinity of the river. If you get the urge to canoe, instead of hike to this location, you should be an experienced canoeist. In his river guide, *Missouri Ozark Waterways,* author Oz Hawksley cautions paddlers about the challenges involved:

> In sharp contrast to the more western Ozark streams, the upper St. Francis cannot be called a "float" stream. It presents a challenge to the experienced canoeist. Due to its boulder-strewn course, it can be run

only during high or moderately high water; that is, in spring or after rather heavy rains. Both the St. Francis and its tributary, Big Creek, run a straighter course than float streams, through narrow defiles of resistant granite rock call shut-ins. Due to their relatively hazardous nature, these sections provide some of the wildest scenic river runs in the state. For shut-in sections it is advisable to carry only lunch and other small items in the canoe and to take life jackets and enough rope to line canoes through bad places if deemed necessary. In high water, decked canoes would be advisable.

As one who enjoys canoeing, I once considered trying to paddle to the area that borders the Wilderness. However, after watching canoe and kayak white-water races in March each year near Silver Mines campground, I decided that my white-water skills wouldn't keep me upright and dry in the state's most challenging rock gardens. I am content to use leg power to keep in close touch with the St. Francis and the beauty to be found up or downstream.

It is the combination of wild water and untamed land that makes this southwestern corner of Rockpile so intriguing. A hike from river's edge into Turkey Pen Hollow is another good adventure. Three years ago, about halfway into the hollow, I found the remains of a deer. The mice had gnawed most every part of the skeleton, but for some reason they had not touched the remains of a single, thick, well-preserved main antler that had only one deformed nub of a point. Whether the deer had been wounded but never found by a hunter or had died of natural causes, I did not know. I stuck the antler tightly in the crotch of an oak tree and hiked deeper into the hollow in hopes of flushing a live deer on the hoof or maybe a turkey. The moist, rich funnel of trees and bottomland looked like ideal wildlife habitat. I expected a whitetail to bust out of cover any minute. But no such luck.

With only one exception, and I'm not really complaining, the hiking and backpacking is as comfortable as it gets under a canopy of trees with forgiving terrain that's not too steep or not too flat. That exception is the switchback hike back up to Little Grass Mountain Trailhead. It was a gut buster even though I had eaten enough provisions out of my pack to lighten the load by two or three pounds. If you've ever had the sensation that your thigh muscles are on fire, that making it to the top is impossible, you know what I mean. But when the burning quits and the heart rate returns to normal, Rockpile is worth it.

11

Wilderness Tips

Away, away from men and towns,
To the wild wood and the downs;
To the silent wilderness
Where the soul need not repress
Its music.

PERCY BYSSHE SHELLEY

MISSOURI'S EIGHT congressionally designated Wilderness Areas offer a wide variety of challenges to anyone who enjoys the freedom of hiking, camping, backpacking, hunting, fishing, or observing wildlife. The public lands represent true outdoor adventure and genuine freedom. Unlike parks and recreation areas with modern conveniences, the Wilderness Areas are notably and beautifully primitive and therein lies their main attraction and value. Nowhere else can you find such "solemn solitude and sweet repose" in unspoiled nature. Nowhere else can we truly express our musical souls in the spirit of Shelley.

If you are already experienced in the outdoors, Missouri Wilderness will offer you new challenges. If you are a beginner, there is no better place to explore nature. This chapter is designed to serve as a guide: For the experienced, it provides a reminder of basic rules of the wilderness. For the newcomer, it offers the information needed to start off on a true and confident course.

Everything you need to know about compass and map, favorable seasons, months, proper clothing and gear, footwear, tents, sleeping bags, backpacks, camp cooking, and sanitation will be discussed in detail. The emphasis will be on low-impact camping and hiking techniques that will help preserve the integrity of the Missouri Wilderness.

The Meaning and Value of Wilderness

According to the U.S. Forest Service, Wilderness is a natural area affected primarily by the forces of nature with little evidence of man's works—where man himself is a visitor. Many outdoor enthusiasts prefer such an area for experiencing the wonders of nature. Wilderness provides outstanding opportunities for primitive or unconfined types of outdoor recreation that allow participants to seek what is valuable to them. While many people may engage in the same activity, no two individuals have exactly the same wilderness experience.

In today's mostly urbanized society, the number of individuals seeking wilderness experience is at an all-time high. At least twenty times as many people visit wilderness now as in the 1930s. The impact of all these new visitors may threaten the very values they seek. To ensure that Wilderness Areas will flourish and be available to future generations, visitors need to practice proper wilderness etiquette.

Wilderness Regulations
The Forest Service has a standard list of rules for all designated Wilderness Areas in the nation. The following practices are not allowed:

1. Possessing or leaving refuge, debris, or litter in an exposed or unsanitary condition.
2. Placing in or near a stream, lake, or waterway any substance which does or may pollute a stream, lake, or waterway.
3. Leaving a fire without completely extinguishing it.
4. Cutting or defacing live or dead standing trees or other vegetation.
5. Possessing or using a motor vehicle, motor boat, motorized equipment, or mechanical transport (including mountain bikes and wagons).

6. Landing an aircraft, dropping, or picking up materials, supplies, or persons by means of aircraft, including helicopters.
7. Building "structures" such as rock fire rings and lean-tos etc.
8. Discharging a firearm or any other implement capable of taking human life or causing injury, in or within one hundred fifty yards of an occupied area, or in any manner or place whereby any person or property is exposed to injury or damage as a result of such discharge.
9. Firing any tracer bullet or incendiary ammunition.
10. Camping in groups of more than ten people.

Wilderness Manners

The Forest Service believes and so do most Wilderness users, that hikers, campers, and backpackers should leave no sign of their presence to disturb those who follow. Tread lightly so nature can endure and replenish. For people used to the disposability of so many modern conveniences, that takes some planning. Here are some guidelines:

Plan your group size. Limit the number of persons to ten or fewer. This reduces impact on soil and ground cover. Camp at least one hundred feet away from the trail or water sources.

Leave your camp cleaner that you found it. Pack out what you pack in. Animals generally dig up what you bury, so avoid burying cans, foil, styrofoam, and plastic. Dispose of human waste at least one hundred feet from campsites, trails, and waterways. Dig a shallow hole—six to eight inches deep—with your boot heel or a small trowel. Cover the hole with soil and leaves.

Use one campfire for warmth, esthetics, and cooking. Small fires are more efficient; bonfires waste wood and are dangerous. Small gas or chemical cooking stoves are recommended.

Seek out campsites that are out of sight and sound of trails and other camps. This will reduce the impact on any one part of the Wilderness. When conditions warrant sharing an area, keep a low profile. Remember that others may have come to the area for the solitude it offers. Avoid overuse of popular areas, and seek out your own special places.

Be prepared for changing weather conditions. Match your equipment and clothing to the season. Carry a dependable compass and corresponding topographical map of the area. Purchase a compact but well-stocked first aid kit. It you do run into trouble, the universal distress signal is three of anything in relatively short duration—shots, shouts, whistles, or puffs of smoke.

When traveling on a primary trail, stay on it rather than creating adjacent trails that could cause erosion and destroy natural vegetation. Always keep your impact to a minimum. One of the joys of hiking is using map and compass for cross-country hiking or bushwhacking off the trails. Making blaze marks on trees with a knife or a hatchet should be avoided. Bright ribbons, reflective markers, or paint detract from the beauty of nature. If the course is complicated, you can mark you way temporarily with toilet tissue. Remember to remove the tissue when you backtrack.

Pack your own shelter, including poles and stakes, rather than trying to improvise with lean-tos. A modern, lightweight backpack tent is worth its weight in gold and much more comfortable as well as more rain- and bug-proof than a "survival lean-to." Anything additional you put up, such as a tarp, should be removed and packed out.

It is not safe to drink unpurified water from springs, streams, ponds, or lakes in any Wilderness, no matter how remote. The curse of giardiasis, commonly called giardia, has spread throughout the world. This disease is caused by a waterborne parasite and is unpleasant, debilitating, and in some cases, chronic. It can completely ruin an outing. For day hikes, carry your own water from home in water bottles or canteens. For extended trips, purchase a brand-name water-purification device that removes impurities found in backcountry water sources. (More about safe drinking water will be discussed later.)

Finding Your Way in the Wilderness

Allow yourself to bond peacefully and confidently with wilderness, even though you may have never been in it before. If there be any doubt in your mind, regard Missouri Wilderness as a safe, peaceful interlude from the complexities and stress of everyday life. It is, in my opinion, far easier to negotiate a steep, unknown wilderness trail than to find your way through a busy city.

Decoding a city map and finding your way through urban and suburban jungles is much more nerve-wracking, complicated, and risky than orienteering—using a topographic map and simple compass to bushwhack your way through forest and glade. Because there are few signs in Wilderness Areas, compass and map proficiency is recommended. Orienteering is an enjoyable and valuable skill. It allows hikers to confidently abandon the beaten path and explore and lets hunters and anglers access unpressured locations.

Some hikers rely on the position of the sun, wind direction, or memory of their surroundings to keep them on course. This reliance on nature and trail familiarity sometimes turns into a guessing game when the sun disappears behind the clouds, the wind changes directions, and multiple trail junctions begin to look alike. Correct compass use eliminates the guesswork. When in doubt, always rely on a compass.

I carry two small, lightweight compasses with me on all hikes. One is easily accessible in my pocket or on a lanyard around my neck. The backup is secured in a pack. I have also seen small, inexpensive compasses called Fisheyes pinned to hikers' clothing. They are a little larger than marbles and enclosed in liquid. While one shouldn't be used as a main compass because of its shape, it would serve well as a direction guide on the trail. Finally, I always carry a small notebook and wooden pencil in a shirt pocket or pack to write down trail notes, compass bearings, and landmark descriptions.

Map and Compass

You, the compass, and the topo map work as a team. A sturdy, reliable compass can be purchased for around twenty dollars. A topographic map of a particular Wilderness Area generally sells for less than four dollars. Using this twenty-four–dollar investment, you can cast away fears of getting lost and quickly build confidence in yourself as a pathfinder.

Topographic maps of Missouri Wilderness Areas can be purchased from personnel at Mark Twain National Forest offices throughout the state. You can also order maps by calling or writing the Forest Supervisor, Mark Twain National Forest, 401 Fairgrounds Road, Rolla, Missouri 65401, phone (573) 364-4621. Maps of Mingo Wilderness, managed by the U.S. Fish and Wildlife Service, can be obtained by writing the Refuge Manager, Mingo National Wildlife Refuge, R.R. 1, Box 103, Puxico, Missouri 63960, phone (314) 222-3589.

Maps may also be ordered through the Map Information Office, United States Geological Survey, Washington, D.C. 20242. You can

first request topographic map general indexes that make it simple
to pick out the maps for specific areas. For maps of areas west of
the Mississippi River, send your order to the Distribution Section,
Geological Survey, Denver Federal Center, Denver, Colorado
80225. For maps east of the Mississippi River, send your order to
Distribution Center, Geological Survey, Washington D.C. 20242.
Some sporting and wilderness outfitting stores also carry topographic maps.

In addition, the Mark Twain National Forest offers free information pamphlets for all seven Wilderness Areas (as does the Mingo
Wildlife Refuge), which feature integrated condensed topo maps.
The Forest Service is in the process of updating and expanding
these pamphlets, some of which may be available at the registration
desks of various trailheads. If you are hiking or camping an area for
the first time, it is best to obtain a pamphlet in advance.

The topo maps that are part of these free pamphlets are generally
adequate for main trail hikes; however, full-size topo maps of each
area, purchased separately, are more detailed, easier to read, and
work better with a compass.

Reading a Compass Bearing

To read the compass bearing of a landmark, squarely face the selected point. Hold your compass level in front of you at about waist
height. Turn the whole compass case in your hand until the needle
points to the letter "N" (north) on the azimuth ring. Now hold the
case and azimuth ring steady, and rotate the capsule only until the
direction arrow on the bottom of the capsule points straight ahead
of you toward the landmark. The number on the azimuth ring that
is opposite the direction arrow is your bearing.

Following a Compass Bearing

After you have your compass bearing, rotate the capsule until the
direction arrow on the bottom points to the given degree figure on
the azimuth ring. Hold the compass level in front of you at waist
height, with the direction arrow pointing straight ahead. Keeping
your eyes on the compass, slowly turn your entire body around
while holding the compass steady until the north end of the compass needle points to the letter "N" on the azimuth ring. The direction arrow points in the direction in which you want to go. Look
straight ahead and pick out some landmark, such as a rock or tree.
By walking directly toward this landmark you are following the

desired compass bearing. Repeat the procedure until you reach your final destination.

Setting a Return Course
After following a compass bearing from one point to another, you can return by simply applying the proper formula:

1. If your outbound compass bearing was between 0 and 180 degrees, add 180 to the bearing followed. For example, if your bearing was 30 degrees, add 180, and return on 210–degree azimuth.
2. If your outbound bearing was between 180 and 360 degrees, subtract 180 from the bearing followed. For example, if your bearing was 210 degrees, subtract 180, and return on a back azimuth of 30 degrees.

Orienteering Your Map with the Compass
Topographic maps have a figure in the margin, a pair of arrows showing the declination, or angle, between magnetic north and true, or map, north for the area covered. Set your compass by twisting the capsule until the direction arrow points to "N" on the azimuth ring. Place the compass over the figure on the map so that the direction arrow on the compass lies directly over the magnetic north line. Leave the compass on the map, and turn the paper until the north end of the magnetized needle points in the same direction as the magnetic north line on the map. Your map will now be "oriented" to the terrain.

Taking a Compass Bearing from a Map
To prepare the map, draw a magnetic north-south line on your map by continuing the magnetic north arrow line, usually found in the bottom margin, across the face of the map. Then add parallel lines at one-inch intervals across the entire area.

1. Locate your present position and your desired destination on the map. Connect these two points with a pencilled line.
2. Rotate the compass capsule so that the direction arrow points to "N" on the azimuth ring. Place the compass on the map with the pivot of the needle directly over the pencil line and the lines on the bottom of the capsule parallel with the magnetic north-south lines you drew on the map, north at the top.

3. Hold the compass case and azimuth ring firmly against the map and rotate the capsule only until the direction arrow points to your destination and is directly above the line that connects your destination with your present position. The direction arrow now points to the compass bearing to be followed. Follow the compass bearing.

For more detailed information on compass and map use, refer to *Be Expert with Map and Compass* by Bjorn Kjellstrom.

The Global Positioning System

Another method of orienteering uses the Global Positioning System (GPS), a constellation of satellites that orbit the earth twice a day, transmitting precise time and position (latitude, longitude, and altitude) information. With a GPS receiver, users can determine their location anywhere on earth. The complete system consists of twenty-four satellites orbiting about twelve thousand miles above the earth and five ground stations to monitor and manage the satellite constellation. These satellites provide constant coverage for both two- and three-dimensional positioning anywhere on earth.

Several companies are currently producing and selling handheld GPS receivers to surveyors, natural resource managers, wildlife managers, geologists, geographers, mappers, forestry managers, search-and-rescue teams, archaeologists, hunters, fishermen, backpackers, and campers. The cost of receivers for sporting applications is about two hundred dollars.

I tried the GPS 2000 Satellite Navigator manufactured by Magellan Systems Corporation in San Dimas, California. The handheld unit was 6.6 inches high, 2.3 inches wide, 1.3 inches deep. It weighed 10 ounces with 4 AA alkaline batteries, which will power the unit for up to 17 hours of continuous operation. Various brands of GPS handheld receivers are available to outdoor adventurers through sporting goods stores specializing in outdoor equipment and by mail order.

Hikers look at the GPS receiver's lighted display screen to see where they are, and the speed at which they're traveling, the distance to their destination, and the direction to travel. The plotter screen draws the picture of the course that is set, the route followed, the location of nearby landmarks stored in memory, and progress to

A GPS unit, for high-tech orienteering. *Author's collection.*

the destination. The unit scrolls through four graphic navigation screens and displays on-screen instructions much like a computer.

It is up to the individual hiker to decide whether to spend twenty dollars for a good compass and necessary maps or two hundred dollars for a portable GPS receiver. For negotiating Missouri Wilderness Areas, compass and map certainly suffice. If you are considering the purchase of a GPS receiver, you should talk to hikers, hunters, or professionals already using one. Ask how the receivers work out in the field, observe them, borrow one if you can. The units are well made and durable.

There are those who will appreciate the new technology that GPS offers, and there are those, myself included, who prefer the simplicity and long tradition of compass and map.

Pedometer

A pedometer is an instrument that records the distance a person covers on foot by responding to the body's motion. There are manual and electronic pedometers available to today's hikers; I have tried both.

Some Forest Service Missouri Wilderness pamphlets and maps print information on the distance from various points and landmarks. While a pedometer is not absolutely necessary for finding your way from one location to another, when properly set to the walking stride of the hiker, the instrument processes valuable and sometimes astounding information.

For instance, it's generally the rule that hikers over-estimate the number of miles they walk in a day. The hotter or colder the temperature or the steeper the terrain, the greater the exaggerated mileage. An accurate pedometer has humbled many a long-distance walker. When mileage is not indicated on a sign or brochure, the pedometer reading serves as a gauge for time needed to reach a landmark or campsite and allows the hiker to plan the return trip.

Whether manual or electronic, the instrument is about the size of a compass, and accuracy varies according to the body motion and stride taken with each step. As reason dictates, consistently spaced strides throughout a half or whole day of hiking are not likely due to variances in walking pace and terrain. The information provided by a pedometer should be taken as a fairly good estimation of distances walked.

Pedometers are available from sporting goods stores, outdoor gear shops, and outlets that sell athletic gear.

Reduce the complexity of life by
eliminating the needless wants of life,
and the labors of life reduce themselves.

EDWIN WAY TEAL

Equipment Selection

Whether you are backpacking in a Wilderness Area or at state or national parks, the best advice is to buy high-quality, name-brand equipment. As is the case with most manufactured products, there are well-designed, long-lasting products available and there are also unreliable, poor-quality imitations. Poorly designed and constructed products can be dangerous.

At first glance, all tents, backpacks, and sleeping bags might look the same to the novice. There is, however, a vast difference in products and in how well they function under the rigors of backpacking and camping. For the backcountry, you want to choose the best gear possible. The investment is well worth the initial outlay.

Tents
The best tents are sold through outdoor specialty shops and mail-

order businesses that specialize in outfitting hikers, campers, back-packers, fishermen, and hunters. You can compare prices and features by referring to magazines like *Outside* and *Backpacker* before purchasing. These publications print special buying and performance guides for tents, sleeping bags, appliances, clothing, and boots. They also list the names, addresses, and phone numbers of manufacturers who provide free product catalogs. Bass Pro Shops retail stores and catalogs sell a video, *Complete Guide to Tent Camping*, which I wrote and hosted. It explains equipment selection, setting up camp, techniques, and where to go to camp.

After comparing for features and cost, you're ready to shop. Don't be swayed by cheap tents that look the same as other, more expensive models. Cheap imitations can bite you. Zippers stick, break, or are too small and hard to work. Fabric is flimsy. It rips, frays, and soaks up moisture. It is not weatherproof, and the rain fly, if there is one, is inadequate. Seams are weak—usually single-stitch—and poorly sewn. Tents are small, uncomfortable, and without ventilation. Poor design means the tent will be hard to put up and will not hold up in strong wind. When you compare tents, you will notice that cheap tents lack extra features, such as gear lofts, wrap-up floors, C-rings, and extra reinforcing at stress points.

Tent Terminology

High-quality tents incorporate features that are not found on lesser tents. Here's a brief guide of features to look for:

1. Double-wall design—Double wall or double-roof design means the tent has a permeable roof that is covered by a double-coated waterproof rainfly. Air circulates between fly and roof to help draw off the water vapor produced by sleeping campers. If the roof is coated, not permeable, this moisture will condense and drip down on the campers. Some tents offer a screened roof vent for additional ventilation.
2. Cross-ventilation—Comfort, rain or shine, depends on cross-ventilation. This includes large screen windows that can be closed with storm flaps. Storm flaps on the inside can be zipped closed to control air flow and also keep out cold, windblown rain and snow. A full-coverage rain fly extends out over the windows so the tent can be adequately ventilated even when it's raining.

3. Waterproof bathtub-type floor—Three- and four-season tents should have a double coated waterproof floor that wraps up the sidewalls so the seam is high above the floor. This means tent floors, sleeping pads, bags, and other gear stay dry.

4. Shock-absorbing design—A quality tent must be able to take the abuse of rain, wind, snow loads, even kids at play. Reliable tents are designed to "give" instead of tearing. Fabrics are light but extremely durable. Frames are made of seamless aluminum, aircraft aluminum, or reinforced fiberglass. Shock-absorbing design is also created by reinforcing layers of fabric where there is extra stress on the tent.

5. Storm rings—Rings attached to the tent and fly that accommodate extra guy ropes are essential for combating occasional or predictable strong winds. They secure the tent and keep it from blowing away.

6. Ring-and-pin assemblies—These speed set-up and reduce stress and abrasion where the frame meets the floor.

7. Flexible suspension—These shock-corded poles work like shock-absorbers to diminish stress and wind loads. Easy, fast set-up is a result of shock-corded poles so that pole pieces can't get mixed-up or lost. Clips that attach the fabric of the tent to the frame assembly decrease set-up time dramatically and are ideal for maintaining a taut tent. Most quality tents set up in fewer than ten minutes.

Tent Choices

There are two basic types of tents to choose from: fairly light and compact backpack tents and traditional camping, or family, tents. Logically, backpack-style tents are better suited to wilderness use in most scenarios for the simple reason they can be easily and comfortably strapped to a pack frame and carried to the camping destination.

Pack tents weigh from two to ten pounds. Family-style tents range from twenty to forty pounds. A thirty-pound family tent can be packed several miles into the wilderness. I have done that, but I needed help from other hikers or hunters in my party who divided up my personal gear and stowed it in their packs. There are benefits to having more floor space and headroom. Family-size tents can also be utilized at wilderness trailheads.

For me, trailhead camping is a second choice, although I have pitched camp near the road several times rather than hauling a full pack into the interior. I prefer putting plenty of space between the trailhead and my wilderness camps.

The Shape of Tents
Backpack and conventional tents come in several different shapes. The shape of a tent has a direct bearing on floor room, height, wind deflection, and overall comfort.

1. Dome—Today's most popular design in tents is the dome style. Domes have 50 percent more internal space than A-Frame tents and shed wind, rain, and snow extremely well. They are freestanding tents, meaning they do not have to be staked.
2. Geodesic Dome—A strong geodesic frame support enables this type of tent to withstand heavy snows and high winds. They may be used as expedition or four-season tents. They are freestanding and as roomy as conventional dome tents.
3. A-Frame—These are based on the old army pup tents, free-standing and light weight, with good ventilation but not as roomy as dome tents.
4. Tunnel—With an elongated, low-profile bivy design, this style is often the choice of solo backpackers and hikers. Tents weigh as little as two pounds. They are basically used for sleeping and protection from the elements, so there is no excess room, and you can't stand up in them, which may be an issue for anyone with claustrophobic tendencies. They shed wind well due to their low profile.
5. Umbrella—This design is used in family tents and offers generous head room and maximum floor space. It does not shed high wind as well as the dome designs but is easy to ventilate.
6. Cabin—The outfitter or military tent design of canvas duck or nylon affords "cabinlike" headroom and floor space. Tents usually require two or more campers to set up, but they are sturdy and dependable when adequately guy-roped.
7. Tepee—A conical Indian design can produce the authentic lodges used by Native Americans or canvas or nylon tents supported by a single center pole and guy ropes. The white man's tepee shelter, sold in some stores and backcountry

outfitting shops, does not withstand the rigors of the elements nearly as well as an authentic Indian tepee.

Important Tip: No matter what kind of tent you get, protect your investment. Never pack and store a tent in its bag when it's wet; make sure it's completely dry. At home, store the tent "high and dry," not on the basement floor. Pitch your tent far enough away from the campfire to prevent fabric "spark holes." A poly tarp under the tent floor prevents punctures.

Sleeping Bags

There are specialized backpack sleeping bags and conventional camp bags. With a few exceptions, which I will discuss later in this chapter, the months of June, July, and August and part of September are not ideally suited for backpacking, hiking, and camping in Missouri Wilderness Areas. Summer is simply too hot and buggy in deep forests and glades unless there are cool, shady streams and lakes nearby.

Knowing this, the recreationist will concentrate primarily on autumn, winter, and spring. In southern Missouri, days may be warm in spring and fall, but nights are cool, and conventional summer-weight sleeping bags lack the insulation and design to provide adequate warmth.

Conventional bags may serve in a pinch during mild weather at trailhead camps, but hikers never know for sure when the weather will turn sour. Standard bags are bulkier, heavier, and difficult to lash to the pack frame. So in the discussion of quality sleeping bags for Wilderness use, the emphasis will be on specialized pack bags that can be used throughout the year.

While conventional sleeping bags are rectangular, most cool and cold weather bags are not. Mummy bag shapes are generally the warmest, lightest, and most compactible. These bags feature built-on insulated hoods with drawstrings or Velcro closures. It is best to choose mummy bags with full-length zippers for ventilation when needed. It takes some getting used to sleeping mummy-style, but the form-fitting design conserves natural body heat better than any other.

The outer shell of a sleeping bag comes in different materials including ripstop nylon, nylon taffeta, and Gore-Tex. Gore-Tex and other waterproof, breathable shells are more expensive than nylon. However, with sensible care, a high-quality pack bag will last indefinitely. I bought a top-name goose-down pack bag in 1968 in preparation for a bighorn sheep hunting in Wyoming. The cost back then was ninety dollars, a considerable sum for a sleeping bag, but I'm still using that same bag for high-country trekking.

When in doubt, buy the warmest backpack sleeping bag you can afford. If it gets too warm, you can always zip open the bag and use it as a comforter or sleep on top of it. You can purchase a zippered fleece liner for warm weather use or add the liner for extra insulation in winter.

Quality bags have comfort-range tags attached. Use the comfort-range information as estimate. Some campers sleep warmer than others. The greater the cold-comfort range, the more the bag will cost. A bag with a comfort rating in the zero to ten below zero range should allow you to stay warm when camping in Missouri during winter's coldest days. Knowing you have the best is comforting when the weather takes a turn for the worse.

Pack Bag Buying Tips
1. Do your sleeping bag homework first by scouring the outdoor adventure magazines and requesting catalogs and information from manufacturers.
2. Mummy bags come in a variety of lengths and widths from short to extra long.
3. Three pounds is considered lightweight, an important consideration when backpacking. There are pack bags that weigh more or less, depending on the insulation, outer shell material, and comfort range.
4. Several types of synthetic and natural insulation, like goose down, are used in today's best pack bags. Down is excellent insulation and compacts easily in a stuff bag for packing. Synthetics also provide excellent warmth. They generally do not compact quite as easily as down, but they do dry faster when wet.
5. Synthetic insulation sleeping bags respond better to regular machine washing than down.
6. A double-pull, two-way zipper is a heavy-duty large-toothed plastic zipper that is self-repairing and is found on quality bags. Metal zippers can freeze shut. Some pack bags can be zipped together to produce one double-size bag.

7. The method by which the filling is attached to the shell is important in reducing or eliminating cold spots. Insulation should not shift or clump. Fabric edges should be double-stitched to prevent unraveling and fraying. Double quilting means that the liner quilting is offset from the shell quilting to eliminate sewn-through seams and cold spots. Some bags feature a trapezoid foot area that allows you the freedom to wiggle your toes without giving up mummy bag heat efficiency.

8. High-quality bags come with a water-repellent, mildew-resistant stuff sack. When attached to the backpack frame, the bag inside the stuff sack is kept clean, protected from moisture and snags. The sack is easily attached to the frame with straps or shock cord. To stuff the bag, start with the foot, or narrow, end of the bag, using hand or fist to compress it as you stuff it into the sack. Do not fold it into the sack.

9. Look for Velcro tabs at the shoulder of the bag to keep the bag closed even if the zipper is open. The tab is handy when a zipper malfunctions or controlled ventilation is desired.

10. Some bags have built-in loops for easy attachment of an optional inner liner. Fleece liners are more comfortable than nylon next to the skin in winter and summer, and they can be easily removed for washing.

Under-Bag Sleeping Pads

To protect the sleeping bag and add a generous measure of ground insulation, the relatively new self-inflating foam air mat takes the lumps and cold out of sleeping on the tent floor. This product is not to be confused with the blow-up air mattress. Three slightly different, but excellent versions of the pad are made by three different outdoor outfitting companies, Basic Designs, Cascade Designs, and Stearns. The pads are lightweight, and compact enough for rolling tight and securing with straps for attachment to backpack frame. These pads will make sleeping easy.

Don't Forget Your Pillow

You can pack your full-size pillow from home when camping from a vehicle, but backpacking has its space limitations. Currently on the market are downsized fleece pillowcases especially made for backpackers that "accept" clothing rather than conventional pillows. Simply load the empty "pillowcase" in your pack. When you're ready for bed, stuff appropriate clothing (T-shirts, sweaters, jackets, etc.) inside the case. The product is designed so that once the clothes are inside, a specially sewn outer tuck of material keeps them in place. Your clothes, stuffed nicely into the fleece case, make a comfortable pillow. And when you wake up in the morning, your clothes are warm! Fleece cases are sold at specialty outdoor equipment shops. Small pack pillows with compact stuff sacks are also an option.

Turtlelike—A Home on Your Back

It's an invigorating and joyous feeling, packing everything you need to live comfortably for a weekend or a week in the wilderness! You have food, shelter, fire, heat, purified water, bedding, clothing, and a new lease on life.

The simple backpack has evolved into a sophisticated cargo carrier for the wilderness explorer. In reality there are no shortcuts, just added comfort and conveniences. It still takes a healthy back and legs—plus a strong desire to live the backcountry experience—to justify packing twenty to fifty pounds on your back.

Your payback for the effort is incomparable scenery and free pieces of scenic real estate on which to set your stakes, shelter, and soul, places worth millions on the "outside" market. Natural sanctuaries where you can confess, heal, ponder, and gain strength and wisdom. Such is the charm, mission, importance, and stature of the blessed and sometimes cursed backpack.

Most of the luxuries, and many of the so called comforts of life, are not only not indispensable, but positive hindrances to the elevation of mankind.

HENRY DAVID THOREAU

Backpacks

Today's modern backpacks are divided into two different designs: The external pack is the one to choose if you do most of your backpacking on developed trails and carry gear for four or more days. An external frame pack places the load over your body's natural center of gravity (upright rather than bent over) and helps conserve energy while carrying heavy loads. The frame holds the pack off the back, allowing air to circulate, and this keeps the hiker cooler— a definite plus when hiking Missouri Wilderness Areas.

Internal frame packs were originally designed for rock climbing, ski touring, snowshoeing, and canoe portaging—activities in which total freedom of movement and balance are critical. Today's designs have taken internal frames out of the specialty realm by adding features that lend the designs to general backpacking as well. Side pockets, for instance, provide areas for organizing small gear. Because internal frames have a narrower profile and ride closer to the body, they place more of the weight on the shoulders than an external frame.

How the pack will be used goes a long way toward determining the style of pack you need. For the average weekend hiker, either an internal or external frame is suitable. If possible, it is best to try both models, possibly borrowing them for a day or two from friends. Proper loading of a pack can also determine the degree of comfort while hiking the trail.

How to Pack a Backpack
The basic concept is to keep heavy objects near the top of the pack and close to your back. Individual compartments in the pack make it possible to control weight distribution. A plain sack, with no compartments, can also be an efficient cargo organizer. Pack the bottom with the sleeping bag or lightweight clothing and add heavier items on top like the food bag, cooking gear, camera, or fishing equipment. Today's backpacks, with padded and contoured shoulder and hip pads, are more comfortable than ever before. Some packs have top or bottom sections that can be zipped off and used as fanny packs for day hiking. A pack with an interior compartment for securing the sleeping bag protects it from rain or snagging on twigs.

Pack Color
A hiker has a choice of earth tones or bright colors. The natural shades are pleasing and fit well into natural surroundings but one word of caution. Some bags blend into the forest floor and trees so well that if taken off, they can be hard to find. If you hike away from your pack to fish or explore, stand the pack up against a tree or rock—some obvious spot. For extra insurance, you can tie a bright-colored bandanna to the pack or a tree limb above it. Losing your backpack in the wilderness, even for a short time, creates an unpleasant rush of anxiety.

Packs for Kids and Adults with Small Torsos
Because of the popularity of backpacking, the availability of

packs designed to fit kids (from ten to fifteen years old) and adults with small torsos has increased dramatically in recent years. There are packs for all sizes, including some with frames that adjust for correct fit. The best way to involve kids in hiking and backpack camping is to buy them their own packs. When they outgrow the scaled-down packs for backpacking, they can use them as daypacks.

Stand Straight

The straighter you can stand with a loaded pack, the more comfortable it is to carry. With a center of gravity that requires little forward lean and a good hip-support system, carrying loads from twenty-five to fifty pounds can be comfortable. You can carry a significant part of the load on your hips by cinching up the padded hip belt. A sternum strap holds the shoulder straps in place and is especially important when using your hips to help support the load.

Hiking Sticks Help

Not everybody who backpacks uses a walking stick or pole, but from personal observation I can tell you that many high-powered long-distance hikers and backpackers use hiking sticks or the new high-tech trekking or walking poles. They provide safety and support through added stability. Sticks or poles force the user to hike or walk in a more upright position, which makes carrying a loaded pack more comfortable. It's also better for back alignment. Manufacturers of seamless aluminum and carbon graphite poles say that trekking poles reduce stress to the knees, joints, and lower back because of the extra support and built-in spring shock absorbers. For crossing streams or rocky terrain, wading fishing, or walking on snow and ice, poles offer extra stability when needed. For walks close to home, they serve nicely to ward off dogs, aggressive park squirrels, and who knows what else.

It is a violation of wilderness regulations to cut down standing trees or saplings, dead or alive. Hikers would have to secure a "green" stick elsewhere or purchase one of the manufactured ones. The aluminum one I use is called a Jacko Pole. It can be telescoped down to twenty-eight inches for storing and transporting. An expander system locks the pole sections tight to the length comfortable for the hiker. For information you can write to Range Finder, Inc., P.O. Box 70216, Tulsa, Oklahoma 74170 or phone (918) 665-8024.

If we are not careful, we shall leave our children a legacy of billion dollar roads leading nowhere except to other congested places like those we left behind.

GENERAL OMAR BRADLEY

Backpack Camping Appliances

Unlike in conventional tent camping, there are limitations to the selection, size, and weight of backpack-camping appliances. For example, a forty-eight–quart polylite cooler or ice chest weighs close to nine pounds empty. What is a very portable and handy convenience when camping from a vehicle is impractical when hiking into the wilderness. It would be nice to ice down drinks and keep fresh meat and produce cold. But for the backpacker, ice, unless it occurs naturally during winter or above timberline in summer, is an unaffordable luxury. Backpacking has defined boundaries. That's one reason not everyone enjoys this specialized mode of travel and out-of-pack living. There is one essential though, that just about every backpacker needs these days, and that's a reliable, single-burner pack stove.

Some backcountry areas do not allow open fires. This is not the case in Missouri Wilderness Areas, unless an emergency situation exists where extremely dry conditions prevent the use of open fires. Individual backpackers are always expected to take common-sense precautions. A tinder-dry forest and moderate to heavy winds can render the use of open fire potentially dangerous. A compact, manageable camp stove provides a sensible, precautionary alternative.

A pack stove also solves a problem in high-use areas where firewood is scarce. Additionally, periods of heavy rain can make starting and maintaining a fire impractical. If nothing else, the wonderful compact technology built into today's pack stoves is ideal for brewing coffee and making tea, hot chocolate, instant soups, noodle or rice dishes, or just plain hot water for washing. The time from cold to boiling water ranges from three to four minutes. Hard plastic cases or soft stuff sacks protect the stove and backpack when hiking. Complementing the stove are backpacker cook kits with all the essentials for two persons. They are compact and weigh about two pounds.

Two examples of lightweight backpack stoves in use. *Author's collection.*

Camp Lighting

Backpacking does not allow for full-size camp lanterns, but there are plenty of alternatives, including campfires, for a bright outlook at night. One of the handiest lighting tools for hands-free trail or camp navigation, cooking, and reading is a strap-on head lamp. The lamps come in a variety of brands and prices. Other light sources include miniature candle lanterns sold at camping supply outlets and scaled-down miniflashlights. Each backpacker should have his or her own light. In the evening, lights can be hung from lanyards that are attached to tree limbs. Small lights can also be hung from tent ceiling C-rings for reading or card playing.

The Coleman Company makes two ultralight and compact butane/propane–powered backpack lanterns, one called the Micro Lantern and the other, Electronic Ignition Lantern. The former is a carried in a stuff sack, and the latter, when unscrewed from the fuel cartridge, is packed in a hard plastic carrying case that measures 6 3/4 inches long by 5 inches wide by 4 1/4 inches deep. Space requirements in the backpack may not allow the luxury of one of the above lanterns on every trip, but when and where possible, the extra light is convenient and helps extend the camping day.

Optional Extras

There are other choices to make, such as whether to use soft, compactible, 420–Denier nylon and closed-cell foam pack chairs that measure 15 by 33 inches and can be folded into a tote sack and attached by straps or bungee cords to the pack frame. The chairs provide ground-level insulation, comfort, and back support.

For cooking over an open fire, there are backpacker cook grids that measure 6 1/2 by 12 1/2 inches and weigh about a pound. An alternative to the grid includes a small, aluminum frying pan with built-on, swing-away aluminum handles. Lightweight fuel bottles, with 17–ounce or 22–ounce capacity that weigh 4.4 ounces and 4.9 ounces, respectively, are necessary when using pack stoves for most cooking chores.

There's even a special backpacker's Lo-polymer plastic trowel that measures 11 inches long and weighs 2 ounces. The trowel has plenty of uses around camp, one of the most important of which is digging a shallow hole, 6 to 8 inches deep, for burying human waste.

Wilderness Sanitation

Developed campgrounds have modern rest rooms with flush toilets, sinks, showers, and hot running water. Designated Wilderness lacks those man-made conveniences. Digging a hole as mentioned above is still considered one of the most sanitary methods for properly disposing of human waste. Covering the hole with a layer of soil initiates a process of biodegradation that works reasonably well for combating odors, flies, and the transmission of disease. Washing hands with soap and hot water after using nature's toilet is just as important as it is when you are at home. Special emphasis should be placed on thorough hand washing during food preparation and before eating. Many of the intestinal problems at camp could be eliminated by regular use of hot water and soap.

While it is impractical to thoroughly delve into this subject here, author Kathleen Meyer uses one hundred seven pages to cover the topic in depth in *How to Shit in the Woods.* Over 300,000 copies of the book are currently in print. A former river guide, she is less squeamish than most of us when it comes to the topic of defecating in the woods. While entertainingly written, the book is also an excellent practical guide on how not to foul our own favorite wilderness nests as well as those of other hikers and campers.

Water Purification

It is no longer advisable to drink water from streams, springs, rivers, ponds, or lakes regardless of how clear and clean they appear. Missouri Wilderness Areas have both continuous and intermittent streams and cold, bubbling springs that are deceptive when it comes to water quality. Certainly, it is tempting to trade the lukewarm, tasteless liquid from a nearly empty water bottle for fresh, frigid springwater, but that tradeoff is risky at best. Giardia and cryptosporidium have infiltrated the continent's waterways.

You can boil water or you can use one of several different purification systems to render water safe to drink. Brands sold at many specialty camping or outdoor outfitting stores are PUR pump/Filters, General Ecology Microlite, First Need Trav-L-Pur, PentaPure Oasis, PentaPure Water Jug, Pocket Travel Well, and Trekker Travel Well. Other water filters include the Katadyn Pocket Filter, MSR WaterWorks, and Basic Designs High-Flow Ceramic gravity feed system with silver-impregnated ceramic filter. An excellent chapter in the Meyer book, "Trekker's Trots," explains water disinfection and filtration devices in detail.

The Earth, like the sun, like the air, belong to everyone—and to no one.

EDWARD ABBEY

Wilderness Food and Nutrition

Hiking and backpacking burn up plenty of calories. There is no need to worry about gaining weight in the wilderness. You can thoroughly enjoy the delights of feasting outdoors. Good, tasty food is a morale booster and keeps you going before and after rigorous exercise. Plan for healthy food choices with extra nutrition and energy. As a backpacker, think of yourself as a finely tuned athlete in training. Your body needs good food.

According to Jane Brody, personal health columnist and science writer for the *New York Times*, what you may perceive as the classic trail lunch could be the antithesis of a healthful diet. Brody has authored several best-selling cookbooks and is also an outdoor enthusiast. She says if you pull a thick salami-and-cheese sandwich with pickles on Italian bread, a bag of chips, a can of soda, and a candy bar from your pack, you may be in for a long day. That lunch, according to Brody, is loaded with fat, sugar, salt, and calories—much more than you can burn on a daylong trek.

She recommends naturally sweet, nutrient-rich fruits, as well as complex carbohydrates (starchy foods) that best serve muscles when they are working long and hard. "These are the nutrients to pack in when you plan to expend a lot of energy," she says.

Carolyn Gunn, who, along with the help of *Backpacker* magazine editors, wrote a fine, forty-six–page booklet titled "Moveable Feast," says, "How carefully you plan the nutritional composition of foods you take to the backcountry depends mainly on the duration of your trip. In general, hikers on trips lasting fewer than five days do not run the risk of developing unbalanced nutrition, especially if adequate calories are consumed daily." Below are Gunn's recommendations regarding the percentage of calories each category should make up in the daily diet:

Carbohydrates provide efficient fuel for the body. Simple carbohydrates include sugar, honey, jellies, and syrups. Complex carbohydrates come from whole foods like rice, cereal, pasta, fruits, and vegetables. Amount: 55 to 60 percent.

Proteins are needed for maintenance, repair, and growth and come from plant and animal foods like lean meats, fish, poultry, eggs, dairy products, cereal grains, beans, peas, nuts, and seeds. Amount: 15 to 20 percent.

Fats, also obtainable from plant or animal sources, provide more than twice the energy of either carbohydrates or proteins. Foods high in fat are vegetable oils, butter, margarine, cheese, nut butters, salamies, beef sticks, and sausage. Amount: no more than 25 to 30 percent.

Please note that vitamins are necessary for chemical reactions to take place in the body. Minerals are components of many body parts. On short backcountry trips, eating a variety of foods will protect against vitamin and mineral deficiencies.

Wilderness Food Tips

1. Use hard bread like bagels for backpacking that won't fall apart like soft loaf bread will.

2. For ease of preparation and cleanup, make one-pot meals, like pasta or rice with sauce.

3. Important items on backpack trips include unsalted sunflower seeds, dried banana chips, and GORP ("Good old raisins and peanuts") to which we add M&Ms and shredded coconut. Instant Cup-O-Soup, Top Ramen beef-flavor noodle soup, granola bars, hot chocolate mix, coffee, tea, and Tang are also considered staples.

4. Good energy boosters are granola bars, Power Bars, and Clif Bars. The Apricot Endurance Bar by Clif is the best I've tasted. Wash down granola and energy bars with water for best results.

5. If you take vitamin supplements at home, continue taking them on the trail.

6. Store food in separate stuff sacks or plastic bags in your pack to keep it organized. When backpacking with others, distribute the food load evenly.

7. Boil water for washing and rinsing plates, utensils, cups, and pots. Use a small amount of biodegradable soap or no soap at all. Nonstick, coated cookware greatly reduces cleanup.

8. You can eat breakfast, lunch, and dinner as usual on most trips. Portions are generally not as large as homemade meals. To keep your energy level high, you will probably be munching more on nutritious food and snacks throughout the day.

9. Drink water throughout the day, even when you don't feel thirsty.

10. According to Lynn Langenberg, registered dietitian at Hammons Heart Institute in Springfield, Missouri, good items to include on backpack trips are instant oatmeal, crunch cereals, dried fruit, nuts, pancake mix that requires only water, cheese, bagels, pocket bread, pasta, peanut butter, instant pudding (made with powdered milk), fig bar cookies, and spices to liven one-pot noodle and rice dishes.

Anatomy of a Commercially Produced Granola Bar

Nutrition Facts: Serving size 1 granola bar = 28 g

1. Calories: 120. Calories from Fat: 45.
2. Total Fat 5g = 8 percent

3. Saturated Fat 2g = 10 percent
4. Cholesterol 0mg = 0 percent
5. Sodium 60mg = 3 percent
4. Total Carbohydrates 19g = 6 percent
5. Dietary Fiber 1g = 5 percent
6. Sugars 11g
7. Sorbitol 1g
8. Protein 2g
9. Vitamin A 0 percent
10. Vitamin C 0 percent
11. Calcium 2 percent
12. Iron 2 percent

Ingredients: Granola, oats, brown sugar, coconut (sulfite treated), corn syrup, vegetable shortening (canola and/or partially hydrogenated soybean oil, honey, soy lecithin, salt), corn syrup, water, crisp rice flour, whey, sugar, barley malt, nonfat milk, carrageenan, peanuts, and almonds.

Source: McKee Foods, Collegedale, Tennessee.

The Importance of Drinking Water

A person normally requires one gallon of water daily. This amount varies according to temperature, humidity, physical exercise, perspiration, and physical makeup. All bodily functions depend on water. One gallon of water weighs eight pounds so it is basically impractical to pack water in a backpack.

Carry water with you when hiking to your destination or returning to the trailhead. You can carry 16- and 32-ounce water bottles in the side compartments of your pack. Some backpacks have special water bottle pouches that make it easy to reach for water when you need it. I prefer plastic, Nalgene water bottles with screw-on, leakproof lids. You can spice up the taste of water with a squirt of fresh lemon or lime juice.

Regular hydration is important; without it dehydration can quickly reduce the amount of blood your heart pumps and force the heart to pump more quickly. This raises your internal temperature and makes exercise feel more difficult. Backpacking, which is supposed to be enjoyable, becomes drudgery under the influence of dehydration. The best advice is to drink water every half hour or so whether you feel thirsty or not.

Water, thou hast no taste, no color, no odor; canst not be defined, art relished while ever mysterious. Not necessary for life, but rather life itself, thou fillest us with a gratification that exceeds the delight of the senses.

ANTOINE DE SAINT-EXUPÉRY

Pack a First Aid Kit and Expertise with You

I'm a believer that solo or group hikers are far safer in a Wilderness Area than they are navigating the streets of a large city, day or night. The occasion of getting injured or sick is greater in today's urban areas due to poor quality air, risky drinking water, close confines indoors with others, car accidents, and crime. So we assume, as hikers, backpackers, hunters, and fishermen, that we will enjoy our backcountry adventures with sound body and mind, knowing full well that we will likely return to our civilized homes in better physical and mental shape than before we left on our journey.

Granted, we lack access to a swift medical treatment at a city's hospitals or doctors' offices. But the mindset, caution, and physical and mental preparation for trekking and camping instills a heightened desire and awareness to protect ourselves from injury or sickness. How many times have you felt poorly immediately prior to a hiking or camping trip only to feel 100 percent better twenty yards down the trail? That's not coincidence. The trail of adventure commonly leads us to renewed vigor—both physical and mental.

Despite the low incidence of injuries and sickness on the trail, preparation is the key to peace of mind. One hiking friend told me that the most important steps hikers and backpackers can take is to sign up for and complete a Red Cross first aid course and CPR class. Compact first aid kits containing most of the essentials for minor cuts and injuries should be packed along on every outing as an essential part of your camp gear. Purchase a kit for the travel vehicle as well as one for the backpack. Select a kit that comes with complete, easy-to-read instructions. Most kits include essentials like scissors, tweezers, forceps, bandages, tape, gauze, and antiseptic. In your kit, you should have the following:

 1. Scissors for cutting clothing, bandages, gauze.
 2. Safety pins for bandage wraps.
 3. Antiseptic for cleaning wounds and bites.
 4. Baking soda for making a paste that soothes insect stings, sunburn, poison ivy, and poison oak. It also makes an effective antacid.
 5. Rubbing alcohol for cleaning and sterilizing cuts and bites.
 6. Sterile gauze pads for cuts.
 7. Soap for hand washing before meals and for food preparation and for cleaning cuts before bandaging.
 8. Antibacterial cleansing wipes are handy for camping and can be burned in a fire.
 9. Aspirin or aspirin substitute for headaches, colds, altitude sickness, and toothaches.
10. Powdered sulfur for dusting inner clothing to prevent chigger bites.
11. Salt for treatment of heat exhaustion—one (1) teaspoon of salt to a quart of cool water.
12. Diarrhea medication as recommended by your doctor.
13. Toothache remedy as recommended by your dentist.
14. Rolls of adhesive bandages 3/4 inch to 2 3/8 inches wide.
15. Tweezers for removing splinters and ticks. Make sure to carefully remove the entire tick, including the head. A firm outward pull generally works best.
16. Clippers for trimming fingernails and loose, dead skin.
17. Adhesive cloth tape for protecting cuts and making emergency splints.
18. Compact first aid handbooks on basic field treatment.

Medicine Cautions

Always apply medicine according to recommended dosages on the bottle for various ages and weights. Many camping and hiking-related ailments can be cured with rest, sleep, water, tea, salt, sugar, aspirin, and kind words. For more comprehensive information about backcountry medical kits, medications, prevention, diagnosis, and treatment, *Wilderness Medicine* is a reliable 124–page "pack-along" reference by Dr. William W. Forgey.

The Trouble with Ticks

Some hikers have allergic reactions to tick bites. A bite at the base of the skull or the back of the neck can cause partial or total paralysis. The good news is that you can expect a total recovery after removing the tick. Another reaction is tick toxicosis. This is a type of poisoning, even though ticks do not inject venom. It begins with redness and swelling at the site of the bite. This is an uncommon reaction, but it can become serious.

Ticks also are carriers of several diseases, including tularemia, Rocky Mountain spotted fever, and Lyme disease. Much has been said about Lyme disease in recent years. Symptoms to watch for in the days and weeks following a tick bite are swelling at the site. With Lyme disease, a raised, target-shaped rash begins to develop within a few days, eventually reaching several inches in diameter. This is followed by unexplained flu-like symptoms: fever, headaches, body aches, and dizziness. When consulting a physician, mention that you were recently bitten by a tick.

Lyme disease researchers have discovered an antibody they say should help doctors quickly determine whether the difficult-to-diagnose infection has invaded the nervous system. Researchers tested patients with clear symptoms of neurological Lyme disease, and 75 percent of them had an antibody the immune system makes almost immediately after the disease invades the spinal fluid. This can happen just days after someone is bitten by one of the ticks that spread the Lyme bacteria from mice and deer to humans and pets.

Prevention, the Best Medicine

Prevention is the best protection against ticks. Wear clothing that is secure around the ankles and wrists. Tucking pant legs into boots helps, as does wearing long-sleeved shirts. Repellents applied to the skin and clothing work to keep ticks away. Inspect for ticks every day out in the field. Most tick-transmitted diseases are not transferred to the host until the tick has been feeding for some time and is full.

How to Remove Ticks

1. Disinfect the area of attachment with alcohol.
2. Grasp the tick with fingers or, better still, with tweezers, as

close to the head as possible, protecting your fingers with tissue or rubber gloves.

3. Remove the tick with a firm outward movement. Never jerk or twist the tick when removing it. It is important that the mouth parts remain attached to the tick, not left imbedded in the skin.

4. Dispose of the tick by crushing it with shoe or boot heel. Do not crush it with your fingers. Disinfect the bite area with alcohol again.

The Right Clothes

Caution: Snug fitting jeans are fine for the saddle,
and look good in town, but for backpacking,
they'll cramp your style and wear you down.

CHARLIE FARMER

Points to Consider When Dressing for Backpacking Trips

1. The cut for trail clothing should be generous for comfort, adequate circulation, and freedom of movement. This means loose fitting as opposed to skintight.

2. Today's choice in materials include new breathable synthetics and traditional wool.

3. Long pants generally get the nod over shorts for leg protection and insect defense. However, it's a good idea to pack a pair of shorts and/or a swimsuit for times when dressing "down" is practical and enjoyable.

4. For moderate to cool climates, even during the summer, long sleeves are a better choice than short ones for protecting the arms from biting insects and scratches. Sleeves can be rolled up for ventilation. There are times however, when hot weather make T-shirts more practical. Polypropylene, Thermax, or Capilene materials are better than standard cotton since they wick moisture away from the body. Some hikers wear T-shirts when hiking and carry a long-sleeved shirt to use for trail breaks and in camp.

5. Colors—the clothing choice is between earth tones and bright colors. Blending into the wilderness has a good feel to

it. But if you have a photographer in the group, the choice would also include some bright colors. You can add color with caps and bandannas.

6. Belts—wear a sturdy belt for harnessing cased belt knife, small camera and case, and water bottles and, of course, for holding up your britches.

7. Socks—polypropylene or Thermax materials work well for light foundation socks that wick moisture away from the feet. Top off these socks with combination polypropylene-and-wool socks of various thicknesses to match seasonal conditions. Avoid cotton socks when hiking. They soak up moisture and cause blisters.

8. Caps—ball-cap style is popular and is made with various materials, including the new synthetics and wool. Caps are handy for warmth and for keeping rain, snow, and sun at bay. Caps keep rain off eyeglasses. Those with ear flaps add extra protection in cold weather.

9. Bandannas—good for keeping sun off the neck and brow as well as for warmth and absorbing perspiration.

10. Underwear—choose long or short styles, depending of the season and weather conditions. Long johns also make ideal camp pajamas. Polypropylene, Thermax, and Coolmax are good wicking fabrics for briefs, boxers, or long johns.

11. Rain suit—one of the most important considerations in camp clothing. Purchase a high-quality brand that offers the waterproof protection plus breathability that you will need when hiking. Always pack your rain gear regardless of the forecast.

12. Parkas—can be worn over shirts, sweaters, or insulated vests. High-quality parkas are rain and wind resistant. Choose parkas with built-on or zip-off hoods.

13. Nylon shells or Anoraks—provide some rain resistance but are mostly used as efficient windbreakers. They come in urethane coated or uncoated nylon models.

14. Gloves—regardless of the season, gloves provide protection for the hands. Insulated and noninsulated models are available. Gloves and mittens are made from synthetics or wool. In addition to keeping your hands warm, gloves are handy for a variety of chores around camp.

Layering
Layer lightweight and medium-weight articles of clothing, synthetics and wool. Add or subtract clothes as temperature and exercise dictates. This system of layering is far superior to wearing a single, heavy, insulated coat that is likely to cause excess perspiration when you are hiking and backpacking. Your pack holds extra layers of clothing. Remove excess clothing when exercising. Add clothes when at rest to prevent chilling.

Synthetics and What They Do Best
Polypropylene, Thermax, Capilene, and Coolmax are excellent for underwear, socks, caps, and gloves. The fabrics are soft, nonbinding, and do not itch. They provide a good foundation when layered with nylon and wool outer garments. Wool does not lose its insulating properties even when wet.

1. Polypropylene—excellent, lightweight, comfortable insulation. It breathes, won't stain or fade, and wicks away moisture.
2. Thermax (Dupont)—good insulation, lightweight, wicks moisture, and has excellent breathability. It's used in parkas, caps, gloves, and boots.
3. Coolmax (Dupont)—soft, yet has excellent breathability and moisture wicking properties, feather-weight and excellent for backpackers and hikers.
4. Supplex (Dupont)—ultralightweight, yet soft and breathable. It resists fading and stains and protects from wind and water.
5. Supplex/Lycra (Dupont)—has the stretch and support of Lycra, which serves to protect muscles during rigorous exercise. It dries quickly, holds colors well, and won't shrink.

Campfire
I sit at your side and you warm me.
You soothe my aches and sweeten my senses.
Your glow mesmerizes and your crackle lulls me to sleep.
Your are more than fire, you are friend.
You keep me company in the black of night.
You are my beacon in the Wilderness.
Your sweet hickory breath saturates me.

I feed you sticks of strength.
You live through me and I through you.
Those who bask in your radiance are mellowed.
Oh, the tales you ignite and witness.
Your spirit ascends on a rising column of smoke.
And when you flicker and die, part of me dies too.
For your tongue is unique and gives special joy.
And when your final ember glows no more.
I bid you farewell.

CHARLIE FARMER

Footwear

More hiking and backpack trips have been spoiled by poorly fitting boots than anything else. Choose hiking boots and shoes with care. Keep your feet happy!

Boot and Shoe Tips to Consider

1. There are more brands and styles of hiking boots on the market than ever before. Choose name-brand manufacturers when selecting boots for the trail.
2. There are all-leather boots; boots made with leather and Cordura nylon; and all-nylon hiking boots. Cordura, nylon, and suede boots are generally lighter than all-leather boots. All-leather boots are more durable and generally offer more foot protection when hiking and climbing rocky terrain.
3. Boot height ranges from low-cut designs to high tops and mid-calf models nine or ten inches high. The disadvantage of low-cut models is they do not keep debris from working its way inside the boot. Calf-high "hunting boot" styles offer good support and protection. Comfort is a major consideration. Some hikers feel better in low-cut shoes and boots. Others prefer high-top boots with built-on scree collars. Boots should provide good ankle support on hills and mountains.
4. The break-in period for leather boots is generally longer than for those made from Cordura nylon and suede. However, current boot construction, materials, and designs have shortened break-in time for most styles. It is still advantageous to wear new boots, with appropriate hiking socks, at

home for several days for a break-in period that prevents foot and blister problems on the trail.

5. Vibram cleated rubber soles are standard on most hiking and hunting boots. Lug soles come in a choice of deep, medium, or shallow. Shallow lugs do not collect as much mud on soggy trails as deep-lug models.

6. When being fitted for hiking boots, wear the socks you will be using for most of your hiking and backpacking trips. Most hikers prefer wearing two pairs of socks—light, inner foundation socks of moisture-wicking polypropylene or Thermax and outer wool or wool/polypropylene combination socks.

7. Gaiters are fabric leg coverings that reach from the instep to above the ankle, mid-calf, or knee. They can be made of Cordura nylon or fleece. They keep snow, moisture, and debris from entering hiking boots. Waterproof gaiters prevent lower pant legs from getting wet and provide lower leg protection when walking through brush and briars. They are used primarily in snow.

Foot Comfort Tip

In addition to your hiking boots, if at all possible, pack another pair of shoes with you. These can be court shoes, boat shoes, moccasins, or sandals. Extra shoes or sandals are comfortable when lounging around camp after a day of hiking. They enable you to air out and dry your hiking boots, while giving your feet a comfort break.

Protect and Waterproof Boots

Most leather boots need to be conditioned and waterproofed on a regular basis. Use a leather conditioner or waterproofing agent recommended by the boot manufacturer. It would be shameful not to mention the properties of Gore-tex lined boots. Gore-tex fabric technology does not permit water droplets to penetrate boot liners (jackets, pants, or caps) but allows moisture vapor to escape from the liner. Rubber boots, for example, are waterproof, but they trap moisture inside the boot, causing wet socks, cold, clammy feet, and the likelihood of developing blisters. Many of today's high-quality hunting and hiking boots are lined with Gore-tex, which eliminates the need for periodic waterproofing.

Finding and Choosing the Right Campsite

Unlike developed campgrounds along the main roads, Wilderness Areas provide a wide variety of primitive campsites. Depending on how far you want to hike, chances are good that your nearest camping neighbors will be miles away. It is up to you to find the locations that satisfy your personal tastes, whether they be pine-studded ridgetops or bottomland close to water. Here are some tips:

1. Locate your camp on high ground (as opposed to bottomland that is flood prone) at least 150 feet from water's edge or an established trail.
2. Set camp at a location that blends in with the natural setting and does not spoil the view for others who may be hiking through the area.
3. Look for natural windbreaks such as live, healthy trees, boulders, and land depressions that block high wind yet allow sufficient breeze for keeping biting insects at bay.
4. Test the ground for slope by laying down prior to pitching the tent. While a slight slope is favorable for drainage in case of rain, too much slope disrupts sleep.
5. Examine favorable exposures. A tent that faces southeast, for example, will be warmed by the rising sun in the morning and shaded in the afternoon.
6. Brush away rocks, sticks, and other objects that could puncture the tent floor or cause uncomfortable sleeping conditions.
7. Whenever possible, choose your campsite and pitch the tent before darkness sets in.

Natural Phenomena to Avoid When Setting Camp

1. Avoid large, dead trees that could topple in heavy wind. Also look for dead limbs on live trees that could pose a hazard.
2. Avoid tall grass, thick brushy areas, swamps, and bottomland during warm weather. Black flies, gnats, chiggers, and mosquitoes commonly breed and thrive in these areas.
3. During periods of little or no rainfall, dry grass and brush can pose fire hazards around camp. Seek out moister, open locations.

4. Avoid gullies and canyon areas. Flash floods can wash away everything, including tents and humans, within minutes.
5. While bluffs or cliffs are immensely beautiful, it's best not to camp directly under them. Rock slides can be dangerous.
6. Be able to identify poison ivy and poison oak in order to prevent setting your camp in the "itchiest" part of the forest.
7. Avoid camping on the tops of primarily bare hills or mountains with one or two tall trees nearby. These spots are susceptible to lightning strikes.

Common Sense Precautions

1. When utilizing trailhead parking areas for extended backcountry trips, make sure all valuables left in the vehicle are hidden out of sight.
2. It's a good idea to tell family, relatives, or friends where you are going and when you plan to be home. Be precise in describing a particular trailhead and camping destination in case of emergency.
3. Pay attention to weather conditions, and use common sense in waiting out severe storms.
4. Stow food bags in places where birds and mammals are not likely to reach and either eat or contaminate your supplies. Unless the Missouri Ozarks suddenly attracts a lot more bears than it has now, bear problems in camp are rare.
5. Set your own hiking or backpacking pace. Choose partners with skill and conditioning levels that closely match your own. Remember to stop and smell the roses. Backpacking is not a race to see who gets there first.
6. Firearms deer season in Missouri opens around the middle of November each year and lasts for eleven days. If you are a hunter, by all means test your skills in the Wilderness Area of choice. If your are a nonhunter, this is probably not the ideal time to plan your camping or backpacking trips. The same advice can also serve for the spring turkey season, which commonly opens the third week in April and lasts for three weeks.

The drumming of wilderness rain is never more soothing than listening to its symphony of rat-a-tat-tats while snug and warm under the roof of a good tent in the midst of fine books and dreamy naps.

CHARLIE FARMER

Young People Are the Future of Wilderness

One of the gifts of parenthood is passing on the backcountry and wilderness tradition to young people. The best plan is to start kids hiking and backpacking as soon as they can walk. Tailor trips to their stamina and skill levels. As parents, you'll be amazed how well, and how quickly, they will grasp outdoor living skills. In the process, at home, in school, and with friends, they will become defenders of Missouri's and our nation's natural resources and wild places. Share with your kids a love for the outdoors and nature that will last a lifetime.

Wilderness Hike and Camp Checklist

I have compiled checklists for conventional camping and wilderness camping. Reason dictates that, for wilderness travel, you discard gear that is impractical when carrying everything in a backpack. Here's my scaled-down version.

Note: This checklist can be used repeatedly if laminated between clear, soft poly-plastic sheets. A grease pencil or felt marker is used to check off items as they are packed. The plastic can then be wiped clean after use. Using the checklist guards against forgetting important items. I should know. One time I forgot the tent. And I can't tell you how many times I failed to pack toilet paper or sunglasses.

1. aspirin or aspirin substitute
2. water bottles filled at home
3. flashlight or head lamp
4. hand and dish soap
5. lip balm
6. maps of camping area
7. plates

8. pocket or belt knife
9. rain jacket and pants
10. fry pan or backpack grill
11. shorts or swimsuit (when appropriate)
12. tea or coffee kettle
13. extra pair of shoes or sandals
14. food bag and food
15. long pants and long-sleeved shirt
16. medicine for insect bite itch, poison ivy, or sunburn
17. small plastic trash bags for packing out litter
18. sleeping pads
19. salt, pepper, and favorite seasonings
20. wooden matches and mechanical lighters
21. pack stove
22. pack lantern (if practical)
23. drinking cups
24. plastic bowls
25. eating utensils
26. insect repellent
27. sunscreen (if appropriate)
28. good book
29. bandanna
30. personal toilet items, including toilet tissue
31. fifty feet of nylon rope
32. sleeping bags
33. sunglasses
34. tent, poles, and stakes
35. small, foldable belt saw for cutting downfall wood
36. floor-saver plastic sheet for under tent
37. backpack pillows that stuff easily into small carry sacks
38. first aid kit with instruction booklet
39. backpacks
40. compass
41. water purification or disinfection filters
42. compact thirty-five–millimeter camera and extra film
43. extra socks and underwear
44. fuel for camp appliances

12

The Future of Missouri Wilderness

Furthermore, a militant minority of wilderness-minded citizens must be
on watch throughout the nation and vigilantly available for action.

ALDO LEOPOLD

THE FUTURE OF Missouri Wilderness belongs to you and me;
it's that simple. As taxpaying citizens of Missouri, we have the
right and the obligation to defend and protect the natural resources of the state, including land already enrolled in the national wilderness preservation system and lands that will be
included in the system within the next several years, by speaking
and writing about our concerns.

The people will prevail in Missouri as long as they speak with
one voice. Even a minority can make itself heard if its members
unite to speak and send their message ringing loud and clear in the
ears and consciences of those who affect the law. For that reason, we
work within the democratic system as writers, editors, orators,
planners, and dreamers with a goal to preserve significant treasures
of our cultural heritage as Wilderness. It takes energy, dedication,
confidence, education, time, money, heart, and soul.

Lest you think the mission of Wilderness impossible, remember
that in this state and throughout the nation, the Wilderness campaigns
of the sixties, seventies, and eighties have already been won. The

blueprint for success, as contained in chapter 2 of this book, can be found in those early campaigns. If a team of one hundred volunteers successfully carried out the first Wilderness mission, think what ten thousand advocates could do. But good intentions alone won't get the job done. Often people who are "for Wilderness" don't go beyond expressing their approval. Complacency is very close to apathy, a deadly enemy of wilderness preservation. What's called for is action.

A Wilderness Job Unfinished

John Kárel, who spearheaded the effort that resulted in the state's eight designated Wilderness Areas, believes there is an "unfinished agenda" for Missouri conservationists. There are seven areas in Mark Twain National Forest needing continued and improved protection: Lower Rock Creek, Van East Mountain, Smith Creek, Big Spring Addition, North Fork, Swan Creek, and Spring Creek.

According to Karel, these choice landscapes were identified during the 1970-1984 Wilderness campaign as part of RARE II studies and were officially endorsed by the Missouri Wilderness Coalition (which includes the Ozark chapter) in 1978. These areas are relatively small, less than fifty thousand acres, but they are very high in quality and value. There is detailed documentation on each area.

Since 1978, the Forest Service has granted a moderate level of administrative recognition for these areas. The service calls them "Sensitive Areas." Since then, there have been no serious ecological violations, despite several threatened Forest Service actions, including timber sales in Spring Creek, vehicular intrusions into Lower Rock Creek, and failure to close roads in North Fork.

The limited protection of areas is the result of longstanding prior campaigns, out of which hard-won, written commitments were obtained from the Forest Service. Our credibility requires that we ensure that no loss of protection be suffered by any of these areas. We should remain alert for opportunities to upgrade their protection.

Wilderness Protection of the Ozark National Scenic Riverways

Since the 1970s, the Missouri Wilderness Coalition (MWC) has advocated protection for three Ozark National Scenic Riverway areas: Cardareva, upper Jacks Fork, and the other half of the Big Spring

Addition. There is detailed documentation for all three. The history of these areas is long and complex.

The 1960 Interior Department studies that led to the creation of the Scenic Riverways specifically identified wilderness preservation as an important objective. It could be argued that the Riverways are the single most important unit of public land in the state of Missouri. Failure by the National Park Service to recognize and protect the superb wild lands of the ONSR is deplorable. Protection afforded the Buffalo National River in Arkansas is a far better example to follow in preserving these unique treasures.

Wilderness Protection of Missouri Conservation Department Land
MDC wild lands have never been the subject of a sustained campaign, but the issue of their preservation has been addressed at various times by prominent Missouri conservationists. With more than 600,000 acres, and in light of promises made during the campaign for passage of the Design for Conservation in 1976, MDC should not exclude wild land protection from its "multiple use" range of options. Many MDC employees concur with this, but no real progress has been made.

Wilderness Protection on State and Federal Lands
This includes not only the Wilderness Areas administered by the Forest Service and the Fish and Wildlife Service, but also state Wild Areas administered by the Department of Natural Resources. Concerns have recently been raised that the DNR may be downgrading its protection for designated Wild Areas through excessive "groomed" or "designer woods" activities. Wild Areas are not to be confused with experimental vegetation manipulation zones. The Missouri Wilderness Coalition has endorsed reintroduction of fire as a natural force in wild land landscapes. MWC does not approve of physical removal of native plants or other management intrusions. Part of MWC's mission is to ensure full compliance with statutory and administrative commitments to wild land resource protection.

Rounding Out Boundaries of Existing Wilderness and Wild Areas
The most important example of the need to extend boundaries is

the undesignated portion of the Irish Wilderness at Tumbling Shoals Hollow. Several other areas have adjacent properties, minor in acreage, which have become public land since designation, and should be added to the protected areas. Another example is the critical acreage at the north end of Rockpile Mountain Wilderness. At Piney Creek, portions of the "Northside" tract are now connected to the Wilderness. Piney would benefit immensely from an added buffer zone.

Karel thinks these adjustments could be made with minimum fuss as slight amendments to other public land legislation, assuming we can restore trust to our relationship with local residents and to the Missouri congressional delegation.

We believe that one cannot enjoy the outdoors without understanding it, and to understand it is to be committed to its preservation.

MARK BRYANT

Mark Twain National Forest Wilderness Candidates

LOWER ROCK CREEK is accessible from Old Woods Road at Wolf Hollow, east of Fredericktown via Highways E and 511.

Lower Rock Creek in Madison and Iron Counties is a tributary to the St. Francis River. Along this stream and on the surrounding knobs of the St. Francois Mountains is one of the finest unprotected resources of the entire Ozark region. With almost fourteen thousand acres, Lower Rock Creek has long been recognized as one of Missouri's wildest and most spectacular scenic areas. The rose-tinted igneous rock canyon walls and the bedrock stream watershed are in superb natural condition. It has massive, continuous exposures of rhyolite along the shut-ins of the steep valley, with sheer cliffs overlooking the creek and rocky terraces on the slopes above. Much of the valley is so steep that there is little or no floodplain at all.

Vegetation includes many communities associated with the St. Francois Mountains. There are a number of endemic Ozark species, including Ozark witch hazel; its yellow blooms may be seen in fall or early spring. Bald eagles are visitors to the area in winter, and in the spring there are spectacular displays of the native rose azalea. A study conducted by the University of Missouri described the area as the most significant remaining example of a St. Francois Mountain watershed landscape.

Lower Rock Creek hosts a steadily increasing number of visitors who value its unspoiled scenery and natural integrity. Recreational use of this unique area is very much dependent upon its wilderness character.

VAN EAST MOUNTAIN is accessible cross-country from Highway D, three miles west of Silver Mines Recreation Area.

A three-knobbed St. Francois Mountain, the Van East wilderness includes about 3,000 acres and reaches 1,330 feet in elevation. An area known as Weiss Shut-Ins is located at the south end of the mountain along Rock Creek. Other small grottoes occur throughout the area. Long Gravel Branch flows through the area, with one spring adding a steady flow of water to the creek. Barren outcrops high on the south flank of the mountain provide superb views of the proposed Lower Rock Creek wilderness to the south. Other outcroppings occur throughout the area from which vistas of surrounding valleys may be admired. Portions of the mountain are known for excellent displays of rose azalea, and Ozark witch hazel flourishes in the narrow streambeds.

Four distinct community types are found in the area. These communities are of such high quality that the University of Missouri identified this area in a special study as one of the outstanding natural areas in southeast Missouri. Several primitive hiking trails found there, along with abandoned logging roads, make the area easily accessible for nature study, day hiking, and extended backpacking trips.

SMITH CREEK is accessible on the Cedar Creek Trail from Highway Y, six miles east of Ashland.

The northern half of the state of Missouri is not traditionally associated with potential wilderness—and with good reason. The northern part of the state has rich soil, and most of this section has been farmed for over a century. Nevertheless, a few small patches of rough, wild land have survived, and some of these are in the public domain. Only one, Smith Creek, is of full wilderness quality. This has made Smith Creek one of Missouri's most cherished wild lands.

Smith Creek, lying mostly in Callaway County with a minor

extension into Boone County, is small, a mere two thousand acres, but what it lacks in size, it makes up for in charm. Named for a tributary of Cedar Creek, which normally flows all year, this stream has carved a beautiful bluff-lined valley through the otherwise level uplands of north-central Missouri. The bluffs are formed of Burlington limestone and have weathered in some places into picturesque pinnacles, buttresses, and gothic arches. Several small tributaries flow along rock-bottom chutes whose surfaces have been worn smooth by the flowing water. Small waterfalls have formed, and sculpted rock ledges line long stretches of the creek. Located north of the Missouri River, the area is not part of the Ozarks. The rare ruffed grouse is found here. On the upland ridges native grasses can be found.

Only twenty minutes from the growing cities of Columbia and Fulton, and perhaps thirty minutes from Jefferson City, Smith Creek is a wilderness oasis for central Missourians. Backpacking is as popular as day hiking in the area. A Boy Scout trail crosses the area. Spring wildflower hikes are often arranged to take advantage of the colorful, seasonal displays. Squirrel hunting is popular.

BIG SPRING is accessible from the Ozark Trail near Van Buren, south from Highway 60, or via Skyline Drive.

Big Spring, rising at the base of a sheer wall of dolomite and flowing into the fabled Current River, is the largest spring in the Ozarks and one of the largest emergences of freshwater on the continent of North America.

In the 1920s, this spectacular natural wonder in Carter County, south of Van Buren, prompted the establishment of a great state park. This park, now incorporated as part of the Ozark National Scenic Riverways, included several thousand acres of rugged and primitive backcountry. It has long been protected from logging and boasts some extremely high quality Ozark forest. The remote backcountry, combined with adjacent, qualified Forest Service lands, constitutes a fine wilderness resource of about six thousand acres. It is a fitting and necessary complement to the heavily developed recreational facilities immediately surrounding Big Spring itself.

The terrain is typical of the Current River hills with a dense oak and oak-pine forest. The area lies entirely within the watershed of the river and includes parts of Kinnard Hollow, Wildhorse Hollow, and Spring Creek Valley. Excellent views of the general area are available from the popular Skyline Drive.

Most of the Park Service portion of this wilderness has not been disturbed for over one hundred years, and some of the white oaks and shortleaf pines are truly majestic. The Park Service portion is also a wildlife refuge, and during winter snow cover, deer and wild turkey tracks are everywhere. Bald eagles use the area during winter.

There are several trails in the area and also a picturesque old fire tower reminiscent of the early days of conservation in the Ozarks. The wilderness is a wonderful monument to the legendary Big Spring.

NORTH FORK is accessible by canoe on the North Fork River from Twin Bridges at Highway 14 to North Fork Campground and by foot via Ridge Runner Trail from North Fork Campground.

The North Fork is one of the finest and most beloved of the Ozark float streams. This tributary of the fabled White River flows south through the plateau country of the Willow Springs unit of the Mark Twain National Forest. The river has cut deeply into this relatively level plateau and carved a twisting, ledge-lined valley flanked by steep hollows and sharp ridges of its smaller tributaries. Nowhere does the North Fork River flow through wilder or more appealing country than in the stretch between Twin Bridges and the old West Plains Road, now called Highway CC.

The block of forestland in this stretch comprises the 6,000–acre North Fork wilderness, mostly in Ozark County but extending into Douglas and Howell Counties. This wilderness is a truly impressive example of the original Ozarks.

As noted, the North Fork wilderness straddles the North Fork River and derives its character from that swift, clear stream. Besides the scenic limestone bluffs, several areas of increasingly rare Ozark bottomland forest are found here. These bottomland forest and open-water river habitats are part of the vital feeding grounds for the endangered gray bat, which finds refuge in caves located in this wilderness.

Besides the popularity of the area for canoeing, the uplands are now traversed by the completed Ridge Runner Trail. The area is also popular as a walk-in turkey-hunting area. Access to the area is conveniently located at the North Fork campground along Highway CC. The established Devil's Backbone Wilderness lies just to the south of the North Fork wilderness, thus forming a vital and logical two-part protection for this priceless Ozark landscape.

SWAN CREEK is accessible cross-country via old, unimproved roads, from Highway UU in Christian County.

The streams of the Ozarks are recognized worldwide for their beauty and recreational quality. Of all these justly famous Ozark streams, none is better known for the clarity of its waters than remote Swan Creek. This ultraclear stream borders an equally remote block of federal land comprising the Swan Creek wilderness.

The Swan Creek area is located in Christian County, thirty-five miles southeast of Springfield near the town of Garrison. As implied by the name, the area lies adjacent to Swan Creek, which forms part of its western border. The topography is characterized by very irregular ridges that are downcut by small streams, or "branches," flowing west toward Swan Creek from higher elevations along the eastern boundary. The forest composition is mostly oak-hickory with much of that in post oak. The forest itself, though not tall, is mature and imparts a feeling of deep solitude. Scattered throughout the area are small open to semi-open cedar glades.

The area harbors several southwestern species of animals, such as the roadrunner and the collared lizard. The numerous glades of the area are a unique feature of the southwestern Ozarks. Hiking and backpacking are popular in the area. Sixteen miles of old, unimproved roads form a trail system. The rugged character of the area and the scenic qualities of Swan Creek give it outstanding recreation potential.

SPRING CREEK is accessible on Ridge Runner Trail from Noblett Lake. Spring Creek is located in one of the most intricately dissected portions of the central Ozarks. The dissecting forces in this case are Noblett and Spring Creeks. Each has carved a deep, narrow, bluff-lined valley. The juncture of the two streams in the heart of the area is a veritable maze of narrow hogback ridges and sheer dolomite bluffs, rising up to 200 feet high. The hogback just above the main juncture offers superb vistas of wild forest in all directions. The double corridor of these narrow, south-flowing valleys forms the scenic core of this area, flanked by the rolling tributary drainages on the east and the west. Elevation ranges from 1,182 feet on the eastern flank to less than 820 feet along Spring Creek. Both Noblett and Spring Creeks are spring-fed permanent streams with deep pools and clear, cold waters. Several springs occur in the area, including Galloway Spring.

Bald eagles winter in the vicinity of Noblett Lake, which is adjacent to the wilderness. Ruffed grouse, listed as rare in Missouri, occur in the area.

National Park Service Wilderness Candidates

CARDAREVA is accessible from Owl's Bend either by canoe on the Current River or by foot via the Ozark Trail.

Most of the Ozark National Scenic Riverways is a relatively narrow strip of public land, but there is one major exception. One of the cornerstone concepts of the original proposal for the Riverways was to incorporate at least one sizeable block of public land in its primitive state in order to preserve a representative example of Ozark wilderness. That block of public land comprises the 12,000–acre Cardareva wilderness. This large, diverse area succeeds in that original intent, perhaps better than the early proponents of the Riverways even foresaw. The Cardareva wilderness includes a superb stretch of the Current River, several imposing bluffs, large expanses of rugged Current River hills, and diversity of forests and wildlife.

Despite this area's outstanding natural merits, its security as a wilderness resource has been clouded by the fact that two public agencies, the National Park Service and the Missouri Department of Conservation, have intermixed holdings inside the wilderness. These agencies will need to cooperate in the best interests of the public, if the unique values of this wilderness resource are to be preserved for the future.

UPPER JACKS FORK is accessible by canoe, beginning at the Highway 17 Bridge at Buck Hollow.

The Jacks Fork River is generally considered to be the finest wilderness-quality canoe float available in the Missouri Ozarks. One of the finest stretches of this float stream ribbons its way from the Highway 17 bridge downstream to Alley Spring.

When the Ozark National Scenic Riverways were authorized in 1964, this section was given a high priority, and a sizeable block of this area is in federal ownership. The finest portion comprises the 4,000–acre Upper Jacks Fork wilderness. This area includes one of the finest float streams in the nation, a bounty of magnificent riverside bluffs, caves, springs and some of the most unique plant communities in the Ozarks.

The Jacks Fork River in this area cuts a virtual canyon through the Salem Plateau. Along the river valley, towering shortleaf pines flank the bluff tops and ridge lines. On some of the north-facing bluffs, extremely rare and lovely flowering plants find a refuge, particularly in the vicinity of the striking Jam Up Cave. This majestic chamber of underground caverns is considered to have one of the most impressive entrances of any in the Ozarks. The area also features good fishing and deer and turkey hunting.

Missouri Department of Conservation Wilderness Candidates

In discussing wild land resources on state-owned property, it is important to understand that these areas are not eligible for inclusion in the federal Wilderness system, short of a transfer of title to the United States. At the time of this writing, no reputable conservation group has recommended any such wholesale transfer.

The Missouri Wilderness Coalition, for example, has recommended that qualified wild lands be protected through special state designation to safeguard those values.

In 1978, the Missouri Department of Natural Resources, to its foresight and credit, inaugurated just such a program. The DNR Wild Areas system is working to protect these unique natural areas, and the concept is well accepted by Missourians and visitors to the state who are enriched by the wild lands experience. Additionally, the Missouri Wilderness Coalition has further recommended that the Missouri Department of Conservation, which has no such system, follow the DNR model and designate qualified areas under a similar program.

BUFORD MOUNTAIN CONSERVATION AREA is accessible eight miles north of Ironton on Highway 21 and one mile north on Highway U.

This magnificent area contains a 3,743–acre forest with a six-mile hiking trail. Primitive camping options are available throughout the area. There is good hunting for deer, turkey and squirrels. Wilderness designation for Buford Mountain would preserve the splendor of the area and prevent the possibilities of recreational development or logging.

CANEY MOUNTAIN CONSERVATION AREA is accessible five miles north of Gainsville on Highway 181, then a half-mile west on an unnamed gravel entrance road.

This 6,674–acre area's dolomite glades, chert savannas, and numerous caves and springs are unique. Caney Creek flows through the area, and 1,330 acres are designated as Caney Mountain Natural Area. Two hiking trails are established along with developed picnic areas and four vistas. Other development includes a parking lot, rest rooms, and an archery range on the area that is accessible to wheelchairs. The developed part of Caney Mountain should be left intact and used as is. However, other undeveloped lands within the conservation area are best protected for the future under designated Wilderness protection. In this case, outdoor enthusiasts, hikers and campers, can have the best of both worlds.

MDC KERR-McGEE LANDS access to these numerous tracts of land are in northern Shannon, Carter, and Wayne Counties.

Combined, the tracts consist of more than 73,300 acres, the biggest block of undeveloped lands in the state. In the spring of 1992, the Nature Conservancy (TNC) bought more than 80,000 acres of land—mostly in Shannon County but some also lies in Carter and Wayne counties—from the Kerr-McGee Corporation. The selling price was 125 dollars per acre, 30 percent below the appraised value. TNC immediately sold 37,543 acres in fee title to the Conservation Department. Another 37,421 acres were sold to the department in the fall of 1993, placing almost 75,000 acres of some of Missouri's most beautiful natural lands under public ownership. MDC has built roads in some of the area, and timber management has been implemented. Of vital importance, according to John Karel, is MDC's preserving a 10,000–acre tract of land near the Current River for state Wild Area designation.

PECK RANCH CONSERVATION AREA is accessible five miles east of Winona on Highway H and another seven miles east on a gravel road (marked with a sign) in Shannon County. This 22,948–acre area has 119 ponds, totaling 125 acres, seven caves, and numerous springs. Designated Natural Areas within the Peck

Ranch area include Mule Hollow Glade (175 acres), Headwater Stream and Roger Creek (6.75 miles long), Stegal Mountain (3,872 acres) and Sinkhole Pond (1 acre). Most of the area is forested. A 9.5–mile stretch of the Ozark Trail goes through the area. Development includes a public contact office and shooting range.

A significant portion of this large and unique area is perfectly suited for designated Wilderness protection in order to preserve its integrity for future generations. The area provides primitive camping, solitude, and good hunting for deer and turkey. Its proximity to the Current River, a jewel of the Ozark National Scenic Riverways system, would also serve to help protect this valuable watershed.

Missouri Department of Natural Resources Wild Area System

INDIAN CREEK WILD AREA is accessible ten miles east of Fruitland off Interstate 55 and Missouri 177 in the northern 1,300 acres of Trail of Tears State Park.

The historically significant land was part of the Cherokees' route on their forced march to the West. The Mississippi River laps the base of towering limestone bluffs in Indian Creek Wild Area. Beyond the river stretches 1,300 acres of majestic hardwood forests, tangled lowland thickets, and floodplain forest of sweet gum and willow. Deeply dissected river hills create a maze of ravines and steep coves with rich forests that possess a distinctly Appalachian flavor.

Features include tulip poplar trees, large sweet gums, native shortleaf pine; high, grassy openings with red cedar and blue ash; and an abundance of wildlife, including deer and turkeys. The ten-mile Peewah Trail winds in several loops through the Wild Area. It includes scenic views of the Mississippi River and many outstanding forest features. Backpackers take advantage of excellent primitive camping opportunities along this trail.

GANS CREEK WILD AREA is accessible seven miles south of Columbia and Interstate 70 on Highway 163 in Boone County.

Natural geologic formations are the principal features of the park. Devil's Icebox Cave, a natural rock bridge, and numerous sinkholes are part of the large limestone cave system dating back thousands of years. A touch of Ozark beauty lies north of the Missouri River where Gans Creek winds its way through the 750–acre Gans Creek Wild Area. Its water ripples over gravel bars to calm pools, washing the feet of cedar-crowned bluffs. Numerous paths lead through surrounding hillsides rich with seasonal displays of columbine, bloodroot, brown-eyed susan, and wild aster. Although much of the area was farmed at one time, nature is reclaiming the fields and pastures with forests of oak, hickory, maple, and wild cherry.

Under DNR Wild Area protection, Gans Creek is open for day-use hiking and nature study. Currently, backpack camping is not allowed by DNR in order to protect the "wilderness setting" of this small but popular area.

ROARING RIVER HILLS WILD AREA is accessible seven miles south of Cassville in Barry County on Highway 112 and Highway F at Roaring River State Park.

Roaring River Hills Wild Area lies within Missouri's glade region and is flavored by many colorful plants and animals typical of drier parts of the country. Its 2,075 acres are a mix of deep narrow valleys and high, sharp ridges. Delightful views open from several lofty glades, expose dry, rugged slopes and deep cove forests. Black bears, armadillos, roadrunners, eastern collared lizards, and scorpions are common, along with white-tailed deer and turkeys.

The 3.5–mile Fire Tower Trail allows easy, although steep, access to the heart of the Wild Area for hikers. The wilderness beyond the trail is rugged, offering adventuresome challenges for the experienced wilderness hiker and backpacker. Primitive off-trail camping is permitted. There is no designated backpack camp for groups .

In addition to the wilderness opportunities at Roaring River Hills, Roaring River State Trout Park offers excellent fishing from March 1 through October 31. The park offers developed campsites, a motel and cabins, and a well-stocked store for campers and anglers.

PATTERSON HOLLOW WILD AREA is accessible from Highways 42 and 134 on the north; Highway 134 and the existing utility corridor on the east; a paved road and the park boundary on the south; and a park boundary on the west at the northern portion of the Lake of the Ozarks State Park.

Wooded ridges rise above forested hollows, spreading like ocean swells in Patterson Hollow Wild Area's 1,275 acres. Small springs and seeps form clear, perennial pools, and hillsides of maples create shimmering color in fall. The scattered fields and old home sites are a fading legacy of the original Ozark mountaineers. Common wildlife include whitetailed deer, five-lined skinks, raccoons, and turkeys. The six-mile Woodland Trail, which winds through the Wild Area, is a secluded pathway through this Ozark environment. A backpack camp is available for small groups. Individual campers often prefer to set tents in the numerous hills and hollows beyond the trail.

NORTHWOODS WILD AREA is accessible approximately sixty miles north of St. Louis at the Cuivre River State Park near Troy in Lincoln County. It is reached via state Highways 47 and 147. Northwoods is that portion of the park north of Highway KK. Access is available at several small pullouts along the north side of KK.

The forested hills within this 1,082–acre Wild Area protect a wilderness quality that is rare in northern Missouri today. White oak forests, numerous springs, and gravel-bottomed creeks lend a distinct Ozark flavor to the landscape. Along Big Sugar Creek are small bluffs where columbine and false hellebore grow. Wildlife is abundant and ranges from pickerel frogs and dark-sided salamanders to turkeys, deer, and woodcock.

The six-mile Lone Spring Trail follows steep, wooded hillsides, parallels Big Sugar Creek, and penetrates impressive forest hollows. A backpack camp overlooks a headwater stream's junction with Big Sugar Creek. From the trail's highest point, the wooded slopes stretch outward through the Wild Area's trailless western half.

COONVILLE CREEK WILD AREA is accessible off Highway 67 in St. Francois County in the St. Francois State Park near Bonne Terre.

Coonville Creek Wild Area's 2,256 acres are heavily forested with a maze of narrow hollows and steep terrain. Moss-covered bedrock ledges, commonly enhanced by cascading spring water, are found throughout the Wild Area. Showy wildflowers grace several open glades, and cool, moist fens abound. One large, picturesque fen is notable for its tallgrass prairie plants and ice-age relics (persistent remnants) such as queen-of-the-prairie. This particular fen has been designated a Missouri Natural Area because of its high quality.

The 11–mile Pike Run Trail leads to many of the Wild Area's rugged hills and hollows. The 2.7–mile Mooner's Hollow Trail follows the steep, narrow valley of Coonville Creek. A backpack camp is available.

EAST FORK WILD AREA is accessible about ten miles southwest of Ironton on Reynolds County Route N. The county road runs through the park and connects with Missouri Highways 49, 72, and 21.

East Fork Wild Area's 1,110 acres preserve a splendid example of the St. Francois Mountain wilderness. The area's hills and valleys, covered with mixed oak, pine, and hickory forests, are dwarfed by sweeping mountain vistas. Multicolored rock barrens, grassy glades, and creeks winding through narrow rock clefts are among the area's unique treasures. The Ozark Trail passes through the area and parallels the narrow chutes and granite boulders of the East Fork of the Black River. Off-trail camping is permitted, but there is no designated backpack camp for groups. The varied relief and soil conditions in East Fork support flora and fauna that are some of the most diverse in the state.

The ancient rock creates a landscape of impressive beauty that is best observed along the East Fork of the Black River, located in the eastern portion. In places, the igneous bedrock confines the stream channel to narrow, canyonlike gorges called "shut-ins." The vertical bluffs and weathered boulders stand as monuments to the area's fiery origin.

WHISPERING PINE WILD AREA is accessible ten miles east of Farmington and about ten miles southwest of Weingarten from Highway 144. The Wild Area is located south of Highway 144 and east of the country road that forms the western boundary of the park.

Whispering Pine Wild Area's 2,080 pine-clad acres feature a deep, igneous gorge, sheer sandstone cliffs, narrow box canyons, and xeric rock barrens, all crowded together in a remarkable puzzle of geology. Sprinkled throughout, visitors find parklike pine groves, deep carpets of ferns, dwarf forests, pink and white azaleas, and delicate woodland orchids. Rich moss and lichen patches carpet and color cliff tops and foregrounds of sweeping vistas.

The ten-mile Whispering Pine Trail, which features two five-mile hiking loops and three backpack camps, winds through this dramatic area.

MUDLICK MOUNTAIN WILD AREA is accessible three miles north of Patterson on Highway 143 in Wayne County. The hiking trailhead is located on the west side of Highway 143, across the road from the Sam A. Baker State Park.

Mudlick Mountain's huge igneous dome dominates this 4,420–acre Wild Area. Around its base, steep talus slopes and sheer 300–foot cliffs rise abruptly from Big Creek's crystal pools. Splendid old-growth forests mantle its slopes, harboring large trees, moss-covered seeps, rocky draws, and boulder gardens.

Mudlick Trail provides an intimate journey into one of the oldest mountain regions of North America, the St. Francois Mountains. It is a moderately strenuous twelve-mile trail, climbing to 415 feet above sea level at the top of Mudlick Mountain. It is open to hiking and backpacking. Most of the trail is located in the Mudlick Wild Area, one of the most significant, undisturbed natural landscapes in Missouri. In November 1980, Secretary of the Interior Cecil D. Andrus designated Mudlick Trail a National Recreation Trail for its importance as an outstanding recreational resource.

The trail begins by ascending the bluffs above Big Creek where three stone hiking shelters, constructed by the Civilian Conservation Corps in the 1930s, offer outstanding views of the surrounding countryside and the "shut-ins" valley below. The trail then drops into Mudlick Hollow, a narrow, rock-strewn valley dotted with pools of clear water. The trail follows Mudlick Hollow for about three quarters of a mile before beginning a gradual climb to the summit of Green Mountain.

The view from Green Mountain is best during the fall and winter when the trees in the thick oak-hickory forest have shed their leaves. From the southern end of Green Mountain, the trail descends rapidly, via a series of switchbacks into Logal Creek valley. A dense stand of red cedar grows in the valley, providing a cool, shaded trail corridor. Once through the valley, the trail begins a steady climb to the top of Mudlick Mountain. It then traverses the rugged eastern slope of the mountain back to the starting point. Currently, the three historic stone shelters mentioned above are open to backpackers from October 1 through May 1.

BIG SUGAR CREEK WILD AREA is accessible three miles east of Troy on Highway 47 in Lincoln County.

The 1,675–acre Big Sugar Creek Wild Area lies south of Camp Derricotte. As in the adjacent Northwoods Wild Area, the landscape and features have been sculpted by Big Sugar Creek. The water has carved through Mississippian limestone to form its rugged watershed. Bluffs along this portion of the creek are much more rugged that anywhere else along the creek. Sugar Bluff towers 90 feet above the creek bed. Several small limestone glades with their unique flora are found on the bluff tops, and on south- or west-facing hillsides. Because of their exposure, lack of moisture, and other qualities associated with the deserts of the southwest, one author has coined the term *desertlettes* to describe these glades.

Hikers in the area also will notice several sinkholes and springs that are characteristic of a distinguishable karst topography. This topography is the result of water percolating through the underlying limestone bedrock over years, dissolving and carrying away some of the subterranean rock. Although common in southern Missouri, karst features in northern Missouri can be found only in the Lincoln Hills region.

Flora and fauna include dogwood, spicebush, Missouri orange coneflower, marbled salamander, and fence lizards. The seven-mile Big Sugar Trail and eight-mile Cuivre River Trail meander through the Wild Area and connect with other park trails leading to nearby Northwoods Wild Area. There are two backpack camps.

Those hikers who are willing to venture from the main trail may find interesting artifacts of cultural history. An Indian burial mound in the vicinity was excavated in 1937 by one of Missouri's noted early archaeologists, Carl Chapman. A cemetery dating back to the 1800s and the cornerstones and last rotting timbers of an old cabin also are located in the Wild Area.

GOGGINS MOUNTAIN WILD AREA is accessible from the north at the Ozark Trailhead along Highway A through Bell Mountain Wilderness; from the south, on the Ozark Trail along Highway N (from the trailhead within Johnson's Shut-Ins in the developed portion of the park). Some access into the area occurs from the east and west along Padfield Branch Road.

Goggins Mountain became a DNR Wild Area on March 31, 1995, the newest and probably the finest in the state. Goggins Mountain Wild Area, 5,000 acres, embraces both Goggins Mountain itself and the south portion of Bell Mountain, extending southward out of the Bell Mountain Wilderness. This range of characteristic St. Francois Mountain domes represents the westernmost terminus of the juncture between the deeply dissected Salem Plateau to the west and the St. Francois Mountain core to the east. The juncture of these mountains is dramatic. In the heart of this area is approximately twelve miles of the Ozark Trail, part of the total thirty-five miles of trail winding continuously across public land.

Within this trail corridor is perhaps the most rugged and superlative wilderness scenery in Missouri. In fact, the natural and harmonious blend of and transitions between glades, savannas, rock barrens, and woodlands mantling the great domes of Goggins and Bell Mountains give this a true presettlement wilderness appearance. Undoubtedly, the wilderness integrity is the highest of all existing state park Wild Areas. Significance of the Goggins Mountain Wild Area becomes even greater when coupled with the 9,027–acre Bell Mountain Wilderness with the total state and federal wilderness landscape close to 15,000 acres.

Goggins Mountain is part of a distinct range of igneous domes situated on the extreme western flank of the St. Francois Mountains. These domes are unique to Missouri, having formed from a region of early volcanic activity. The Wild Area encompasses four dome summits, the tallest being 1,484 feet. Goggins Mountain ridge is oriented north-south, with drainage off to the east flank into Shut-in Creek and to the west into the Middle Fork of the Black River.

Between Bell and Goggins Mountains is a deep valley drainage called Padfield Branch, which forms a huge, mile-wide amphitheater valley. It is here that impressive wildness prevails, particularly in the view to the northeast, looking onto Lindsey Mountain, which looms into the sky like a distant volcano.

The National Wilderness Preservation System must be expanded promptly, before the most deserving of Federal lands are opened to other uses.

PRESIDENT JIMMY CARTER

Mark Twain Forest Plan Should Include More Wilderness

President Carter's proclamation is as true today as it was in 1977. Unfinished Wilderness business, unique lands deserving full protection, are documented in this chapter. It is now up to Wilderness conservationists, elected representatives, and personnel of the Mark Twain National Forest, National Park Service, MDC, and DNR to save the best of what we have left for us and future generations.

This could very well be the final Wilderness campaign. And

when it is completed, Missourians can stand proud, knowing that a small but significant part of the state's cultural heritage and unspoiled beauty have been saved from "other uses." The pure, quiet, dramatically beautiful land and water—a legacy we pass on to those who follow—are natural treasures that would grow more valuable with each passing year.

In October 1997, the first issue of the *Mark Twain National Forest Planning Journal* was sent to professionals and citizens who value their public lands and national forests. In that issue, Forest Supervisor Randy Moore is quoted on page one: "The mission of the Forest Service as well as the Mark Twain National Forest, is to achieve quality land management and meet a variety of public needs." That being the case, the Forest Service is well aware that recreation and wildlife have replaced mining, timber, and livestock grazing as the most important and economically feasible uses of the National Forest System.

In 1996, Assistant Secretary of Agriculture Jim Lyons told a group of outdoor retailers just that. Speaking to the Outdoor Retailer Summer Market show in Salt Lake City, Lyons said that national forests (192 million acres) contribute 130.7 billion dollars annually to the U.S. economy. Of that, recreation generates 97.8 billion; hunting, fishing, and other wildlife-related activities, 12.9 billion; mineral production, 10.1 billion; and timber, 3.5 billion. However, Lyons said, these facts are relatively unknown in Washington, D.C. because the outdoor recreation industry is not an outspoken lobby and not well respected by the current Congress. Consequently, he said, investments in outdoor recreation by the Forest Service make up only 21 percent of the agency's budget.

"More and more, our business is recreation," Lyons said. "We need to help give Congress a better understanding of the need to invest in the Forest Service programs that provide that recreation." Secretary of Agriculture Dan Glickman said, "It's high time the natural splendor of our public lands got the respect it has earned."

By the year 2000, the Forest Service estimates that outdoor recreation on Forest Service land will contribute seven times more to the economy than mining and foresting combined. In fact, in that year, 75 percent of the gross domestic product created by Forest Service activities will be from outdoor recreation.

Yet in fiscal year 1996, recreation programs accounted for less than 20 percent of the Forest Service budget. Trail maintenance backlogs are almost insurmountable, and our national forests and parks, including the Mark Twain Forest, are strapped for cash and personnel. A case in point, currently the Mark Twain Forest employs only one person to patrol the seven congressionally designated Wilderness Areas in Missouri.

Mark Twain Forest's New Forest Plan Due by 2001

The Mark Twain, like other forests throughout the system, is obligated to follow the federal laws and regulations that apply to National Forest management and planning. These regulations require the Mark Twain Forest to revise the Forest Plan every ten to fifteen years. The last Forest Plan was finalized in 1986 and must be revised by 2001.

The current plan is revised in order to make improvements and to reflect changes in information, knowledge, and expectations that lead to better management of the Mark Twain National Forest. In this case, there should be major emphasis, regarding the remarks of Lyons and Glickman, concerning the economic power of outdoor recreation.

Those responsible for coordinating the revision of the Mark Twain Plan are currently working full time on the project. The planning team leader is Rich Hall. The resource specialist for the team is Garry Houf. Mike Shanta is the team analyst, and Laura Watts is responsible for the human aspects of forest resources, such as recreation and heritage resources. She will also be coordinating the public involvement activities for the plan revision. Watts has a degree in landscape architecture. Hall and Schanta have degrees in forestry. Houf has a degree in wildlife biology. These key personnel can be reached at the Mark Twain Forest Headquarters in Rolla. The phone number is (573) 364-4621.

In February 1998, I received the second issue of the *Mark Twain National Forest Planning Journal*. In a nutshell, the new Forest Plan was being delayed for the following reason. For several years, U.S. Department of Agriculture and the Forest Service have considered changing the regulations that guide the revision of forest plans. To encourage the development of new planning regulations, Congress included an amendment in its 1998 funding bill for the National Forests that prohibits the Forest Service from spending money on any new Forest Plan revisions until new planning regulations are developed and implemented.

Now the plan revision is on a later time schedule, depending on when the new regulations are issued. The Forest Service expects to complete new planning direction in early 1999. This means Mark Twain Forest will not publish its Notice of Intent in the fall of 1998 as planned. And the assessment phase, which was due early in 1998, will also be delayed.

Until the committee of scientists who are evaluating the Forest Service planning process reach a conclusion and make recommendations to the secretary of agriculture and the chief of the Forest Service, the new plan and the quest for more Missouri Wilderness is on hold. Hopefully the delay will be in favor of outdoor recreation, specifically the purest kind, which realizes the recreational and monetary worth of the Wilderness experience.

In the meantime, Mark Twain Forest personnel at Rolla headquarters are encouraging Missourians to get involved in revising the planning regulations by making written comments to the Forest Supervisor or Planning Team members. The time frame is close. The blueprint for success, as John Karel and others initially pioneered for Missouri Wilderness victories, is contained within this text. I hope you do not feel it presumptuous of me to believe that this book can help the cause.

For more Forest Plan information at the national level, contact Bob Cunningham, who is the designated federal official to the committee, at (202) 205-2494. Written comments may be submitted to: Committee of Scientists, Mail Stop 1104, Forest Service, USDA, P.O. Box 96090, Washington, D.C. 20090-6090.

How to Make Positive Public Comment to the Forest Service

Many potentially good comment letters to the Forest Service regarding Forest Plans, Notice of Intent Publication and Scoping, Draft Environmental Impact Statement, Final Revised Forest Plan, and Final Environmental Impact Statement are dismissed because they contain too much emotion and not enough hard, well-thought-out facts. Avoid conjecture! Eliminate sentimentality, "family stories and personal experiences." Study the issues and comment specifically on the subject matter at hand. Stick to the facts pertaining to

1. land use
2. public needs
3. citizens' rights
4. outdoor recreation
5. fish and wildlife
6. flora
7. environmental concerns
8. proven solutions to environmental concerns
9. historical and cultural heritage
10. economics
11. endangered species
12. clean air
13. clean water
14. soil erosion
15. timber extraction
16. mineral extraction
17. grazing
18. forest roads
19. archaeological and geological preservation

Letter Format

1. Type or computer print out all comment letters.
2. Use business-size stationary (8½ X 11 inches) and business-size envelopes.
3. Use formal business style.
4. Try to keep your comments to one page.
5. Avoid severe criticism, anger, and vulgarity in the comment letter.
6. Utilize facts that prove to the Forest Service you are familiar with the issues.
7. Check the letter for correct spelling and grammar.
8. Sign the letter.
9. Make a copy of the letter for your files.
10. Make extra copies of the letter to send to your elected representatives.
11. Type correct Forest Service address and your return address on the envelope.
12. If you have professional credentials in any of the eighteen issue areas listed above, briefly state your expertise.

13. Send letter to: Planning Team, Mark Twain National Forest, 401 Fairgrounds Road, Rolla, MO 65401, phone (573) 364-4621. Fax (573) 341-7475.
14. There is the option of using fax machines for making comment deadlines.
15. Comments sent to elected representatives should receive the same attention to detail and business courtesy as those sent to the Forest Service.
16. Personally touring forestlands in question and attending Forest Service open meetings is an effective way to find answers.

A Word of Advice

According to Forest Service personnel, it is best to comment individually with a personal business letter. Some environmental, conservation, and sportsmen's groups use form letters or petitions, where only a signature is required, stating the organizations' desires or criticisms when making public comment. This method of group comment is most often discarded by the federal agencies and not recorded on official comment records.

Can the Public Trust Forest Service Decisions regarding Wilderness?

In the first round of Wilderness campaigns in the 1970s and 1980s, conservationists eventually prevailed. But early on, there was resistance from the commodity-oriented Forest Service as to what areas qualified for federal enrollment and whether those areas should be protected from timber or mineral management methods during the identification and study periods. Some of the areas were threatened by timber sales. Fortunately the Missouri Wilderness Coalition kept a tight rein on the Wilderness study areas and prevented overzealous superintendents and district rangers at the time from tampering with various areas.

Seven Wilderness Areas are presently in the system, but seven additional areas, as already documented in this chapter, were not accepted by the Forest Service, despite outstanding qualities. It is hoped that Mark Twain Forest administrators and their superiors will join the campaign to add these remaining seven lands to Missouri's Wilderness legacy. The hope is for mutual trust and professionalism in reaching agreements that preserve these lands forever.

Reasons for More Congressionally Designated Wilderness Areas

1. Wilderness is established as a place to allow natural processes to occur without the influence of man.

2. Wilderness has a vital place in ecosystem management, a place where the natural variability of ecosystems can be measured, giving Wilderness managers a barometer to measure the effects of their activities.

3. Wilderness sets the standard for measuring air quality, water quality, and plant inventories against "outside" standards—so scientists can distinguish good from poor standards as time passes and conditions change.

4. Wilderness protects certain species of wildlife, including bears, wolves, mountain lions, and fish. For instance, a trout species named after Lewis and Clark is on the brink of extinction because of logging and development that followed the explorers into the Pacific Northwest. The rare Lewis and Clark species of cutthroat trout are only found in cold, clear streams on national forest and other public lands, primarily in designated Wilderness and other roadless areas where logging and other development have not occurred.

5. A 1996 Fish and Wildlife Service survey shows a significant increase in the popularity of fishing, hunting, and wildlife observation. Many outdoor recreation areas today are at full capacity throughout most of the year. Wilderness provides additional high-quality areas for hiking, camping, backpacking, wildlife observation, fishing, and hunting in a setting of solitude and natural progression.

6. Wilderness serves as a unique, irreplaceable "living laboratory" for medical and scientific research. Already numerous plant and animal species have played major roles in the development of heart drugs, antibiotics, anticancer agents, and anticoagulants. More than one quarter of all prescriptions sold in America each year contain active ingredients from plants.

7. In the state of Missouri, population growth of cities, many of them in the Ozarks, is at an all-time high. If the remaining Wilderness candidates are not added to the system in the near future, they may be lost or transformed into highly developed

Jack Ward Thomas, a former chief of the Forest Service and trained wildlife biologist. Thomas is an outstanding representative of the career Forest Service professional.

and manipulated "forest parks" that lack the purity, solitude, and character of presettlement wilderness.

8. There is a permanency in designated Wilderness that can be trusted, unlike unprotected federal, state, or private lands, where timber cutting, road building, chemical spraying, commercial development, mineral extraction, and gravel dredging can destroy the beauty of a major forest environment in less than a year. Wilderness stifles man's destructive impulses and surprises and keeps developers at bay.

9. Jack Ward Thomas, a former chief of the Forest Service, said in a speech to the Outdoor Writers Association of America in June 1995, "The future of your public lands ain't little stuff. It may be the biggest stuff in conservation this century. Not only for you and your kids, but for generations to come." Thomas cited as threats to the American tradition of public lands both the budget cuts by Congress and the efforts to convert ownership to private entities or local government. In the case of existing designated federal Wilderness, the chance of privatization is remote. And this is one of the strongest reasons for setting aside more Missouri Wilderness.

10. Americans are spending more time and money on old-fashioned pleasures such as fishing, hunting, and watching wild animals, a 1996 survey by the Fish and Wildlife Service

revealed. Americans spent more than 100 billion dollars in 1996 pursuing the nation's wildlife with fishing rods, rifles, shotguns, cameras, binoculars, and spotting scopes, the survey of 32,400 citizens shows. That was an increase of 33 percent from 1991. Among public lands and waters to pursue those pleasures, the nation's designated Wilderness Areas, including the eight treasures in Missouri, rank the highest in terms of solitude, unspoiled resources, good hunting and fishing, unique and abundant bird and plant life—the complete quality outdoor experience.

11. Wilderness protects watersheds upon which many cities and rural communities depend for clean water.

12. Wilderness serves as critical habitat for wildlife threatened by extinction.

13. Wilderness improves the quality of our air because of the filtering action of green plants and forest.

14. Wilderness provides protection for geological resource values. Undisturbed, naturally occurring geologic phenomena are protected for present and future generations to use in pursuit of knowledge about the origin of this planet and the universe.

15. Wilderness serves as a haven from the pressure of fast-paced industrialized society. It is a place where humans can seek relief from the noise and speed of machines, confines of steel and concrete, and the crowding of people.

16. Wilderness is a unique repository for cultural resource values. Artifacts and structures protected by the Archaeological Resources Protection Act or other laws take on a new perspective when experienced within the context of the wilderness. These features tell a valuable story about the human relationship with wilderness.

17. For all its uses, values, and scenic wonders, wilderness is a land heritage that is uniquely American. In the words of Pulitzer Prize–winning novelist Wallace Stegner, "Something will have gone out of us as a people if we ever let the remaining wilderness be destroyed."

Wilderness Facts

A majority of the nation's Wilderness, 62.3 percent of the system, is in Alaska. Almost 30 million acres, or one-third of the entire Wilderness system, is in eleven western states. Thus, 95.3 percent of all the protected Wilderness in the United States is in the eleven western states or Alaska. Only 4.7 percent of the nation's Wilderness lies east of the one hundredth meridian, and almost half of that can be found in just two areas: Everglades National Park in Florida and the Boundary Waters Canoe Area in Minnesota. Nationwide, there are 474 Wilderness Areas—43 in Alaska and 431 in the rest of the United States. Federal Wilderness Areas are found in every state except Connecticut, Rhode Island, Delaware, Maryland, Kansas, and Iowa.

The nation's largest Wilderness, 8.7 million acres, is Wrangell–St. Elias National Park in Alaska. The largest Wilderness Area in the lower 48 states is the Frank Church–River of No Return Wilderness in Idaho, which totals 2.3 million acres. The nation's smallest Wilderness, just five acres, can be found at Oregon Islands off the coast of Oregon.

Important Dates

1917—Landscape architect Frank Waugh surveys the recreational potential of National Forests and concludes that the "enticing wilderness" of the forest has "direct human value" and should be given parity with economic consideration when determining the forests' future.

1919—Arthur Carhart, a planner for the Forest Service, recommends that the Trapper Lake areas in Colorado's White River National Forest not be developed for summer homes but be allowed to remain wild. Regional office approves Carhart's plan.

1924—Noted ecologist Aldo Leopold, a Forest Service forester and one of the Wilderness Society's eight cofounders, urges the Forest Service to protect the Gila National Forest in New Mexico. On June 3, 1924, 574,00 acres are set aside as a preserve for Wilderness recreation, the first step in a forty-year administrative and legislative journey that is to culminate in passage of the 1964 Wilderness Act.

1926—Forest Service Chief William B. Greeley issues a national policy statement on Wilderness and instructs his assistant, Leon F. Kneipp, to prepare an inventory of all de facto Wilderness on the National Forests, the first such survey of its kind in American history.

1929—Forest Service issues the L-20 Regulations to establish "primitive" areas within the national forests.

1930—Robert Marshall, another Wilderness Society cofounder and later Forest Service manager, publishes "The Problem of the Wilderness" in *Scientific American*. "The preservation of a few samples of undeveloped territory," Marshall writes, "is one of the most clamant issues before us today. Just a few more years of hesitation and the only trace of Wilderness which has exerted such a fundamental influence in molding American character will lie in the musty pages of pioneer books."

1930—Congress enacts the Shipstead-Newton-Nolan Act to protect the more than one million acres of interconnected waterways that make up the Superior Primitive Area in northern Minnesota—the first federal law in American history to protect a Wilderness Area.

1935—Marshall, Leopold, Benton MacKaye, Bernard Frank, Harold Anderson, Ernest Oberhoklyzer, and Robert Sterling Yard launch the Wilderness Society on January 21, an organization devoted to preserving wilderness.

1939—At the urging of Marshall, the Forest Service issues the U Regulations, which supplant and strengthen the L-20 Regulations and direct that the "primitive" areas be reviewed and reclassified as "wilderness," "wild," or "roadless," depending on size.

1950–1956—Conservationists rally to prevent a proposed dam at Echo Park in the Dinosaur National Monument. Howard Zahniser, executive director of the Wilderness Society, becomes convinced of the need for statutory protection of wilderness and writes the first draft of a wilderness bill.

1956—Senator Hubert Humphrey of Minnesota introduces the bill in the U.S. Senate, June 7, 1956. Congressman John Saylor of Pennsylvania introduces a companion bill in the House of Representatives just a few days later.

1963—U.S. Senate passes the Wilderness bill, 73 to 12, on April 9.

1964—House of Representatives passes the Wilderness bill by a resounding 373 to 1 on July 30. President Lyndon Johnson signs the Wilderness Act at a White House garden ceremony on September 3.

1964—After eight years, eighteen hearings, and some sixty-six different versions of the Wilderness bill it eventually becomes a law. Upon passage of the Wilderness Act, all National Forest areas that had been administratively designated as "wild," "wilderness," or "canoe" areas immediately become part of the national wilderness preservation system, a total of 9.1 million acres. But the act also directs the Forest Service to study all of its remaining "primitive" areas to determine which of these should also be preserved. The act also directs the National Park Service and the Fish and Wildlife Service to study their lands for possible Wilderness designation.

1971—The Forest Service begins a Roadless Area Review and Evaluation (RARE I) of national forestlands to assess their Wilderness suitability. Using a stringent "purity" standard for Wilderness eligibility, the agency holds that in order for roadless areas to qualify as Wilderness, they must be totally pristine, removed from even the "sights and sounds" of civilization. No roadless areas in the East qualify as Wilderness because eastern forests have been impacted by roads and timber cutting.

1975—Following court challenges of the RARE study, Congress enacts the Eastern Wilderness Act of 1975, designating sixteen National Forest Wilderness Areas in thirteen eastern states.

1976—Congress passes the Federal Land Policy and Management Act, giving the Bureau of Land Management its Wilderness mandate. The law directs the agency to inventory and study all of its roadless lands in the lower forty-eight states to determine which lands should be recommended for Wilderness. The BLM later determined that approximately twenty-five million acres are to be studied for possible Wilderness designation.

1976—Missouri's first two designated Wilderness Areas, Hercules Glades (Forest Service) and Mingo (Fish and Wildlife Service) are enrolled in the national wilderness preservation system under Public Law 94-557, October 1976.

1978—Congress passes the Endangered American Wilderness Act, which designates significant Wilderness Areas in the West. The law makes clear that Wild Areas could not be disqualified simply because cities or towns could be seen or heard from them.

1979—The Forest Service completes a more extensive Roadless Area Review and Evaluation (RARE II) of sixty-two million acres of roadless forestlands, required by the 1978 Endangered American Wilderness Act. It recommends that 15.4 million acres be designated as Wilderness, 10.6 million acres be set aside for further study, and 36 million acres be released for development. RARE II also results in appeals and legal challenges. Despite controversy, the RARE II study has served as a starting point for Congress to designate Wilderness on a state-by-state basis for thirty-one states during the 1980s.

1980—Six Wilderness candidates in Missouri—Devil's Backbone, Paddy Creek, Bell Mountain, Piney Creek, Rockpile Mountain, and Irish are enrolled into the national wilderness preservation system during the 1980s. Irish Wilderness is the last to be designated under Public Law 98-289, on May 21, 1984.

1980—The historical Alaska National Interest Lands Conservation Act of 1980 more than triples the size of the Wilderness system. It increases Wilderness acreage in National Parks in Alaska to 56.5 million acres and that on National Wildlife Refuges to 18.7 million acres.

Future Challenges

The future of Wilderness in America can be characterized on two fronts. The growing pressure for uses of public lands that is not compatible with Wilderness will make designation of more Wilderness as controversial as it has been for the last twenty-five years. The second and increasingly important challenge for the future will be how to protect and preserve the Wilderness that has been designated. The value to future generations will not come through designation alone. Humans must learn to properly care for the land that has been set aside as "an enduring resource of Wilderness."

The intangible values of Wilderness are what really matter, the opportunity of knowing again what simplicity really means, the importance of the natural and the sense of oneness with the earth that inevitably comes within it. These are spiritual values. They are, in the last analysis, the reasons for its preservation.

SIGURD F. OLSON

TOTAL PUBLIC LANDS

Agency	Units	Federal Acres
Forest Service, USDA	399	34,678,493
National Park Service, USDI	44	42,302,023

Fish and Wildlife Service, USDI	75	20,685,341
Bureau of Land Management, USDI	137	5,241,042
Grand Total:	655	103, 721,133

NATIONAL WILDERNESS PRESERVATION SYSTEM (EXCLUDING ALASKA)

Agency	Units	Federal Acres
Forest Service, USDA	380	28,925,594
National Park Service, USDI	36	9,322,653
Fish and Wildlife Service, USDI	54	2,009,021
Bureau of Land Management, USDI	137	5,241,042
Total:	607	45,498,310

ALASKA WILDERNESS PRESERVATION SYSTEM

Agency	Units	Federal Acres
Forest Service, USDA	19	5,752,899
National Park Service, USDI	8	32,979,370
Fish and Wildlife Service, USDI	21	18,676,320
Bureau of Land Management, USDI	0	0
Total:	48	57,408,589

Local, State and National Environmental and Conservation Groups

1. American Hiking Society—is the only national nonprofit organization dedicated to promoting hiking and to establishing, protecting, and maintaining foot trails in America. The address is 1422 Fenwick Lane, Silver Spring, MD 20910, phone (301) 565-6704
2. Conservation Federation of Missouri—is an affiliate of the National Wildlife Federation. It is dedicated to protecting and enhancing fish, wildlife, and wildlife habitat. Members include sportsmen and conservationists. The address is 728 West Main, Jefferson City, MO 65101-1534, phone (573) 634-2322.
3. Forest Keepers—is dedicated to protecting and enhancing the Mark Twain National Forest, near Shell Knob, Missouri, including the protection of the nearby Piney Creek Wilderness. The address is Plaza Shopping Center, P.O. Box 27, Shell Knob, MO 65747, phone (417) 858-6126.
4. Missouri Coalition for the Environment—is a citizens'

watchdog organization. It is a not-for-profit, nonpartisan, member-funded, and member-directed group. It promotes public information and education on environmental issues that directly affect the entire state of Missouri. It is the most vocal and oft-quoted environmental organization in the state. The coalition supports Wilderness values and campaigned mightily on those issues in the 1970s and 1980s. The Missouri Coalition for the Environment and the Sierra Club are considered the most effective environmental organizations in the state. The address is 6267 Delmar Boulevard, St. Louis, MO 63130, phone (314) 727-0600.

5. Missouri Department of Natural Resources, Parks and Historic Preservation Division—manages state park Wild Areas that are large tracts of undeveloped land where space and solitude are preserved and where wilderness heritage can be enjoyed. Ten Missouri state parks contain Wild Areas totaling more than 18,000 acres. The address is P.O. Box 176, Jefferson City, MO 65102, phone (573) 751-2479.

6. Missouri Department of Conservation—manages, protects, and enhances the fish, wildlife, and timber of the state. Currently it does not have a wild lands program but owns several large tracts of land that would qualify as state Wild Areas. The address is P.O. Box 180, Jefferson City, MO 65102-0180, phone (573) 751-4115 or (department ombudsman) (573)-751-4115, ext. 250.

7. Mark Twain Forest Watchers—husband-and-wife team that has forced less clear-cutting and large old-growth tree destruction on the Mark Twain Forest. When critical and potentially damaging Forest Service management methods threaten the Mark Twain Forest, this small but mighty force of two environmentally minded citizens rises to the occasion in a sensible, knowledgeable, and effective manner. The address is 17918 Rocky Top Road, Elk Creek, MO 65464.

8. Missouri Parks Association—An extremely important organization, this group performs a watchdog role over state parklands, including those lands in the Wild Area system. The Missouri Parks Association played a key role in the all-important designation of Goggins Mountain Wild Area.

9. Missouri Wilderness Coalition—a cohesive team of citizen Wilderness conservationists who banded together statewide

in the 1970s and 1980s and developed into the most formidable and successful campaigners for Wilderness preservation in the state. Members proved adept at negotiating with resource agencies and elected representatives for promoting and securing the eight Missouri Wilderness Areas now enrolled in the National Wilderness Preservation System. Still active, MWC will be involved in round two when the New Forest Plan embraces additional Wilderness Areas for the state in the near future. Volunteers are welcome. The address is 299 Seraphin Street, Ste. Genevieve, MO 63670, phone (573) 883-5919.

10. Izaak Walton League of America—was founded in 1922 and dedicated to the enhancement of water and air quality. It protects wetlands and public lands, fish and wildlife habitat, and areas for outdoor recreation and promotes sound outdoor ethics. The address is 707 Conservation Lane, Gaithersburg, MD 20878-2983, phone (301) 548-0150.

11. National Audubon Society—is an effective and highly visible conservation organization with prime interest in wild birds and their habitats. While "birding" is a major pleasure among society members, there is also strong emphasis on air, water, and soil quality and forest and Wilderness preservation. Audubon Nature Centers across the country educate citizens about wild birds, their needs, and how they fit into nature's scheme. An active regional group, Greater Ozarks Audubon Society represents twelve southern counties in the Ozarks. The address is P.O Box 3231 GS, Springfield, MO 65808. Headquarters are located at 700 Broadway, New York, NY 10003, phone (212) 979-3000, and 666 Pennsylvania Ave. S.E., Washington D.C. 20003, phone (202) 547-9009.

12. National Park Service—manages National Scenic Riverways and wild land corridors in the Ozarks, including the upper Jacks Fork, Current, and Eleven Point Rivers. Currently manages lands in the state that have National Wilderness Preservation qualifications. Address letters to Superintendent, P.O. Box 490, Van Buren, MO 63965, phone (573) 323-4236.

13. National Wildlife Federation—believes the preservation and acquisition of Wilderness lands and the protection of wildlife habitat have been central to the federation's mission

since its founding in 1936. NWF believes that the survival and quality of life of all people is inextricably linked to the health of the earth's environment and its natural resources. The preservation of Wilderness is critical to maintaining a healthy environment. The address is 1400 Sixteenth Street, N.W., Washington, D.C. 20036-2266, phone (202) 797-6800.

14. Sierra Club—is a nonprofit, member-supported, public interest organization that promotes conservation of the natural environment by influencing public policy decisions—legislative, administrative, legal, and electoral. Founded in 1892, its first president was John Muir. The Sierra Club has proven to be one of the most effective environmental groups of all times—mirroring perhaps the tenacity of its first president. The club has 550,000 members, 65 chapters, and 396 groups. Its mission is "To explore, enjoy and protect the wild places of the earth; to practice and promote the responsible use of the earth's ecosystems and resources; to educate and enlist humanity to protect and restore the quality of the natural and human environment; and to use all lawful means to carry out these objectives." Local and regional chapters of the Sierra Club in Missouri paved the way for all Wilderness currently enrolled under the national wilderness protection system. And there is little doubt the Sierra Club will play a vital role in forthcoming Missouri Wilderness campaigns. The address is 85 Second Street, San Francisco, CA 94105, phone (415) 977-5500.

15. U.S. Fish and Wildlife Service—is responsible for one of the eight designated Wilderness Areas in the state—the uniquely beautiful and haunting Mingo Wilderness. Today, the Fish and Wildlife Service manages 20.7 million acres under the national wildlife refuge system. The smallest Wilderness Area in the system is two-acre Wisconsin Islands Wilderness, Green Bay. The address is Fish and Wildlife Service, 4401 N. Fairfax Drive, Webb Building, MS 130, Arlington, VA 22203, phone (202) 208-4131.

16. U.S. Forest Service—Internal proposals as well as outside pressure led the Forest Service into Wilderness management. Three Forest Service employees who later gained prominence as environmental and recreational masterminds were Aldo Leopold, Arthur Carhart, and Robert

Marshall. In the 1920s and 1930s, these three men designed and helped implement a wilderness policy for the Forest Service. While today the Forest Service commonly is in the middle of Wilderness discussions and sometimes between a rock and hard spot due to Washington D.C. directives, the service is most often an ally of Wilderness preservation. Address letters to Forest Supervisor's Office, 401 Fairgrounds Road, Rolla, MO 65401, phone (573) 364-4621.

17. The Wilderness Society—conceived and most vigorously promoted the Wilderness Act of 1964, a dream of preservation that had begun with the organization's founding in 1935. The Wilderness Society is a nonprofit membership organization devoted to preserving Wilderness and wildlife, protecting America's prime forest, parks, rivers, deserts, and shoreland, and fostering an American land ethic. It is one of the strongest and most effective environmental organizations in the world. 900 Seventeenth Street, N.W., Washington, D.C. 20006, phone (202) 833-2300.

A Word from Former Mark Twain Forest Supervisor B. Eric Morse

B. Eric Morse started his career in the Forest Service in 1961 on the Gifford Pinchot National Forest in Washington. He served subsequently on the Mt. Hood, Umpqua, and Willamette National Forests in Oregon. He returned to Mt. Hood in 1976 for his first district ranger assignment on the Bear Springs District. He was moved to the Willamette National Forest in 1979 as district ranger on the Rigdon Ranger District. From there he was moved to the Mark Twain National Forest in June 1982 as deputy forest supervisor. He was promoted to Mark Twain Forest supervisor in January 1985, where he served until his retirement in 1994.

Eric Morse admits that he had no role in the creation of Missouri Wilderness and was only vicariously involved in the development of management plans for them. By the time he became a deputy forest supervisor on the Mark Twain in 1982, all but the Irish Wilderness had been enrolled in the national wilderness preservation system.

Today, living with his wife, Karen, in Rolla, Missouri, the thirty-three-year Forest Service veteran reflects back upon those Wilderness campaigns. He says, "The designation of Wilderness is a political process and decision based on limited resource information and skilled compromise. To that end major credit in Missouri goes to former Senators Tom Eagleton and John Danforth; and on the public side to John Karel and the Sierra Club."

Early on, when I was contemplating writing a book on Missouri Wilderness, I wrote to Eric and asked his opinion. He replied, "I think your Missouri Wilderness book idea is a good one and would find a warm welcome. I can offer you assistance in gathering historic, geologic, cultural, cartographic and other support information, as well as making personnel available to help you figure it all out. You are embarking on an ambitious, exciting, fun, and rewarding endeavor. I wish you the best!"

In a letter I received from him in February 1996, he offered this suggestion. "Leave room in your book for more Wilderness. The last page is yet to be turned. The Irish Act precluded further consideration of Wilderness for the first planning period. That period has all but ended and the Forest Plan Revision for the next period must consider Wilderness. Your book perhaps can become an important resource in the debate . . . and rest assured there will be a debate."

A few days before concluding this book, I talked with John Karel. I wanted to know if the Missouri Wilderness Coalition was alive and indeed ready to initiate another successful campaign in order to finish Wilderness business it had begun in the 1970s. His affirmative reply left no doubt.

The last great debate for remaining Missouri Wilderness could very well be the most satisfying and enlightening for those who cherish sanctuaries of peace, solitude, introspection, and natural adventure and the physical, mental, and spiritual health derived. We could bestow on future generations a lasting legacy of trust and beauty.

For us the Wilderness and human emptiness of this land is not a source of fear but the greatest of its attractions. We would guard and defend and save it as a place for all who wish to rediscover the nearly lost pleasures of adventure, adventure not only in the physical sense, but also mental, spiritual, moral, aesthetic and intellectual adventure. It is a place for the free.

EDWARD ABBEY

Recommended Reading

IN THE TEXT, I mentioned books that have been useful to me and might be helpful to readers. For convenience they are also listed below. In a few cases, when I think the guides are essential for hikers and campers, I have also listed ordering information.

Some general information about Wilderness can be found in *The Wilderness Movement and the National Forests* by Dennis M. Roth (College Station, Tx.: Intaglio Press, 1988); and in *These American Lands* by Dyan Zaslowsky, T. H. Watkins, and the Wilderness Society (Washington, D.C.: Island Press, 1994).

A guide to canoeing in Missouri is *Missouri Ozark Waterways* by Oz Hawksley (Missouri Department of Conservation, 1997). *One Hundred Nature Walks in the Missouri Ozarks* by Alan McPherson (Vienna, Ill.: Cache River Press, 1998) is a good trail guide. If you're interested in knowing what to look for and identifying what you see as you hike along, I recommend *Geologic Wonders and Curiosities of Missouri* by Thomas H. Beveridge (Missouri Department of Natural Resources, 1990); *Missouri Wildflowers* by Edgar Denison (Missouri Department of Conservation, 1998); and *Paradigms of the Past: The Story of Missouri Archaeology* by Michael J. O'Brien (Columbia: University of Missouri Press, 1996).

For help finding your way when you leave the trail, try *Be Expert*

263

with Map and Compass: The Complete Orienteering Handbook by Bjorn Kjellstrom (New York: Collier Books, 1994).

Finally, I suggest taking the following three references along with you when you hike or camp: *Wilderness Medicine* by William W. Forgey, M.D. (Merrilville, Ind.: ICS Books, 1994) is available from the publisher at One Tower Plaza, Suite 107, Merriville, IN, 46410, phone (219)-769-0585. "Moveable Feast" by Carolyn Gunn and the editors of *Backpacker* magazine is a pamphlet that will help you pack and eat the right foods for energy and good health on the trail. *How to Shit in the Woods* by Kathleen Meyer (Berkeley, Calif.: Ten Speed Press, 1994) is an excellent practical guide and is available from the publisher at Box 7123, Berkeley, CA, 94707, or by calling (800)-841-BOOK (you'll need a credit card if you're calling). It is also usually available in bookstores.

About the Author

CHARLES J. FARMER is a full-time writer who specializes in accounts of outdoor adventures for various magazines and for the *Springfield News-Leader*. A resident of Ozark, Missouri, he has written books about fishing, hunting, camping, canoeing, backpacking, outdoor cooking, and history and is cohost of the popular radio program *Outside Story*. Farmer also wrote the introduction for *Images of the Ozarks*, available from the University of Missouri Press.